William Harvey Wells

A Grammar of the English Language

For the use of schools

William Harvey Wells

A Grammar of the English Language
For the use of schools

ISBN/EAN: 9783337087227

Printed in Europe, USA, Canada, Australia, Japan

Cover: Foto ©Paul-Georg Meister /pixelio.de

More available books at **www.hansebooks.com**

WELLS'S SCHOOL GRAMMAR.—REVISED EDITION.

A GRAMMAR

OF THE

ENGLISH LANGUAGE.

FOR THE USE OF SCHOOLS.

BY

W. H. WELLS, M.A.,

SUPERINTENDENT OF PUBLIC SCHOOLS, CHICAGO; AND LATE PRINCIPAL OF THE
STATE NORMAL SCHOOL, WESTFIELD, MASS.

TWO HUNDRED AND TWENTY-FIFTH THOUSAND.

CHICAGO:
S. C. GRIGGS & CO., 39 & 41 LAKE ST.
NEW YORK: IVISON, PHINNEY & COMPANY.
BOSTON: BROWN, TAGGARD & CHASE. PHILADELPHIA: SOWER, BARNES
& CO., AND J. B. LIPPINCOTT & CO. CINCINNATI: MOORE, WILSTACH,
KEYS & CO. SAVANNAH: J. M. COOPER & CO. ST. LOUIS: KEITH
& WOODS. NEW ORLEANS: BLOOMFIELD, STEEL & CO.
DETROIT: F. RAYMOND & CO.

1860.

Entered, according to Act of Congress, in the year 1858, by
IVISON & PHINNEY,
In the Clerk's Office of the District Court for the Southern District of New York.

PREFACE TO THE REVISED EDITION.

When the first edition of this Grammar was published, it contained more principles and exercises in Grammatical Analysis than had appeared in any work previously issued in this country. It would have been easy to embody the more abstruse principles of Analysis which are contained in the works of Kühner, Crane, De Sacy, and other foreign writers, but it was feared that such a system would rather confuse than aid the pupils in our schools. All the fundamental principles of Analysis were presented, and teachers were urged to introduce their pupils as early as practicable to this important branch of grammatical study. It was not, however, intended to recommend that Grammatical Analysis should supersede the essential exercises of Etymological and Syntactical Parsing.

The tendency of our schools is to reach at once toward that which is called *higher*, and neglect that which has the misfortune to be regarded as *lower;* while it is obvious that the lower departments of study are at least equally important with the higher, and that neither should be allowed to take the place of the other. It is not then remarkable, that many teachers should have gone from a mere routine of common parsing to the opposite extreme, and devoted their attention almost exclusively to Analysis. Hence we find at the present time not a few schools in which pupils know very little of Etymological and Syntactical Parsing, while they are able to recite with uncommon fluency in all the forms of technical Analysis.

It is this tendency to an extreme, that has in so many instances brought the whole system of Grammatical Analysis into disrepute. The experience of the last few years has satisfied intelligent Teachers and Boards of Education that pupils need to be thoroughly instructed both in the elements of Etymological and Syntactical Parsing, and in the principles of Grammatical Analysis; and it is to be hoped that each department will hereafter receive its due share of attention in the study of our mother tongue.

In the present edition of the School Grammar, that portion of the work which is devoted to Analysis has been re-written and greatly enlarged. It will now be found characterized by completeness in the presentation of principles, and by copiousness in the illustrations. The remarks which accompany the illustrative examples explain a great variety of idioms and forms of construction, and will be found more useful to the learner than the same number of special rules.

The chapter on the Grammatical Connection and Relation of Words, p. 134, has met with special favor among intelligent teachers. It has been carefully revised in the present edition.

Several pages of the Grammar have heretofore been devoted to the *Sounds of the Letters*. As this subject is now fully illustrated in all the principal series of School Readers, it is omitted in the present edition.

CHICAGO, February 27, 1858.

ORIGINAL PREFACE.

About nine years since, while engaged in the instruction of a class of Teachers, the author commenced a critical examination of several grammatical works, in connection with a systematic course of English reading. All the important principles of the language were familiarly discussed before the class. The definitions and rules of different grammarians were carefully compared with one another, and tested by constant reference to the usage of standard writers. In conducting the exercises of successive classes of Teachers, a similar course has been repeated from year to year till the present time. The result of these labors is embodied in the work now offered to the public.*

English Grammar is too often taught as if it were merely the art of *Parsing*. It is hoped that instructors will find the present work adapted to teach "the art of *speaking* and *writing*." Copious exercises and illustrations have been introduced, and the learner is required to make constant application of the principles as he advances.

The essay on Oral Instruction was prepared at the request of Henry Barnard, Esq., Commissioner of Public Schools for the State of Rhode Island, and first appeared as one of his series of Educational Tracts.   W. H. W.

Phillips Academy, Andover, Mass., 1846.

---

* In pursuing these investigations, the author has collected more than four hundred different treatises on English Grammar, and noted above twenty thousand illustrative examples in the productions of the best English writers.

CATALOGUE OF ENGLISH GRAMMARS.

[The catalogue here given embraces only those Grammars to which special reference is made in the pages of the following work.

Adams, Rev. Charles, A. M., 12mo, Boston; 1838.
Adams, Daniel, 3d ed. 12mo, Montpelier, Vt.; 1814.
Ainsworth, Luther, 12mo, Providence; 1837.
Alden, Abner. A. M., 12mo, Boston; 1811.
Alexander, Caleb, A. M., 10th ed., 12mo, Keene, N. H.; 1814.
Alexander, Samuel, 4th ed., 18mo, London; 1832.
Allen, Rev. William, 2d ed., 12mo, London; 1824.
Allen and Cornwell, 3d ed., 18mo, London; 1841.
Angell, Oliver, A. M., 12mo, Providence; 1830.
Angus, William, M. A., 2d ed., 12mo, Glasgow; 1807.
Arnold, T. K., M. A., 2d ed., 12mo, London; 1841.
Ash, John, LL. D., new ed., 18mo, London; 1785.
Badgley, Jonathan, 12mo, Utica; 1845.
Balch, William S., 12mo, Boston; 1839.
Baldwin, Edward, 2d ed., 18mo, London; 1824.
Barnard, F. A. P., A. M., 12mo, New York; 1836.
Barrett, John, 2d ed., 18mo, Boston; 1819.
Barrett, Solomon, 10th ed., 18mo, Utica; 1845.
Barre, Alexander, 9th ed., 18mo, Edinburgh; 1800.
Beall, Alexander, 12mo, Cincinnati; 1841.
Bell, John, 12mo, Glasgow; 1769.
Bicknell, Alexander, 12mo, London; 1790.
Bingham, Caleb, A. M., 12th ed., 24mo, Boston; 1801.
Blair, Rev. David, 15th ed., 18mo, London; 1826.
Booth, David, 12mo. London; 1837.
Brace, Joab, 18mo, Philadelphia; 1839.
Brightland, John, 5th ed., 12mo, London; 1728.
British Grammar, 12mo, London and Boston; 1784.
Brittain, Rev. Lewis, 2d ed., London: 1790
Brown, Goold, stereotype ed., 12mo, New York; 1846.
Buchanan, James, 12mo, London; 1767. — Philadelphia, 179
Bucke, Charles, 18mo, London; 1829.
Bullions, Peter, D. D., 15th ed., 12mo, New York; 1846.
Burn, John, 7th ed., 18mo, Glasgow; 1799.
Burr, Jonathan, A. M. 3d ed., 18mo, Boston; 1818.
Butler, Noble, A. M., 12mo, Louisville, Ky.; 1845.
Cardell, William S., 3d ed., 18mo, Hartford; 1827.
Chapin, Joel, 12mo, Springfield; 1842.
Churchill T. O., 12mo, London; 1823.
Coar, Thomas, 12mo, London; 1796.
Cobb, E., 2d ed., 12mo, Boston; 1821.
Cobbett, William, 12mo, London; 1818. — New York; 1833

Cochran, Peter, A. B., 18mo, Boston; 1802
Comly, John, 15th ed., 18mo, Philadelphia; 1838
Connel, Robert, 2d ed., 18mo, Glasgow; 1834.
Connon, C. W, M. A., 12mo, Edinburgh; 1845.
Cooper, J. G., 12mo, Philadelphia; 1831.
Coot, C., LL. D., 8vo, London; 1788.
Cornell, William M., 4to, Boston; 1840.
Crane, George, 12mo, London; 1843.
Crombie, Alexander, LL. D., F. R. S., 4th ed., 8vo, London; 1836.
Cutler, Andrew, 12mo, Plainfield, Ct.; 1841.
Dalton, John, 2d ed., 12mo, London; 1843.
Davenport, B., 18mo, Wilmington, Del.; 1830.
Davis, Pardon, 12mo, Philadelphia; 1845.
Day, Parsons E., 2d ed., 18mo, Ithaca, N. Y.; 1844.
Dearborn, Benjamin, 12mo, Boston; 1795.
Del Mar, E., 12mo, London; 1842.
Dilworth, Thomas, 26th ed., 12mo, London; 1764.
D'Orsey, Alexander J. D., 12mo, Edinburgh: 1842.
Earl, Mary, 18mo, Boston; 1816.
Elmore, D. W., A. M., 18mo, Troy, N. Y.; 1830.
Elphinston, James, 12mo, London; 1766.
Emmons, S. B., 12mo, Boston; 1832.
Everest, Cornelius B., 12mo, Norwich; 1835.
Farnum, Caleb, A. M., 2d ed., 12mo, Boston; 1843.
Farro, D., 12mo, London; 1754.
Felch, W., 12mo, Boston; 1837.
Felton, O. C., 2d ed., 12mo, Salem; 1843.
Fenning, D., 12mo, London; 1771.
Fisher, A., 28th ed., 12mo, London; 1795.
Fletcher, Levi, 12mo, Philadelphia; 1834.
Flint, John, 18mo, New York; 1837.
Flower, M. and W. B., 18mo, London; 1844.
Fowle, William B., 12mo, Boston; 1842.
Frazee, Rev. Bradford, 12mo, Philadelphia; 1844.
French, D'Arcy A., 12mo, Baltimore; 1831.
Frost, John, A. M., 12mo, Philadelphia; 1842.
Fuller, Allen, 12mo, Plymouth, Mass.; 1822.
Gilbert, E., 18mo, New York; 1835.
Giles, Rev. T. A., M. A., 2d ed., 12mo, London; 1838
Goldsbury, John, A. M., 12mo, Boston; 1842.
Goodenow, S. B., 2d ed., 12mo, Boston; 1843.
Graham, G. F., 12mo, London; 1843.
Grant, John, A. M., 12mo, London; 1813.
Granville, George, 12mo, London; 1827.
Green, R. W., 5th ed., 18mo, Philadelphia; 1834.
Greenleaf, J., 20th ed., 4to, New York; 1837.
Greenwood, James, 2d ed., 12mo, London; 1722.
Gurney, David, A. M., 2d ed., 18mo, Boston; 1808.
Hall, Rev. S. R., 2d ed., 12mo, Springfield; 1833.
Hallock, Edward J., 12mo, Andover; 1842.
Hamlin, L. F., stereotype ed., 12mo, New York; 1832
Hart, John S., A. M., 12mo, Philadelphia; 1845.
Hazen, Edward, A. M., 12mo, New York; 1842.

Hazlitt, Wm., 18mo, London; 1810.
Hendrick, J. L., A. M., 18mo, Syracuse; 1844.
Higginson, Rev. T. E., 12mo, Dublin; 1803.
Hiley, Richard, 3d ed., 12mo, London; 1840.
Hodgson, Rev. Isaac, 12mo, London; 1770.
Hornsey, John, 6th ed., 12mo, York, England; 1816.
Hort, W. Jillard, 18mo, London; 1822.
Howe, S. L., 18mo, Lancaster, Ohio; 1838.
Hull, J. H., 4th ed., 12mo, Boston; 1828.
Ingersoll, C. M., 12mo, Philadelphia; 1835.
Jaudon. D., 4th ed., 18mo, Philadelphia; 1828.
Jenkins, Azariah, 12mo, Rochester, N. Y.; 1835.
Joel, Thomas, 12mo, London; 1775.
Johnson, Samuel, LL. D., (prefixed to Dictionary), 4to, London; 1775.
Johnson, Ben, 8vo, London; 1640. — 1816.
Jones, Joshua, 18mo, Philadelphia; 1841.
Judson, Adoniram, A. B., 12mo, Boston; 1808.
Kennion, Charlotte, 12mo, London; 1842.
King, Walter W., 18mo, London; 1841.
Kirkham, Samuel, 36th ed., 12mo, Rochester, N. Y.; 1834.
Latham, R. G., A. M., 12mo, London; 1843.
Lennie, William, 13th ed., 18mo, Edinburgh; 1831.
Lewis, William G., 18mo, London; 1821.
Lindsay, Rev. John, A. M., 18mo, London; 1842.
Locke, John, M. D., 18mo, Cincinnati; 1827.
Lovechild, Mrs., 40th ed., 18mo, London; 1842.
Lowth, Robert, LL. D., 18mo, London; 1763. — Cambridge, U. S.; 1838
Lynde, John, 18mo, Woodstock, Vt.; 1821.
Maittaire, Michael, 12mo, London; 1712.
Marcet, Mrs., 7th ed., 18mo, London; 1843.
Martin, Benjamin, 12mo, London; 1754.
M'Cready, F., 12mo, Philadelphia; 1820.
M'Culloch, J. M., D. D., 7th ed., 18mo, Edinburgh; 1841.
Meilan, Mark Anthony, 12mo, London; 1803.
Menye, J., 12mo, New York; 1785.
Milligan, Rev. George, 2d ed., 18mo, Edinburgh; 1839.
Morgan, Jonathan, A. B., 12mo, Hallowell, Me.; 1814.
Morely, Charles, A. B., 18mo, Hartford; 1836.
Murray, Lindley, 8vo, Holdgate, England; 1795. — New York; 1814.
Nutting, Rufus, A. M., 3d ed., 12mo, Montpelier, Vt.; 1826.
Oliver, Edward, D. D., 12mo, London; 1807.
Oliver, Samuel, 8vo, London; 1825.
Parker and Fox, 5th ed., 12mo, Boston; 1837.
Parkhurst, John L., 18mo, Andover; 1838.
Peirce, Oliver B., 12mo, New York; 1839.
Perley, Daniel, M. D., 18mo, Andover; 1834.
Perry, William, (prefixed to Dictionary), 12mo, Edinburgh; 1801.
Picket, A. and J. W., 12mo, Cincinnati; 1837.
Pinnock, W., 12mo, London; 1829.
Pond's Murray, 6th ed., 12mo, Worcester; 1835.
Powers, Daniel, A. M., 12mo, West Brookfield, Mass.; 1845.
Priestley, Joseph, LL. D., 3d ed., 18mo, London; 1772.
Pue, Hugh A., 18mo, Philadelphia; 1841.

Pullen, P. H., 2d ed., 12mo, London; 1822.
Putnam, J. M., 18mo, Concord, N. H.; 1831
Reed, Caleb, A. M., 18mo, Boston; 1821.
Robbins, Manasseh, 12mo, Providence; 1826.
Ross, Robert, 7th ed., 12mo, Hartford; 1782.
Russell, J., D. D., 10th ed., 18mo, London; 1842.
Russell, William E., 2d ed., 18mo, Hartford; 1819.
Sanborn, D. H., 12mo, Concord, N. H.; 1836.
Simmonite, W. J., 12mo, London; 1841.
Skiffern, R. S., A. M., 2d ed., 12mo, Gloucester, England, 1808.
Smart, B. H., 12mo, London; 1841.
Smetham, Thomas, 12mo, London; 1774.
Smith, Eli, 18mo, Philadelphia; 1812.
Smith, Peter, A. M., 18mo, Edinburgh; 1826.
Smith, R. C., stereotype ed., 12mo, Philadelphia; 1845.
Snyder, W., 12mo, Winchester; 1834.
Spear, M. P., 12mo, Boston; 1845.
Staniford, Daniel, A. M., 2d ed., 18mo, Boston; 1815.
Stearns, George, 4to, Boston; 1843.
St. Quentin, D., A. M., 12mo, London; 1812.
Story, Joshua, 3d ed., 12mo, Newcastle, England; 1783
Sutcliffe, Joseph, A. M., 2d ed., 12mo, London; 1815.
Swett, J., A. M., 2d ed., 12mo, Claremont, N. H.; 1844.
Ticken, William, 12mo, London; 1806.
Ticknor, Elisha, A. M., 3d ed., 18mo, Boston; 1794.
Todd, Lewis C., 2d ed., 18mo, Fredonia, N. Y.; 1827.
Trinder, William M., 12mo, London; 1781.
Ussher, G Neville, 12mo, London; 1787. — Exeter, N. H. 1804.
Waldo, John, 18mo, Philadelphia; 1814.
Walker, John, 12mo, London; 1805.
Wallis, John, D. D., (in Latin), 6th ed., 8vo, London; 1765.
Ward, H., 12mo, Whitehaven, England; 1777.
Ward, John, LL. D., 12mo, London; 1758.
Ward, William, M. A., 3d ed., 12mo, Northampton, England; '771
Webber, Samuel, 12mo, Cambridge, Mass.; 1832.
Webster, Noah, LL. D., 12mo, New Haven; 1831.
Weld, A. H., M. A., 12mo, Portland; 1846.
Whiting, Joseph, A. M., 12mo, Detroit; 1845.
Wilbur, Josiah, 2d ed., 12mo, Bellows Falls; 1822.
Wilcox, A. F., 18mo, New Haven; 1828.
Willard, Samuel, 18mo, Greenfield, Mass; 1816.
Wilson, George, 18mo, London; 1777.
Wilson, J. P., D. D., 8vo, Philadelphia; 1817.
Worcester, Samuel, 18mo, Gloucester, Mass.; 1827.
Wright, Joseph W., C. E., 12mo, New York; 1838.
Brown, Goold, 8vo, New York; 1851.
Barton, Rev. J. G., A. M., 18mo, New York; 1855.
Barnes, William, B. D., 8vo, London; 1854.
Clark, S. W., A. M., 12mo, New York; 1856.
Fowler, William C., 8vo, New York; 1855.
Goodwin, Thomas, A. B., 12mo, London; 1855.
Mulligan, John, A. M., 12mo, New York; 1852.
Pinneo, T. S., M. A., 12mo, Cincinnati; 1850.

1*

TO TEACHERS.

That portion of the work which is printed in the largest type, is designed for beginners; and the corresponding questions are printed in Roman characters. That which is printed in type of the second size, is designed for pupils more advanced; and the corresponding questions are in Italics. That which is printed in the smallest type, is designed for occasional reference.

The Exercises which occur in different portions of the work are intended to be modified or extended at the discretion of teachers.

ORAL INSTRUCTION
IN
ENGLISH GRAMMAR.

[The following outline of Oral Instruction is designed to furnish practical suggestions to teachers engaged in imparting a knowledge of the rudiments of English Grammar.

By adopting a familiar, inductive method of presenting this subject, it may be rendered highly attractive to young learners; and the practice of introducing illustrative exercises in composition, will be found to afford great assistance to pupils in comprehending and retaining the principles presented, while it also leads them to cultivate the habit of expressing their thoughts with facility and accuracy.

It is not expected that teachers will confine themselves strictly to any particular system; but it is hoped that the *general* features of the sketch here presented will be found to meet the wants of all classes of beginners.]

PARTS OF SPEECH.

§ 1. The *classification* of words may be introduced by referring to the different kinds of trees; to the different kinds of animals; or to any other collection of objects that admits of a regular division into distinct classes. Thus, when we go into a forest, we find that the number of trees about us is greater than we can estimate. But we soon observe that a portion of them have certain striking resemblances, while they differ essentially from all the rest. We also observe that others, which differ materially from these, have similar resemblances to one another. And by extending our observation, we find that this countless multitude of trees all belong to a very few simple classes, which are easily distinguished from one another. Those of one class we associate together, and call them *Oak* trees: those of another class we call *Pine* trees; and in this manner we proceed with all the different kinds.

Just so it is with the words of our language. Though their number is about eighty thousand, yet we find, on a careful examination, that they all belong to less than a dozen different classes, called Parts of Speech; so that we have only to learn the character of these divisions, and we shall be able to tell the class to which any word in the language belongs.

By some such introductory illustration, the curiosity of a class of beginners may be easily excited, and they will thus be prepared to enter with eagerness upon the labor of learning to distinguish the different parts of speech.

The teacher should lead his pupils to take an active part in these lessons from the beginning; not only by proposing frequent questions for them to answer, but also by encouraging them to ask such questions as their own curiosity may suggest.

THE NOUN.

§ 2. Having prepared the way for the consideration of *words*, the teacher next requests his pupils to mention the *names* of any objects that occur to them. As they proceed to give the words *book*, *desk*, *inkstand*, etc., the teacher writes them in a column on the blackboard.

The teacher now asks a variety of questions, similar to the following: — Are all words names? Can you mention any words that are not names? Are *good* and *bad*, names? Why not? Can you think of any object that has not a name? Do any objects that you cannot *see* or *touch* have names? Is *wise* a name? Is *wisdom*? *Virtue*? *Virtuous*? *Knowledge*?

After these questions have been disposed of, the pupils are informed that the *names* of all objects, whether material or immaterial, are called *Nouns;* and the teacher proceeds at the same time to write this title over the column of names on the board.

One or more sentences are now placed in the hands of the pupils, or written on the board; and each member of the class proceeds to select all the nouns, and write them in a column on a slate or piece of paper. The teacher should commence with sentences of the simplest construction, and afterwards introduce more difficult forms of expression as the learners advance.

Model I.*

The earth is a large globe or ball. — Virtue is better than riches.

> Nouns.
> Earth
> Globe
> Ball
> Virtue
> Riches

Exercises of this description should be continued till the pupils are able to point out the nouns of any common sentence with readiness.

The teacher next writes several nouns on the black-board, and calls on the class to construct one or more sentences embracing the words which he has placed before them.

Model II.

Sun, bird, idleness, night.

The hawk is a bird of prey. — Idleness often leads to vice. — The sun shines by day, and the moon by night.

After going through with several exercises of this kind, the pupils may be required to construct a variety of sentences, and write the letter *n* over all the nouns embraced in them.

Model III.†

In w$\overset{n}{i}$nter the p$\overset{n}{o}$nds and r$\overset{n}{i}$vers are generally covered with i$\overset{n}{c}$e. — R$\overset{n}{u}$ssia is the largest c$\overset{n}{o}$untry in E$\overset{n}{u}$rope.

---

* See Frazee's Grammar. † See Greenleaf's Grammar.

THE ADJECTIVE.

§ 3. When the pupils have become sufficiently acquainted with the nature of nouns, they may be introduced to the class of *Adjectives* in a similar manner. The teacher directs the attention of the pupils to a book, and asks if they can mention any words that express its *character* or *quality*. To this they will readily answer, that it is a *good* book, a *large* book, an *interesting* book, etc. The teacher then calls on them to name as many words as they can, that express the *qualities* of objects. As they proceed to enumerate words of this class, the teacher writes them in a column on the board as before.

Such expressions as "These books," "A wise man," "Ten days," are next written on the board; and the learners are requested to point out the words which serve to *define* or *limit* the nouns, but do not strictly *qualify* them. After this is done, they proceed to mention others of the same character, which are written under the column of *qualifying* words already commenced. It is now time to inform them that all words which are used to *qualify* or *define* nouns, belong to the class called *Adjectives;* and this title is accordingly placed at the head of the column of words on the board.

The pupils may also be told in this connection, that the words *a* or *an* and *the* are distinguished from other definitives by the title of *Articles.*

Simple sentences are again placed before the pupils, and they are required to select all the adjectives, writing them in a column as before. They should also distinguish the articles, by underlining them in the column.

MODEL IV.

Great men are not always wise. — *The climate of Egypt is hot in summer, but delightful in winter.*

ADJECTIVES.
Great
Wise
The

Hot
Delightful

Other sentences are now given to the pupils, from which they select the nouns and adjectives, writing them in separate columns; and distinguishing the articles as in the previous exercise.

Model V.

There are very few plants that will grow in all countries. — Ivory is a hard solid, and firm substance, of a white color.

Nouns.	Adjectives.
Plants	Few
Countries	All
Ivory	A
Substance	
Color	Hard
	Solid
	Firm
	A
	White

The teacher next writes a number of adjectives on the board, and the pupils proceed as before to form the sentences which embrace them.

Model VI.

Diligent, cold, warm, sweet.

Charles is a diligent scholar. — In cold weather we protect ourselves by the use of warm clothing. — The rose is sweet, but it is surrounded with thorns.

After this, the pupils write sentences containing adjectives of their own selection. In exercises of this character, the learners should distinguish, by their several abbreviations, all the parts of speech to which they have attended.

Model VII.

$\overset{n}{\text{Copper}}$ is $\overset{ar}{\text{a}}$ very $\overset{adj}{\text{useful}}$ $\overset{n}{\text{metal}}$, which is found in almost $\overset{adj}{\text{all}}$ $\overset{n}{\text{parts}}$ of the $\overset{n}{\text{world}}$. It is of $\overset{ar}{\text{a}}$ $\overset{adj}{\text{red}}$ $\overset{n}{\text{color}}$, and may be drawn out into $\overset{adj}{\text{fine}}$ $\overset{n}{\text{wire}}$, or beaten into $\overset{adj}{\text{thin}}$ $\overset{n}{\text{leaves}}$.

THE VERB.

§ 4. This part of speech may be introduced by a few simple questions and answers.

Teacher. What part of speech is *horse?*
Pupil. A *noun.*
T. Why?
P. Because it is a *name.*
T. Can you think of any words that tell what the horse *does?*
P. *Runs, walks,* etc.
T. Are *runs* and *walks* nouns?
P. They are not.
T. Why not?
P. Because they are not *names.*
T. Are they *adjectives?*
P. They are not.
T. Why not?
P. Because they do not *qualify* or *define* any thing.
T. Will you name as many words as you can recollect, that tell what any thing *does*, or express some kind of *action?*
P. *Speak, read, study, sing, play,* etc.

These words are written in a column on the board, after which the questions are continued.

T. In the sentence, "The sea is calm," does the word *is* express any degree of *action?*
P. It does not.
T. Does it express the *being* or *existence* of any thing?
P. It does.
T. Can you name any other words that are used to express the *being* or *existence* of objects?
P. *Am, was, live,* etc.

These words are placed under the column already commenced on the board, and the pupils are informed that all words which express *action*, and those which express *being* or *existence*, are called *Verbs.*

A number of sentences are next placed before the pupils, from which they select all the verbs, writing them by themselves as in previous exercises.

Model VIII.

Birds fly in the air. — The earth shook and trembled. — Boston is the capital of Massachusetts. — I wrote a letter to my friend last week, and received an answer this morning.

VERBS.
Fly
Shook
Trembled
Is
Wrote
Received

Other sentences are now given to the learners, from which they select all the nouns, adjectives, and verbs; writing them in separate columns, and distinguishing the articles.

MODEL IX.

He came in the morning, and went away at night. — Truth never fears examination. — Venus is the brightest of all the planets. It is sometimes visible at mid-day.

NOUNS.	ADJECTIVES.	VERBS.
Morning	The	Came
Night	The	Went
Truth		Fears
Examination	Brightest	Is
Venus	All	Is
Planets	The	
Mid-day	Visible	

Several verbs are next placed before the learners, and they are required to form sentences which include them. See Models II and VI.

After this, the pupils write sentences containing several verbs of their own choice; and distinguish all the verbs, adjectives, and nouns.

MODEL X.

   ar *n* *ar* *n*   *v*   *n*   *v* *n*
In the spring the farmer ploughs his ground and sows his seed; in
ar *n*   *n*   *v*   *n*   *ar* *n*
the summer and autumn he gathers his harvest; and in the winter he
v *n*   *v*   *n*
cuts his wood and threshes his grain.

The teacher should make frequent suggestions and explanations during these exercises. It is highly important that learners become thoroughly acquainted with the nature of verbs, before advancing to consider the other parts of speech.

THE PRONOUN.

§ 5. *Teacher.* In the sentence, "John is diligent, and he will improve," for what name does the word *he* stand?

Pupil. John.

T. Can you mention any other names for which *he* is sometimes used?

P. George, Charles, man, boy, etc.

T. For what nouns does *she* stand?

P. Jane, Susan, girl, woman, etc.

T. What words besides *he* and *she* are used in the place of nouns?

P. Him, her, I, who, etc.

These words are written on the board, under the title of *Pronouns*; and the pupils are informed that this term applies to all words which are used to supply the place of nouns.

Sentences are now placed before the learners, from which they select all the pronouns, writing them in a column by themselves. See Models I and IV.

Other sentences are also given them, from which they select all the nouns, adjectives, verbs, and pronouns, writing them in columns as before. See Models V and IX.

After this, the teacher writes several pronouns on the board, and the pupils form sentences embracing them. See Models II and VI.

They then write sentences including a number of pronouns of their own choice.

MODEL XI.

When the wind blows violently among the trees, they bend, and almost break. Though their roots are very strong, they sometimes yield to the force of the wind, and fall to the ground.

In this manner the pupils secure by frequent repetition what they have before learned, and also cultivate habits of careful comparison and discrimination, by examining the different parts of speech in connection.

THE ADVERB.

§ 6. *Teacher.* In the sentence, "The horse runs very rapidly," what word tells *how* the horse runs?

Pupil. Rapidly.

T. What word, then, does *rapidly* modify?

P. Runs.

T. What part of speech is *runs?*

P. A *verb.*

T. What word in the sentence modifies *rapidly?*

P. Very.

T. In the sentence, "He is an exceedingly diligent scholar," what word modifies *diligent?*

P. Exceedingly.

T. What part of speech is *diligent?*

P. An *adjective.*

T. The words *rapidly, exceedingly,* and *very,* all belong to the same class, and are called *Adverbs. Rapidly* modifies a *verb; exceedingly* modifies an *adjective;* and *very* modifies an *adverb.* Remember, then, that all words which modify *verbs, adjectives,* or *adverbs,* belong to the class of *Adverbs.*

T. Can you think of any other words that are used in this manner?

P. Wisely, here, now, when, etc.

These words are written in another column on the board, under the title of *Adverbs.* When this is done, sentences are again placed before the pupils, from which they select all the adverbs, (Models I and IV,) and others from which they select all the nouns, adjectives, verbs, pronouns, and adverbs. See Models V and IX.

The teacher next writes a number of adverbs on the board, and the learners form sentences which embrace them. See Models V and VI.

After this, they construct sentences containing adverbs selected by themselves, and distinguish all the parts of speech to which they have attended, as in former exercises. See Models VII, X, and XI.

THE PREPOSITION.

§ 7. *Teacher.* When I say, "My hand is over the table," what word expresses the relation of my hand to the table?

Pupil. Over.

T. When I say, "My hand is under the table," what word then expresses the relation between my hand and the table?

P. Under.

T. Mention any other words that express the relation of different things to each other.

P. On, between, in, above, etc.

These words are written in a column on the board, under the word *Prepositions.* The pupils are told, at the same time, that every word which is used to express the relation of one word to another belongs to this class.

Sentences are now given to the pupils, from which they select the prepositions; and others, from which they select all the classes of words which they have learned. See Models VIII and IX.

They then proceed to construct sentences containing prepositions assigned by the teacher; and others embracing examples of their own selection. See Models VI and XI.

THE CONJUNCTION.

§ 8. *Teacher.* In the sentence, "I saw James or his brother," what word connects *James* and *brother?*

Pupil. Or.

T. What word connects the different parts or clauses of the sentence, "James went to school, but John remained at home?"

P. But.

T. Can you think of any other words that are used to connect words, or clauses of a sentence?

P. And, nor, if, etc.

These words are written on the board in a column, under the word *Conjunctions;* and the pupils are told that all words used merely as *connectives* belong to this class.

They are then required to select all the conjunctions from given sentences; and afterwards to write sentences containing conjunctions, and others embracing all the parts of speech which they have yet learned. See previous Models.

THE INTERJECTION.

§ 9. *Teacher.* In the expression, "Alas! I am undone," what word is used merely to express strong *feeling* or *emotion?*

Pupil. Alas.

T. Can you name any other words that are used to express strong or sudden *emotion?*

P. Oh, ah, ho, etc.

These words are written in a column on the board; and the pupils are told that they form a class called *Interjections.* They are then directed to write a few sentences containing examples of this part of speech.

GENERAL EXERCISES ON ALL THE PARTS OF SPEECH.

§ 10. Having considered the several classes of words separately, the learners are now prepared to take up a variety of selections from their reading lessons, and classify the different words as they occur; writing those of each part of speech in a column by themselves. See Models V and IX.

They should also devote several lessons to the writing of sentences which embrace copious examples of all the parts of speech; placing an abbreviation over each word, to indicate the class to which it belongs. See Models X and XI.

All exercises of this kind should be made *progressive.* From simple sentences, the learners should advance to the construction of those which are more difficult; from difficult sentences, to short compositions; and from short compositions, to those of greater length.

By pursuing the course here described, the pupils will soon become familiar with the nature of words in common use, and be able to classify them with facility.

MORE PARTICULAR EXAMINATION OF THE PARTS OF SPEECH.

§ 11. The subdivisions of the parts of speech, and their most important offices, may now be brought under consideration.

Nouns.

§ 12. The distinction between *proper* and *common* nouns, and the distinctions of *gender*, *person*, *number*, and *case*, may be severally introduced by familiar interrogative exercises, similar to those which have already been given to aid in distinguishing the parts of speech.

As soon as the pupils understand the nature of proper and common nouns, they may be required to select all the nouns from given sentences, writing the proper nouns in one column and the common nouns in another. They should then construct sentences which embrace examples of both proper and common nouns. (See previous Models.) The other distinctions of nouns may be illustrated and enforced by similar exercises.

Adjectives.

§ 13. The *degrees of comparison* are now taken up, and made the basis of a familiar oral exercise. The distinction between *descriptive* and *definitive* adjectives should also receive some farther attention. These distinctions are next exemplified in written exercises.

Verbs.

§ 14. The *verb* is the most difficult and important of all the parts of speech, and the teacher should make special effort to impart clear and correct views respecting its principal uses.

The assertion or affirmation expressed by the verb may now be explained to the young learner.

The division of verbs into *regular* and *irregular*, and into *transitive* and *intransitive*, with the distinction between the *active* and the *passive voice*, should be introduced and illustrated by practical inductive exercises.

The government of the objective case by a transitive verb, and the agreement of a verb with its subject or nominative, may be explained in this connection.

The writing of illustrative sentences, on the part of the pupils, follows next in order. See previous Models.

It is generally better not to attempt a full exhibition of the *modes* and *tenses*, till pupils have advanced farther in the study. They should, however, be taught at this period to distinguish between *declaratory*, *conditional*, and *interrogative* sentences; and to determine whether the time denoted by a verb is *present*, *past*, or *future*.

A general idea of *participles*, and of *auxiliary* and *compound* verbs, may also be communicated at this time.

Each of these subjects should be explained in the familiar, conversational manner already described; and accompanied by practical exercises in the construction of sentences.

Pronouns, Prepositions, and Conjunctions.

§ 15. The remaining points which demand special consideration in these introductory lessons, are the division of pronouns into *personal*, *relative*, and *interrogative*, together with the *person*, *number*, and *case* of pronouns; the *connection* of words and sentences by conjunctions; and the *relation* expressed by prepositions. These modifications, like those before presented, should be introduced in a familiar and practical manner, and made the basis of exercises in the construction of illustrative sentences.

§ 16. Before closing this course of lessons, the learners should prepare several exercises in composition, exemplifying all the important principles to which they have attended. The first exercise may embrace the different modifications of the noun; the second, those of the adjective; the third, those of the verb; the fourth, those of the pronoun; and the fifth, the principles relating to the remaining parts of speech.

Model XII.

Modifications of the Noun.

I am highly gratified, my dear friend, to learn of your safe return from

Ohio. My brother and sister expect to leave Boston in about two weeks. They will spend a few days at Springfield, in compliance with your father's kind invitation.— I, Thomas Smith, have written this short composition.

Common Nouns. — Friend, return, brother, sister, weeks, days, compliance, father's, invitation, composition.

Proper Nouns. — Ohio, Boston, Springfield, Thomas Smith.

Noun in the Masculine Gender. — Brother, father's, Thomas Smith.

Noun in the Feminine Gender. — Sister.

Nouns in the Neuter Gender. — Return, Ohio, Boston, weeks, days, Springfield, compliance, invitation, composition.

Noun in the Common Gender. — Friend.

Noun in the First Person. — Thomas Smith.

Noun in the Second Person. — Friend.

Nouns in the Third Person. — Return, Ohio, brother, sister, Boston, weeks, days, Springfield, compliance, father's, invitation, composition.

Nouns in the Singular Number. — Friend, return, Ohio, brother, sister, Boston, Springfield, compliance, father's, invitation, Thomas Smith, composition.

Nouns in the Plural Number. — Weeks, days.

Nouns in the Nominative Case. — Brother, sister, Thomas Smith.

Noun in the Possessive Case. — Father's.

Nouns in the Objective Case. — Return, Ohio, Boston, weeks, days, Springfield, compliance, invitation, composition.

Noun in the Case Independent. — Friend.

§ 17. After the pupils have in this manner exemplified the various modifications of all the parts of speech, they should be required to write several compositions of considerable length, and parse each word by itself. Thus, in parsing a noun, the learner should tell why it is a noun; whether it is proper or common, and why; its gender, and why; person, and why; number, and why; case, and why. If it is in the nominative case, he should point out the verb of which it is the subject; if in the possessive, the noun denoting the object possessed; if in the objective, the word which governs it. A similar course should be adopted in parsing all the other parts of speech.

ENGLISH GRAMMAR.

§ 18. GRAMMAR is the science which treats of the principles of language.

English Grammar teaches the art of speaking and writing the English Language correctly.

§ 19. Grammar is divided into four parts; — *Orthography, Etymology, Syntax,* and *Prosody.*

Orthography treats of letters, and the proper method of combining them to form syllables and words.

Etymology treats of the classification of words, their derivation, and their various modifications.

Syntax treats of the construction of sentences, according to the established laws of speech.

Prosody treats of accent, quantity, and the laws of versification.

PART I.
ORTHOGRAPHY.

§ 20. ORTHOGRAPHY treats of letters, and the proper method of combining them to form syllables and words.

LETTERS.

§ 21. A *letter* is a mark or character used to represent an elementary sound of the human voice.

The word *letter*, like many other terms used in orthography, is often applied to the sound represented, as well as the written character.

The letters of a language, taken collectively, are called its *Alpha-*

What is grammar? What does English grammar teach? How is grammar divided? Of what does Orthography treat? Etymology? Syntax? Prosody? What is a letter? What are the letters of a language called?

bet. The English alphabet consists of twenty-six letters, which have the following different forms: —

Roman.		Italic.		Old English.		Script.		Names.
Capital.	Small.	Capital.	Small.	Capital.	Small.	Capital.	Small.	
A	a	*A*	*a*	𝔄	𝔞	𝒜	𝒶	A.
B	b	*B*	*b*	𝔅	𝔟	ℬ	𝒷	Bee.
C	c	*C*	*c*	ℭ	𝔠	𝒞	𝒸	See.
D.	d	*D*	*d*	𝔇	𝔡	𝒟	𝒹	Dee.
E	e	*E*	*e*	𝔈	𝔢	ℰ	ℯ	E.
F	f	*F*	*f*	𝔉	𝔣	ℱ	𝒻	Eff.
G	g	*G*	*g*	𝔊	𝔤	𝒢	𝑔	Jee.
H	h	*H*	*h*	ℌ	𝔥	ℋ	𝒽	Aitch.
I	i	*I*	*i*	ℑ	𝔦	ℐ	𝒾	I.
J	j	*J*	*j*	𝔍	𝔧	𝒥	𝒿	Jay.
K	k	*K*	*k*	𝔎	𝔨	𝒦	𝓀	Kay.
L	l	*L*	*l*	𝔏	𝔩	ℒ	𝓁	Ell.
M	m	*M*	*m*	𝔐	𝔪	ℳ	𝓂	Em.
N	n	*N*	*n*	𝔑	𝔫	𝒩	𝓃	En.
O	o	*O*	*o*	𝔒	𝔬	𝒪	ℴ	O.
P	p	*P*	*p*	𝔓	𝔭	𝒫	𝓅	Pee.
Q	q	*Q*	*q*	𝔔	𝔮	𝒬	𝓆	Kue.
R	r	*R*	*r*	𝔕	𝔯	ℛ	𝓇	Ar.
S	s	*S*	*s*	𝔖	𝔰	𝒮	𝓈	Ess.
T	t	*T*	*t*	𝔗	𝔱	𝒯	𝓉	Tee.
U	u	*U*	*u*	𝔘	𝔲	𝒰	𝓊	U.
V	v	*V*	*v*	𝔙	𝔳	𝒱	𝓋	Vee.
W	w	*W*	*w*	𝔚	𝔴	𝒲	𝓌	Double-u
X	x	*X*	*x*	𝔛	𝔵	𝒳	𝓍	Eks.
Y	y	*Y*	*y*	𝔜	𝔶	𝒴	𝓎	Wy.
Z	z	*Z*	*z*	ℨ	𝔷	𝒵	𝓏	Zee.

U and *v* were formerly considered the same letter, and were used indiscriminately, the one for the other; as, *haue* for *have*, and *chvrch* for *church*.

The sounds of *i* and *j* were both originally represented by the letter *i*; as, *Iames* for *James*.

When the diphthongs *æ* and *œ* have either of the sounds of *e*, the letters are united in printing.

Examples: — Ægis, diæresis, œsophagus, antœci.

CAPITALS AND ITALICS.

§ 22. The following classes of words should commence with capital letters: —

1. The first word of a sentence.
2. The first word of every line in poetry.
3. The first word of a direct quotation.

Examples: — And Nathan said unto David, " *Thou* art the man."— Remember the ancient maxim, " *Know* thyself."

An *indirect* quotation may be introduced without the use of a capital.

Example: — It is recorded of him who " *spake* three thousand proverbs," that " *his* songs were a thousand and five."

4. Words used as names of the Deity.

Examples: — " Our *Father*, who art in Heaven." — " Remember now thy *Creator*, in the days of thy youth."

5. Proper names and titles of honor or distinction.

Examples: — The city of *Boston*; — The *Honorable Daniel Webster*; Sir *Matthew Hale*; — *Pliny* the *Younger*.

6. Common nouns personified.

Examples: — " If *Pain* comes into a heart, he is quickly followed by *Pleasure*; and if *Pleasure* enters, you may be sure that *Pain* is not far off."—*Addison*.

" And *Discipline* at length,
O'erlooked and unemployed, fell sick and died.
Then *Study* languished, *Emulation* slept,
And *Virtue* fled." — *Cowper*.

What are the several classes of words which commence with capitals?

7. Every important word in a phrase used as a title or caption.

Examples: — "*Prescott's History* of the *Conquest* of *Mexico.*" — "*Virtue* the only true *Source* of *Nobility.*" — "The *American Board* of *Commissioners* for *Foreign Missions.*" — "The *New York Historical Society.*" — "The *American Revolution.*"

The pronoun *I* and the interjection *O* should also be written in capitals.

Examples: — "Must *I* endure all this?" — "Come forth, *O* ye children of gladness, come!"

Most adjectives derived from proper names should commence with capitals.

Examples: — "A *Grecian* education was considered necessary to form the *Roman* orator, poet, or artist." — *Whelpley.* "The *Copernican* system is that which is held to be the true system of the world." — *Olmsted.*

A personal pronoun referring to the Deity is sometimes commenced with a capital.

Examples: — "All that we possess is God's, and we are under obligation to use it all as *He* wills." — *Wayland.*

"Will *He* not hear thee
Who the young ravens heareth from their nest?
Will *He* not guard thy rest?" — *Hemans.*

There are also numerous cases in which words may commence either with capitals or small letters, according to the taste of the writer.

Short, detached pieces of writing, are often composed entirely of capitals. For examples, see title-pages, heads of chapters and sections, monumental inscriptions, cards, etc.

§ 23. *Italic* letters are those which stand *inclining.* (See the Alphabet, p. 26.) *This sentence is printed in Italics.*

When an author wishes to distinguish any particular word or phrase, for the sake of emphasis, or for any other purpose, it is generally printed in Italics.

[The questions and directions which are printed in Italics, are designed to be omitted by beginners.]

What two words of one letter are always written and printed in capitals? What adjectives usually commence with capitals? What are Italic letters? For what purpose are they employed?

Examples: — "If we regard enunciation and pronunciation as the *mechanical* part of elocution; inflection, emphasis, and pausing, may be designated as its *intellectual* part." — *Russell.* "To be perfectly polite, one must have great *presence of mind*, with a delicate and quick *sense of propriety*." — *Mrs. Chapone.*

When a word is used merely as a *word*, it should generally be printed in Italics.

Examples: — "The adjective *same* is often used as a substitute." — *Webster.* "*Who* is applied to persons, and *which* to animals and inanimate things." — *Murray.*

Words and phrases introduced into English writings from foreign languages, are generally expressed in Italics.

Examples: — "An adjournment *sine die*, is an adjournment without fixing the time of resuming business." — *Webster's Dict.* "The White Pine is, *par excellence*, a New England tree." — *N. A. Review.*

Sentences of special importance are often printed entirely in Italics.

When a particular word, phrase, or sentence, is designed to be made still more conspicuous than it would be if expressed in Italics, it is printed in capitals.

Examples: — "OBSERVATION and EXPERIMENT constitute the basis of the science of Mechanics." — *Olmsted.* "To the numerous class of young men in the United States, who are mainly dependent on their own resources for knowledge, or respectability, one of the most important counsels of wisdom which can be addressed, is, STUDY YOUR OWN CHARACTER AND PROSPECTS." — *B. B. Edwards.*

When a word or phrase, embraced in an *Italic sentence*, is to be distinguished from the rest, it is generally printed in *Roman* letters. If it is particularly important, it should be expressed in capitals.

Examples: — "*The grand clew to all syntactical parsing is* the *sense.*" — *G. Brown.* "HYDROSTATICS *is that branch of Natural Philosophy which treats of the mechanical properties and agencies of* LIQUIDS." — *Olmsted.* "*To find the surface of a* REGULAR SOLID." — *Day.*

Select examples. Specify the several circumstances which require the use of Italics. How is a word or phrase rendered still more conspicuous than it would be if expressed in Italics? How is a word or phrase distinguished from the rest, in an Italic sentence?

In the common English version of the Scriptures, Italics are used to indicate those words which are not found in the original.

Examples: — "After two days was *the feast of* the passover;" — in the original, "After two days was the passover." "There are yet four months, and *then* cometh the harvest;" — in the original, "There are yet four months, and the harvest cometh."

§ 24. In *writing*, it is customary to underline such words as would be italicized in printing.

Example.

"*It does not seem possible, even after the testimony of our senses.*"

EXERCISES.

[After studying attentively the rules respecting the use of capitals and Italics, pupils should be required to select from other works a variety of examples to which they respectively apply. The following directions will serve as a guide in performing this exercise. Those which are printed in Italics, are designed to be omitted by beginners.]

§ 25. Point out examples of words commencing with capitals at the beginning of a sentence; — *at the beginning of a direct quotation.* Select several names representing the Deity, which commence with capitals; — several examples of proper names and honorary titles. *Examples of common nouns personified; — of important words in a title or caption.* Examples of the pronoun *I* and the interjection *O*. *Examples of adjectives derived from proper names.* Examples of short pieces of writing, printed entirely in capitals.

Point out examples of important words and phrases, printed in Italics. *Examples of entire sentences in Italics. Examples of words, phrases, and sentences, in capitals. Examples, in Italic sentences, of words, and phrases, printed in capitals or small Roman letters.* Examples of words used merely as words. *Examples of foreign words and phrases employed in English writings. Examples of Italic words in the Scriptures.*

For what purpose are Italics employed in our translation of the Scriptures? Select examples. How are important words and phrases distinguished in *writing?*

Write a sentence containing some prominent word or phrase, and distinguish it from the rest by underlining it.

VOWELS AND CONSONANTS.

§ 26. The most general division of letters is into *vowels* and *consonants*.

A *vowel** is a letter which represents a free and uninterrupted sound of the human voice. The vowels are *a, e, i, o, u,* and sometimes *w* and *y*.

A *consonant*† is a letter which represents a sound that is materially modified by some interruption during its passage through the organs of speech.

The consonants are *b, c, d, f, g, j, k, l, m, n, p, q, r, s, t, v, x, z,* and sometimes *w* and *y*. *H*, which is a simple breathing, is also classed with the consonants.‡

What is the most general division of letters? What is a vowel? Enumerate the vowels. What is a consonant? Enumerate the consonants.

---

* "A vowel is an utterance of the voice receiving its peculiar character from the *position* of the organs; and a consonant is an *action* of the organs of speech, accompanied by breath or voice." — *Smart.*
"A vowel is an elemental sound which may be formed without bringing the articulating organs into contact with any part of the mouth. A consonant is an elemental sound which cannot be formed but by some contact between the parts of the mouth." — *Day.* See also Walker's Principles of English Pronunciation, Webster's Dictionary, and Wright's Orthography.

† A consonant has commonly been defined "a letter which cannot be perfectly sounded without the aid of a vowel;" but this seems not to be the true idea of this class of letters. In pronouncing a syllable commencing with a consonant, a distinct sound is always uttered before the vowel sound is commenced; and we have many syllables in which the vowel though written, is not heard at all in pronunciation, as in the words *taken, burdened,* which are pronounced *tak-n, burd-nd.* There are instances, also, in which a consonant is sounded as a distinct syllable, without the use even of a written vowel, as in the words *chas-m, rhyth-m.* See Fowler.
The etymology of the term *consonant* (*sounding with*) seems to have misled many grammarians, and thus aided in perpetuating the error here alluded to.

‡ "The claims of *h* to be regarded as a letter have been denied by many

W is a consonant when it is not preceded by a vowel in the same syllable; as in *win, swift, thwart.*

W is usually considered as a vowel, when it follows another vowel in the same syllable; as in *new, how.*

Y is a consonant when it begins a syllable, and is immediately followed by a vowel in the same syllable; as in *yet, youth.*

In all other cases, *y* is a vowel; as in *very, rhyme, beryl.*

§ 27. Vowel sounds are called *open* or *close*, according to the relative size of the opening through which the voice passes in forming them. Thus, *a* in *father*, and *o* in *nor*, are called *open* sounds, because they are formed by a wide opening of the organs of speech; while *e* in *me*, and *u* in *rule*, are called *close* sounds, because the organs are nearly closed in uttering them.

§ 28. Two vowels combined in the same syllable, are called a *diphthong;* as in *coil.*

A diphthong in which both vowels are sounded, is called a *proper* diphthong; as in *oil, boy.*

A diphthong in which only one of the vowels is sounded, is called an *improper* diphthong, or *digraph;* as in *rain, eat, believe.*

§ 29. Three vowels combined in the same syllable, are called a *triphthong;* as in *eye, awe, lieu, beauty.*

§ 30. Those consonant sounds which are formed by the vocal organs, during the passage of a mere *breathing*, are called *aspirates.* They are represented by *p* in *map, t* in *hut, k* in *book, f* in *fine, s* in *see, th* in *thin, sh* in *ash, ch* in *church*, and *h* in *hero.*

When is w a consonant? Examples. When a vowel? Examples When is y a consonant? Examples. When a vowel. Examples. Explain the terms open *and* close, *as applied to vowels.* Define a diphthong. Examples. *A proper diphthong. Examples. An improper diphthong. Examples.* A triphthong. Examples. *What consonants are called aspirates? Enumerate them.*

---

grammarians; and certainly, when it is remembered that the sound of this letter is produced by a mere emission of the breath, without any conformation of the organs of speech, this opinion would seem well-founded. There are others, however, who insist that there is no feature in the sound or qualities of this letter, which it does not possess in common with some other consonants; and consequently any attempt to invalidate its claim to the distinction, militates equally against them "— *B*…*de's Ene*

VOWELS.

§ 31. The cognate or corresponding sounds, which are respectively formed by a similar disposition of the organs, during the passage of the *voice*, are called *vocal* consonants. They are represented by *b* in *but*, *d* in *did*, *g* in *go*, *v* in *vain*, *z* in *zero*, *th* in *that*, *z* in *azure*, and *j* in *just*. In a natural whisper, these sounds cannot, of themselves, be readily distinguished from the corresponding aspirates. *H* has no cognate.

Cognates,
{ Vocal   *b*, *d*, *g*, *v*, *z*,* *th*,† *z*,§ *j*.
{ Aspirate *p*, *t*, *k*, *f*, *s*, *th*,‡ *sh*, *ch*.

§ 32. The remaining sounds, *m* in *man*, *n* in *no*, *ng* in *sing*, *l* in *look*, *r* in *race*, *w* in *world*, and *y* in *youth*, though produced by the voice, may also be distinctly uttered in a whisper. They are hence called *intermediate* or *neutral* consonants. In forming the first three of these, — *m*, *n*, and *ng*, — the voice is made to pass principally through the nose, and they are on this account called *nasal* consonants.

WORDS AND SYLLABLES.

§ 33. A *word* is a letter or combination of letters, used as the sign of an idea; as, *I, man, science, extemporaneous.*

§ 34. A *syllable* is a word or a part of a word, which is pronounced by a single impulse of the voice; as, *art, ar-tic-u-la-tion.*

Most syllables are written with at least one vowel; but in many words the vowel of the final syllable is silent, as in *sea-son, whis-tle, hap-pened.*

What are vocal consonants? Enumerate them. What aspirate is the cognate of b *?—of* d *?—of* g *in* go *?—of* v *?—of* z *in* zero *?—of* th *in* that *?—of* z *in* azure *?—of* j *in* just *? Which of the aspirates has no cognate? What are intermediate or neutral consonants? Enumerate them. Which are the nasal consonants? Why so called? What is a word? Examples. What is a syllable? Examples. Name a syllable which has no vowel sound?*

---

* *Z* in *zero*.   † *Th* in *that*.   ‡ *Th* in *thin*.   § *Z* in *azure*

A word of one syllable is called a *monosyllable;* one of two syllables, a *dissyllable;* one of three, a *trisyllable;* and one of more than three, a *polysyllable;* as, in, intend, intention, intentionally.

§ 35. Words are divided into two general classes;—*primitive* and *derivative.*

A *primitive* or *radical* word is one that is not derived from any other word or words in the language; as, *hill, tree, kind, consider.*

A *derivative* word is one that is formed from some primitive word or words in the language; as, *hillock, kindness, inconsiderate.*

§ 36. Words are also divided into two other classes, called *simple* and *compound.*

A *simple* word is one that is not formed by uniting other words; as, *hand, fortune.*

A *compound* word is one that is formed by joining two or more simple words, without materially modifying either; as, *book-seller, rail-road, common-place book.*

Division of Words into Syllables.

§ 37. As a general principle, it may be observed, that the syllables of a word are those divisions which are made in a correct pronunciation of it. See § 275, Note.

The following are perhaps the only *definite* rules that can be given on this subject:—

1. Two consonants forming but one sound, as *ng, ch, th, sh, ph, wh,* are never separated. Thus, we write *church-es, wor-thy, feath-er, ring-ing, a-while.*

2. Compound words are commonly separated into the simple words of which they are composed; as, *care-less, bee-hive, rail-road.*

3. In expressing the past tense and perfect participle of regular verbs, the termination *ed,* though not always pronounced separately, is regarded in writing as a distinct syllable; as, *lov-ed, burn-ed.* See § 86, Rem. 2.

What is a word of one syllable called?—of two?—of three?—of more than three? Into what two general classes are words divided? What is a primitive word? Examples. A derivative word? Examples. A simple word? Examples. A compound word? Examples. What are the syllables of a word? What three rules are given respecting the division of words into syllables?

PART II.

ETYMOLOGY.

§ 38. ETYMOLOGY treats of the classification of words, their derivation, and their various modifications.

PARTS OF SPEECH.

§ 39. The different classes into which words are divided are called *Parts of Speech.*

There are in English *eight** parts of speech; namely, the *Noun*, the *Adjective*,† the *Pronoun*, the *Verb*, the *Adverb*, the *Preposition*, the *Conjunction*, and the *Interjection*.

A *Noun* is a word used to express the *name* of an object; as, *America, man, book, wisdom.*

An *Adjective* is a word joined to a noun or pronoun, to qualify or define its meaning; as, *honest* men; *ten* days; *this* book.

A *Pronoun* is a word used to supply the place of a

Of what does Etymology treat? What are the different classes of words called? Enumerate the parts of speech. What is a noun? Examples. An adjective? Examples. A pronoun? Examples.

---

* "I adopt the usual distribution of words into eight classes, because, if any number, in a thing so arbitrary, must be fixed upon, this seems to be as comprehensive and distinct as any." — *Priestley.*

The division of words into eight classes is also adopted by Butler, Frazee Swett, Fowle, E. Oliver, Lindsay, Hort, M'Culloch, Connon, D'Orsey, Willard, Robbins, S. Barrett, Fowler, Barnes, Whiting, Weld, Greene, and others.

† For note respecting the articles, see p. 58.

noun; as, "When Cæsar had conquered Gaul, *he* turned *his* arms against *his* country."

A *Verb* is a word that expresses an assertion or affirmation; as, I *am;* I *love;* I *am loved.*

An *Adverb* is a word used to modify the sense of a verb, an adjective, or another adverb; as, "He is *not* understood;" — "A *remarkably* diligent boy;" — "She reads *very correctly.*"

A *Preposition* is a word used to express the relation of a noun or pronoun depending upon it, to some other word in the sentence; as, "He went *from* Boston *to* Albany;" — "Washington was the father *of* his country."

A *Conjunction* is a word that is used to connect words or sentences; as, "Seven *and* five are twelve;" — "Straws swim on the surface; *but* pearls lie at the bottom."

An *Interjection* is an exclamatory word, used merely to express some passion or emotion; as, *Oh! ah! alas!*

THE NOUN.

§ 40. A *Noun** is a word used to express the *name* of an object; as, *America, man, book, wisdom.*

This part of speech not only embraces the names of *material* objects, as *horse, tree, carriage;* but it also includes the name of every thing that can be *conceived to exist,* as *hope, virtue, strength.*

What is a verb? Examples. An adverb? Examples. A preposition? Examples. A conjunction? Examples. An interjection? Examples. What is a noun? Examples. What names, besides those of **material** objects, are embraced under this part of speech? Examples.

---

* *Noun* is derived from the Latin word *nomen,* which signifies *a name.*

§ 41. Nouns are of two kinds; — *proper* and *common*.

1. A *proper noun* is a name used to distinguish an *individual* object from others of the same class; as, *George, Boston, Ontario, Vesuvius, January*.

Rem. — The particular names of nations, ranges of mountains, and groups of islands, are generally classed with proper nouns; as, The *Jews*, The *Andes*, The *Azores*.

Observation. — The pupil should be careful to discriminate between a proper name used to distinguish an *individual* object, and the same word used to denote a *class* or *species*. Thus, when we say, "The *Prussians* are distinguished for their system of free schools," *Prussians* is a *proper* noun, because it is used to distinguish a *particular* nation from all other nations; but, in the sentence, "I saw several Prussians in Paris," the word *Prussians* becomes a *common* noun, because it may be applied in the same sense to any other portion of the whole *class* of individuals composing the kingdom of Prussia. So also in the expression, "He is the *Cicero* of his age," the word *Cicero* is employed to denote a *class*, and is applicable in this sense to other individuals in common with the celebrated Roman orator.

2. A *common noun* is a name that may be applied to any one of a whole *class* of objects; as, *desk, house, town, scholar*.

§ 42. Common nouns embrace also the particular classes, termed *abstract, participial*, and *collective*.

1. An *abstract noun* is the name of a quality considered apart from the object to which it belongs; as, *hardness, strength, wisdom, benevolence*. Thus, in the phrase, *beautiful flower*, the quality denoted by the word *beautiful*, when considered as separated from the object *flower*, is expressed by the abstract noun *beauty*.

Into what classes are nouns divided? What is a proper noun? Examples. *What of the particular names of nations, groups of islands, &c.? Examples. Show how the same word may be either a proper or a common noun. Examples.* What is a common noun? Examples. *What particular classes are embraced under common nouns? What is an abstract noun? Illustrate. Examples.*

2. A *participal noun* is a word that has the form of a participle, and performs the office of a noun; as, "They could not avoid sub- mitting to this influence."

Rem.—There are a few words ending in *ing*, as *morning, evening*, which are not embraced in this class, since they are not derived from verbs.

3. A *collective noun*, or *noun of multitude*, is a name that denotes a collection of many individuals; as, *school, flock, people, assembly*.

EXERCISES.

§ 43. Ship, London, army, Alps, virtue, industry, Palestine, mountain, field, pleasure, France, assembly.

Which of the foregoing nouns are common? Which proper? *Which abstract? Which collective?*

"Paris is the metropolis of France."—"In the days of youth, the multitude eagerly pursue pleasure as their chief good."—"Industry is the law of our being. It is the demand of nature, of reason, and of God."—"This was said in the hearing of the witness."

Mention the nouns in the foregoing sentences. Which are common? Which proper? *Which are abstract? Which participial? Which collective?*

Write a sentence containing both a common and a proper noun. *One containing an abstract noun; — a participial noun; — a collective noun.*

PROPERTIES.

§ 44. The properties belonging to nouns are *gender, person, number*, and *case*.

GENDER.

§ 45. Gender is the distinction of objects in regard to sex.

There are four* genders;— the *masculine*, the *feminine*, the *common*, and the *neuter*.

What is a participial noun? Examples. What is a collective noun? Examples. What properties have nouns? What is gender? What are the different genders?

---

* Since there are but two sexes, some critics have contended that we

1. Nouns that denote males, are of the *masculine gender;* as, *man, brother, king, father.*

2. Nouns that denote females, are of the *feminine gender;* as, *woman, sister, queen, mother.*

3. Nouns that are applicable alike to both sexes, are of the *common gender;* as, *parent, child, friend.*

4. Nouns that denote objects neither male nor female, are of the *neuter gender;* as, *rock, wind, paper, knowledge.*

REM. 1.—Nouns of the masculine or feminine gender are frequently used in a general sense, including both sexes; as, "And with thee will I break in pieces the *horse* and *his* rider."—*Jer.* 51 : 21. "Go to the *ant,* thou sluggard; consider *her* ways, and be wise."—*Prov.* 6: 6.

REM. 2.— When we speak of males and females of our own species without regard to sex, we generally employ a term in the masculine gender; as, "*Man* is mortal;"— "The *authors* and *poets* of the age."

REM. 3.— In speaking of young children, and of animate objects whose sex is unknown, we often employ the neuter pronoun *it;* as, "The child was well when I saw *it;*"—"He caught the bird, but *it* soon escaped from him."

REM. 4. — In the English language, the gender of nouns follows the order of nature; but in the Greek, Latin, and German tongues, the grammatical genders are frequently assigned without regard to sex; while in the French, Italian, etc., which have no neuter gender, every object is, of necessity, regarded as grammatically masculine or feminine.

REM. 5. — By a figure of speech called *Personification,* gender is sometimes attributed to objects without sex. Thus, the *sun, time, death,* etc., are usually considered as masculine; and *the earth, a ship, virtue,* etc., are commonly characterized as feminine.

OBS. 1.— This figurative mode of expression, by which we give life

---

What nouns are of the masculine gender? Examples. What of the feminine? Examples. What of the common? Examples. What of the neuter? Examples.

---

have properly no more than two genders. This reasoning would be satisfactory if the word *gender* were synonymous with *sex;* but the best grammarians have uniformly employed it in a less restricted sense, to express "distinction in regard to sex." As some names denote males, some females, some objects of either sex, and some objects of no sex, it is obvious that, in regard to sex, there must be four distinct classes of nouns. In designating these classes, grammarians have found it convenient to employ the terms *masculine, feminine, common,* and *neuter* gender. See Frazee, Goldsbury, Hall, R. C. Smith, Parker and Fox, Pickett, Goodenow, Fowle, Parkhurst, Sanborn, Willard, Webber, Perley, Felch, Barrett, C. Adams, Cooper, Granville, Beall, Booth, Crane, Pinnock, Smart, Sutcliffe, Weld, Fowler, Pinneo, Mulligan, Goodwin, and De Sacy.

and sex to things inanimate, contributes greatly to the force and beauty of our language, and renders it, in this respect, superior to the polished languages of Greece and Rome.

OBS. 2. — No fixed rule can be given to determine, in all cases, which gender should be assigned to inanimate objects personified. Those which are distinguished for masculine qualities, as energy, boldness, or strength, are generally regarded as masculine; and those which are distinguished for feminine qualities, as beauty, mildness, or timidity, are generally characterized as feminine. Abstract nouns, and the names of ships, cities, and countries, are usually considered as feminine.

Examples: — "They arrived too late to save the *ship;* for the violent current had set *her* more and more upon the bank." — *Irving.*

"Statesmen scoffed at *Virtue,* and *she* avenged herself by bringing their counsels to nought." — *Bancroft.*

"*Earth,* with *her* thousand voices, praises God." — *Coleridge.*

"Where rolls the *Oregon,* and hears no sound,
Save *his* own dashing." — *Bryant.*

"The *oak*
Shall send *his* roots abroad and pierce thy mould." — *Ibid.*

"And see where surly *Winter* passes off,
Far to the north, and calls *his* ruffian blasts." — *Thomson.*

§ 46. The distinction between males and females is expressed in three different ways.

1. By the use of different words: —

Masculine.	Feminine.	Masculine.	Feminine.
Beau	belle	Lad	lass
Boy	girl	Landlord	landlady
Brother	sister	Lord	lady
Buck	doe	Male	female
Drake	duck	Man	woman
Earl	countess	Master	mistress
Father	mother	Master	miss
Friar *or* monk	nun	Nephew	niece
Gander	goose	Papa	mamma
Gentleman	lady	Son	daughter
Hart	roe	Stag	hind
Horse	mare	Uncle	aunt
Husband	wife	Wizard	witch
King	queen		

2. By a difference of termination: —

Masculine.	Feminine.	Masculine.	Feminine.
Abbot	abbess	Adulterer	adulteress
Actor	actress	Ambassador	ambassadress
Administrator	administratrix	Arbiter	arbitress

In what three ways is the distinction between males and females expressed? Examples of each.

NOUNS.

Masculine	Feminine	Masculine	Feminine
Author	authoress	Landgrave	landgravine
Baron	baroness	Lion	lioness
Bridegroom	bride	Marquis	marchioness
Benefactor	benefactress	Margrave	margravine
Caterer	cateress	Negro	negress
Chanter	chantress	Patron	patroness
Conductor	conductress	Peer	peeress
Count	countess	Poet	poetess
Czar	czarina	Prior	prioress
Dauphin	dauphiness	Prophet	prophetess
Deacon	deaconess	Protector	protectress
Don	donna	Priest	priestess
Duke	duchess	Prince	princess
Emperor	empress	Shepherd	shepherdess
Enchanter	enchantress	Songster	songstress
Executor	executrix	Sorcerer	sorceress [tana
Giant	giantess	Sultan	sultaness *or* sul-
Governor	governess	Tailor	tailoress
Heir	heiress	Testator	testatrix
Hero	heroine	Tiger	tigress
Hunter	huntress	Tutor	tutoress
Host	hostess	Viscount	viscountess
Instructor	instructress	Votary	votaress
Jew	Jewess	Widower	widow

3. By prefixing another word: —

Masculine.	Feminine.	Masculine.	Feminine.
Man-servant	*maid*-servant	*He*-goat	*she*-goat
Male-child	*female*-child		

Some words are used only in the feminine; as, *Amazon, brunette, dowager, shrew, syren, virago.*

PERSON.

§ 47. *Person*, in grammar, is that property which distinguishes the speaker, the person or thing addressed, and the person or thing spoken of.

Nouns have three persons; — the *first*, the *second*, and the *third*.

1. The *first person* denotes the speaker; as, "The salutation of *me, Paul*, with *mine* own hand."

2. The *second person* denotes the person or thing spoken

What is person? Name the persons. What does the first person denote? Examples. The second? Examples.

to; as, "These are thy glorious works, *Parent* of good;" "Come, gentle *Spring.*"

3. The *third person* denotes the person or thing spoken of; as, "*Dependence* and *obedience* belong to *youth.*"

REM. — The third person is occasionally employed for the first or second. Thus, Solomon, addressing the Deity, says of himself, "Thy servant is in the midst of thy people, which thou hast chosen." So also, Moses, in narrating the events of his own life, speaks of himself just as he would speak of any other person. In the following example, the third person is employed for the second: — "And Jonathan spake good of David unto Saul his father, and said unto him, Let not the *king* sin against *his* servant, against David."

EXERCISES.

§ 48. Mention the gender of each of the following nouns: —

Bell, uncle, cherry, girl, neighbor, sister, tree, rose, grass.

Mention three nouns in the masculine gender; — three in the feminine; — three in the common; — three in the neuter. Give an example of a noun in the first person; — in the second; — in the third.

Write a sentence containing a noun in the masculine gender; — in the feminine; — in the common; — in the neuter. One containing a noun in the first person; — in the second; — in the third.

NUMBER.

§ 49. Number is the distinction of *one* from *more than one.*

Nouns have two numbers; — the *singular* and the *plural.*

1. The *singular number* denotes but one object; as, *day, book, volume.*

2. The *plural number* denotes more objects than one; as, *days, books, volumes.*

What does the third person denote? Examples. What is number? What numbers have nouns? What does the singular number denote? Examples. What does the plural number denote? Examples.

§ 50. The plural of nouns is generally formed by adding *s* or *es* to the singular.

1. Words ending in a sound which will unite with the sound of *s*, form the plural by adding *s* only; as, *herd, herds; tree, trees.*

2. Words ending in a sound which will not unite with the sound of *s*, form the plural by adding *es;* as, *fox, foxes; lash, lashes.*

Rem. 1. — But words ending in silent *e*, whose last sound will not combine with the sound of *s*, add *s* only for the plural; as, *rose, roses; voice, voices.*

Rem. 2. — Most nouns ending in *o* preceded by a consonant, form the plural by the addition of *es;* as, *cargo, cargoes; hero, heroes;* but the following nouns are commonly written in the plural with *s* only:— *canto, grotto, junto, memento, portico, quarto, octavo, solo, two, tyro, zero.* There are also a few others, with respect to which, usage is not uniform.

Rem. 3. — Several nouns ending in *f* or *fe*, form the plural by substituting *ves*, for the termination in the singular; as, *loaf, loaves; life, lives; beef, beeves; shelf, shelves; knife, knives.* Others, as *chief, dwarf, fife, grief, gulf, handkerchief, hoof, proof, roof, reproof, safe, scarf, strife, surf, turf,* and most of those ending in *ff*, form the plural regularly; as, *gulf, gulfs; muff, muffs. Staff* has *staves* in the plural, but its compounds are regular; as, *flagstaff, flagstaffs.*

Rem. 4. — Nouns ending in *y* after a consonant, form the plural by changing *y* to *ies;* as, *lady, ladies.* But nouns ending in *y* after a vowel, form the plural regularly; as, *day, days.*

Obs. — Many words ending in *y* were formerly spelled with *ie* in the singular; as, *glorie, vanitie.* The termination *ie*, in the singular, is now laid aside for *y*, while the old plural termination *ies*, is retained; as, *glory, glories; vanity, vanities.*

Rem. 5. — The plurals of the following nouns are variously formed: — *man, men; woman, women; child, children; ox, oxen; mouse, mice; tooth, teeth; goose, geese; foot, feet; brother, brothers* (when applied to persons of the same family); *brother, brethren* (when applied to persons of the same society or profession); *die, dies* (stamps for coining); *die, dice* (small cubes for gaming); *genius, genii* (aërial spirits); *genius, geniuses* (men of genius); *pea, pease* (the species); *pea, peas* (the seeds as distinct objects); *penny, pence* (in computation); *penny, pennies* (as distinct species of coin).

How is the plural of nouns generally formed? What words form the plural by adding s *only? Examples. What words by adding* es *? Examples Give the plural of the following nouns:* — *Man, woman, child, ox, mouth, tooth, mouse, foot, brother, die, genius, pea, penny.*

REM. 6. — *Spoonful, mouse-trap, camera-obscura, Ave-Maria,* and other similar compound nouns, form the plural regularly; as, *spoonfuls, mouse-traps, cameras-obscuras, Ave Marias.* But words composed of an adjective and a noun, or of two nouns connected by a preposition, generally form the plural by adding *s* to the first word; as, *court-martial, courts-martial; knight-errant, knights-errant; aid-de-camp, aids-de-camp; cousin-german, cousins-german; son-in-law, sons-in-law.*

Examples: — " Those who are carried down in *coachfuls* to Westminster-Hall." — *Addison.* " Captains Orme and Morris, the two other *aids-de-camp,* were wounded and disabled." — *Sparks.* " The lunacy as to *knights-errant* remaining unabated." — *Hallam.*

REM. 7. — Letters and numeral figures generally form the plural by adding an apostrophe with the letter *s;* as, Twelve *a's;* three 5's. The plural of words, considered as words merely, is formed in the same manner.

Examples: — " I busied myself in crossing my *t's* and dotting my *i's* very industriously." — *Willis.* "The dividend contains two *x's,* two *y's,* and two *z's.*" — *Young's Algebra.* " Cast all the 9's out of the sum of the figures in each of the two factors." — *Hutton's Mathematics.* " Who, that has any taste, can endure the incessant, quick returns of the *also's,* and the *likewise's,* and the *moreover's,* and the *however's,* and the *notwithstanding's ?* " — *Campbell's Phil. of Rhet.*

REM. 8. — Many nouns adopted from foreign languages, retain their original plurals: —

Alumnus	alumni	Beau	beaux
Amanuensis	amanuenses	Calx	{ calces
Analysis	analyses		calxes
Animalculum	} animalcula*	Cherub	{ cherubim
Animalcule (*Eng.*)			cherubs
Antithesis	antitheses	Chrysalis	chrysalides
Apex	{ apices	Crisis	crises
	apexes	Criterion	{ criteria
Appendix	{ appendices		criterions
	appendixes	Datum	data
Arcanum	arcana	Desideratum	desiderata
Automaton	{ automata	Diæresis	diæreses
	automatons	Dogma	{ dogmas
Axis	axes		dogmata
Bandit	{ banditti	Effluvium	effluvia
	bandits	Ellipsis	ellipses
Basis	bases	Emphasis	emphases

What rule is observed in forming the plural of letters, numerical figures, and words considered merely as words? Examples.

---

* " Animalculæ is a barbarism." — *Smart, adopted by Worcester.*

NOUNS.

Encomium	encomiums / encomia	Memorandum	memoranda / memorandums
Ephemeris	ephemerides	Metamorphosis	metamorphoses
Erratum	errata	Miasma	miasmata
Focus	foci	Momentum	momenta / momentums
Formula	formulas / formulæ	Monsieur	messieurs
Fungus	fungi / funguses	Nebula	nebulæ
Genus	genera	Oasis	oases
Gymnasium	gymnasia / gymnasiums	Parenthesis	parentheses
Hypothesis	hypotheses	Phasis	phases
Ignis fatuus	ignes fatui	Phenomenon	phenomena
Index	indices (referring to algebraic quantities)	Radius	radii
		Scoria	scoriæ
		Scholium	scholia / scholiums
		Seraph	seraphim / seraphs
Index	indexes (pointers, or tables of contents)	Speculum	specula
		Stamen	stamens / stamina
Lamina	laminæ	Stimulus	stimuli
Larva	larvæ	Stratum	strata
Medium	media / mediums	Thesis	theses
		Vortex	vortices

REM. 9. — Some nouns have the same form in both numbers; as, *deer*, *sheep*, *swine*, *trout*, *salmon*, *congeries*, *series*, *species*, *means*, *odds*, *bellows*; *ethics*, *mathematics*, *metaphysics*, *pneumatics*, *optics*, and other similar names of sciences.

REM. 10. — There are also several nouns of number, which do not commonly vary their forms in the plural; as, "Six *dozen*;" "Three *score* and ten."

REM. 11. — The words *horse*, *foot*, and *infantry*, denoting bodies of soldiers, are singular in form, but plural in signification. *Cavalry* is often used in the same manner. The words *cannon*, *sail*, and *head*, are also frequently employed in a plural sense.

Examples: — "Nelson now proceeded to his station with eight *sail* of frigates under his command." — *Southey*. "A body of a thousand *horse* was sent forward to reconnoitre the city." — *Prescott*. "He ordered two *cannon* to be fired." — *Irving*.

REM. 12. — The following words, though sometimes used as singular nouns, are more properly plural: — *alms*, *amends*, *pains*, *riches*, *wages*.

REM. 13. — The following are used only in the plural: —

Annals	Calends	Goods	Lungs
Archives	Clothes	Hatches	Manners
Ashes	Drawers (an article of dress)	Hose (stockings)	Minutiæ
Assets		Hysterics	Morals
Billiards	Dregs	Ides	Nippers
Bitters	Embers	Lees	Nones
Bowels	Entrails	Letters (literature)	Orgies
Breeches	Exuviæ	Literati	Pincers

Pleiads	Shears	Thanks	Vespers
Politics	Snuffers	Tidings	Victuals
Scissors	Statistics	Tongs	Vitals
Shambles			

REM. 14. — Nouns denoting objects which do not admit of plurality, are used only in the singular; as, *gold, silver, wheat, molasses, wine, flour, industry, pride, wisdom.*

OBS. — When, however, different *kinds* or *varieties* are spoken of, words of this class sometimes take the plural form; as, "The *teas* of China."— "He also acquired a lucrative monopoly of *wines.*" — *Bancroft.* In these examples, the different species or classes are signified, and not a number of individual objects of the same class.

REM. 15. — The word *news* is now regarded as singular, though it was formerly used in both numbers. Shakspeare has it most frequently in the plural.

REM. 16. — Proper names are sometimes pluralized like other nouns; as, The two *Scipios*, The *Howards*, The *Johnsons;* but these plural names are not used to designate individuals, and may with more propriety be classed with common nouns.

REM. 17. — Proper names ending in *y* preceded by a consonant, are sometimes pluralized by adding *s* to the singular, as The *Henrys*, The *Ptolemys;* but the regular form, as The *Henries*, The *Ptolemies*, is to be preferred. Proper names ending in *o* preceded by a consonant, are most frequently pluralized by adding *s* to the singular; as, The *Catos*, The *Ciceros.*

REM. 18. — In expressing the plural of a proper name and a title, taken as one complex noun, good writers most frequently annex the plural termination to the title only; as, "The *Misses* Smith." This form is therefore to be preferred.*

Examples: — " The *Misses* Barrett." — *Graham's Magazine.* " The *Misses* Vanhomrigh." — *Edinb. Journal.* "The *Misses* Wood." -- *Boston Courier.* " The *Misses* Fellows." — *H. Winslow.* " The *Messrs.* Carey." — *J. G. Palfrey.* " The *Messrs.* Abbott." — *Judge Hubbard.* " The *Messrs.* Harper." — *N. A. Review.* " *Messrs.* Percy." — *Southey.* " The celebrated *Misses* Davidson." — *R. W. Griswold.*

What of proper names, pluralized? How do writers most frequently form the plural of a proper name and a title, taken as a complex noun? Examples

---

* In forming the plural of proper names to which titles are prefixed, usage is still unsettled. While a majority of our popular writers pluralize the title and not the name, as " The *Misses* Smith," there is also

NOUNS. 47

REM. 19. — The proper names of nations, societies, groups of islands, and chains of mountains, are generally plural; as, *The French, The Moravians, The Azores, The Alps, The Andes.*

EXERCISES.

§ 51. Give the number of each of the following nouns: —

Cloud, vices, knives, life, lyceum, mirth, men, feet, brother.

Give the plural of the following nouns: —

Month, lion, church, poet, woman, thought.

Give the number of the following nouns: —

Oxen, brethren, die, cherubim, data, hypotheses, beaux, analysis, series, means, mathematics, alms, wages, ashes, scissors.

Give the plural of the following nouns: —

Penny, pailful, father-in-law, amanuensis, focus, stratum, erratum, genus, phenomenon.

Write a sentence containing two or more nouns in the singular number; one containing two or more nouns in the plural.

CASE.

§ 52. Case denotes the relation of nouns and pronouns to other words.

Nouns have four cases; — the *nominative*, the *possessive*, the *objective*, and the *independent.**

What is case? What cases have nouns?

---

a large class of writers equally reputable, that pluralize the name and not the title, as "The Miss *Smiths.*"

Examples: — "The Miss *Byleses.*" — *Miss Leslie.* "The Miss *Hornecks.*" — *Irving.* "The two Miss *Flamboroughs.*" — *Goldsmith.*

Besides the two forms already exhibited, there is still another, in which the plural termination is annexed to both the name and the title; as, "The *Misses Smiths.*" This form, though not very common, is occasionally employed by the best writers.

Examples: — "The *Messrs. Harpers.*" — *N. A. Review.* "The *Misses Mores.*" — *B. B. Edwards.* "The two *Misses Beauvoirs.*" — *Blackwood's Magazine.*

* The *nominative* case is defined by the best grammarians, to be "that form or state of a noun or pronoun which denotes the subject of a verb;" and since a noun or pronoun, used *independently,* cannot at the same time

§ 53. The *nominative case* denotes the subject of a finite verb; as, " *Birds* fly; " — " *Life* is short."

All parts of the verb are called *finite*, except the infinitive and the participle.

§ 54. The *possessive case* denotes *ownership* or *possession;* as, " *John's* book; " — " The *sun's* rays."

§ 55. The possessive singular of nouns is generally formed by adding an apostrophe, with the letter *s*, to the nominative; as, nom. *man;* poss. *man's*.

REM. 1. — The possessive of singular nouns ending in the sound of *s* or *z*, is sometimes formed by adding only the apostrophe; as, " *Achilles'* shield." In poetry, this omission of the apostrophic *s* is fully sanctioned by usage; though the regular form is also frequently employed. In prose writings, the *s* may be omitted when its use would occasion a disagreeable succession of hissing sounds.

Examples: — " But we are *Moses'* disciples."—*John* 9 : 28.
" *Achilles'* shield his ample shoulders spread,
Achilles' helmet nodded o'er his head."—*Pope.*
" A train of heroes followed through the field,
Who bore by turns great *Ajax'* seven-fold shield."—*Ibid.*
" As for *Tibullus's* reports,
They never passed for law in courts."—*Swift.*

OBS. — The learner will observe that in pronouncing the word *Moses s*, with the additional *s*, the sound of *z* occurs *three times* in immediate succession; while in such expressions as " Davies's Surveying," the sound of *z* occurs only *twice*, the third *s* retaining its proper sound.

REM. 2. — When the use of the additional *s* does not occasion an

---

What does the nominative case denote ? Examples. The possessive ? Examples. How is the possessive singular generally formed ? Examples. *Under what circumstances is the additional* s *omitted ? Examples.*

---

be employed as " the subject of a verb," there is a manifest impropriety in regarding it as a *nominative.*
" Is there not as much difference between the *nominative* and *independent* case, as there is between the *nominative* and *objective?* If so, why class them together as *one* case ? "—*S. R. Hall.*
" Nouns have four cases ; — the *nominative, possessive, objective,* and *independent."—Felton.*
So also Kenrion, Fowle, J. Flint, Goodenow, Bucke, Hazen, Goldsbury, Peirce, Chapin, S. Alexander, P. Smith, Clark, Pinneo, Dearborn, and Weld.

unpleasant succession of hissing sounds, the regular form is generally to be preferred.*

Examples:—"Mrs. *Hemans's* fine lines on the death of Fergus."—*N. A. Review.* "*Collins's* Odes."—*Southey.* "The character of *Douglas's* original poetry."—*Hallam.* "The original remained in manuscript until *Sands's* writings were collected."—*R. W Griswold.* "*Edwards's* work on the Will."—*Channing.* "*Stephens's* Incidents of Travel."—*N. A. Review.* "*Erasmus's* Dialogues."—*Macaulay.* "*Sandys's* Sermons."—*Hallam.*

OBS.—In some expressions of frequent occurrence, usage has decided in favor of rejecting the additional s, contrary to the general rule. Thus, we say, "For *conscience* sake," and not "For *conscience's* sake."

REM. 3.—Plural nouns ending in s, form the possessive by adding an apostrophe only; as, nom. *fathers;* poss. *fathers'.*

REM. 4.—Plural nouns that do not end in s, form the possessive by adding both the apostrophe and s; as, nom. *men;* poss. *men's.*

REM. 5.—The import of the possessive may, in general, be expressed by the preposition *of.* Thus, for "*Man's* wisdom," we may say, "The wisdom *of man.*"

REM. 6.—The sign 's is a contraction of *es* or *is.* Thus, *man's, king's,* were formerly written *mannes, kinges.*†

How do plural nouns ending in s, *form the possessive?* *Examples.* *How do plural nouns that do not end in* s, *form the possessive?* *Examples.*

---

* With respect to the manner of forming the possessive of singular nouns ending in *s*, the usage of good writers is, to a considerable extent, divided. In a collection of nearly a thousand examples, from the productions of several hundred different authors, about two thirds of the number retain the additional *s*, while the rest reject it. The rule given above has, therefore, for its support, a decided preponderance of reputable usage. It may, however, be remarked, that the apostrophic *s* is at present more frequently omitted than formerly; and it is not improbable, that in the course of another century, usage may require the uniform rejection of the *s* in prose, after words ending in the sound of *s* or *z*.

† Several respectable authors and critics have fallen into the error of regarding this possessive termination as a contraction of the pronoun *his*. "The same single letter (*s*) on many occasions, does the office of a whole word, and represents the *his* or *her* of our forefathers."—*Addison.*

It is true that the word *his* was frequently written after words to form the possessive, by Spencer, Dryden, Pope, and other popular authors, during a period of two or three centuries, as, "*Christ his* sake," "*Socrates his* rules;" but the present contracted form of the possessive was in use still earlier, and our ablest philologists have uniformly referred its origin to the old Saxon termination.

"From the introduction of the Saxons into this island, to the Norman

§ 56. The *objective case* denotes the object of a transitive verb or a preposition; as, " Boys love *play;* "— " The queen of *England.*"

§ 57. The *independent case* denotes that the noun or pronoun is used *absolutely*, having no dependence on any other word; as, " Your *fathers,** where are they ? " — " The *treaty* being concluded, the council was dissolved ; " — " There is no terror, *Cassius,* in your threats; "— " Webster's *Dictionary ;* "— " *Liberty !* *Freedom !* Tyranny is dead ! "

REM. — The nominative, objective, and independent cases of nouns are the same in form, being distinguished only by their relation to other words.

  Nom. *Obj.*   *Nom.* *Obj.*
 John struck James. James struck John.

Here the meaning is reversed by the interchange of the nouns ; the nominative or agent being indicated by its *preceding* the verb, and the object of the action by its *following* the verb. A noun in the independent case is distinguished by its denoting neither subject, object, nor possessor.

DECLENSION.

§ 58. To *decline* a noun, is to express its cases and numbers.

	Singular.	Plural.	Singular.	Plural.
Nom.	Father	fathers	Man	men
Poss.	Father's	fathers'	Man's	men's
Obj.	Father	fathers	Man	men
Ind.	Father	fathers	Man	men

What does the objective case denote ? Examples. What does the independent case denote ? Examples. *What is it to decline a noun ?*

---

conquest, the Saxon genitive was in universal use. From the latter period to the time of Henry II. (1170), though the English language underwent some alterations, we still find the Saxon genitive. In Gavin Douglass, who lived in the beginning of the sixteenth century, we find *is* instead of *es*, thus, *fœderis hands.* In the time of Henry the Eighth, we find, in the works of Sir T. More, both the Saxon and the English genitive; and in a letter written in 1559, by Maitland of Lethington, the English genitive frequently occurs. Had this genitive, then, been an abbreviation for the noun and the pronoun *his,* the use of the words separately would have preceded their abbreviated form in composition. This, however, was not the case."— *Crombie*

See also Wallis's Grammatica Linguæ Anglicanæ, Hickes's Thesaurus, Brightland, Fisher, British Grammar, Fenning, Lowth, Priestley, Ash, Brittain, Grant, Sutcliffe, Latham, Johnson, and Webster.

* For a particular description of the different classes of words in the independent case, see the Remark under the 4th Rule of Syntax.

Rem. — "Susan used Eliza's book." *Susan* is here the subject of the verb, and is therefore in the *nominative* case; *Eliza's* is in the *possessive* case, because it denotes the *owner* of the book; *book* is the object of the action expressed by the verb *used*, and is therefore in the *objective* case.

EXERCISES.

§ 59. "Romulus founded the city of Rome." — "The king's heart is in the hand of the Lord." — "The prophets, do they live forever?" — "A wise man's anger is of short continuance." — "Genius lies buried on our mountains and in our valleys." — "Columns, arches, pyramids, — what are they but heaps of sand?" — "As virtue is its own reward, so vice is its own punishment." — "Venerable men! you have come down to us from a former generation."

Point out the nouns in the foregoing sentences, and give the case of each, with the reason. Give also the gender, person, and number of each, with the reasons.

Write the possessive singular and the possessive plural of the following nouns:
Man, child, body, day, needle.

Write one or more sentences, containing examples of nouns in all the different cases.

THE ADJECTIVE.

§ 60. An *Adjective** is a word joined to a noun or pronoun, to qualify or define its meaning; as, *honest* men; *ten* days; *this* book.

§ 61. Adjectives may be classed under two general divisions; — *descriptive* and *definitive*.†

What is an adjective? Examples. What are the principal classes of adjectives?

---

* The term *adjective* is derived from the Latin word *adjectus*, which signifies *added to*.

† "Adjectives are of two kinds, *defining* and *describing* adjectives.' — *Cardell.* See also Butler, R. W. Green, and Goodenow.

1. A *descriptive adjective* is one that expresses some quality or property of the noun or pronoun to which it belongs; as, a *dutiful* child; a *faithful* friend; *large* trees.

2. A *definitive adjective* is one that defines or limits the meaning of the noun or pronoun to which it belongs; as, *three* days; *these* books; *the** lesson; *all* men.

§ 62. These two general classes of adjectives may also be divided into several others, of which the following are the most important: —

1. A *proper adjective* is one that is derived from a proper name; as, American, Ciceronian.

2. A *numeral adjective* is one that is used to express number; as, one, two, three; first, second, third.

One, two, three, etc., are also denominated *cardinal* adjectives; and *first, second, third*, etc., *ordinal* adjectives.

3. A *pronominal adjective* is a word that partakes of the nature of the pronoun and the adjective.

REM. 1. — When used to define a noun expressed, it is parsed as an adjective; but when employed as a substitute for a word or phrase, it is parsed as a pronoun. Thus, in the sentence, "Some cried *one* thing, and some another," *one* is to be regarded as an adjective; but, in the expression, "Every *one* has his peculiar trials," *one* performs the office of a pronoun or substitute.

REM. 2. — The principal pronominal adjectives are *each, every, either, neither, this, that, these, those, all, any, one, other, another, none, some, such, same, both, several, few, much, many*.

REM. 3. — *Each, every, either*, and *neither*, are called *distributives*, because they denote the persons or things that make up a number, considered separately; as, "*Each* man in his order."

What is a descriptive adjective? Examples. What is a definitive adjective? Examples. *Into what other classes are adjectives divided? What is a proper adjective? Examples. A numeral adjective? Examples. A pronominal adjective? When is a pronominal adjective parsed as an adjective, and when as a pronoun? Illustrate. What are some of the principal pronominal adjectives? Which of the pronominal adjectives are called distributives, and why?*

---

* See note respecting the articles p 53.

Rem. 4. — *This, that, these,* and *those,* are called *demonstratives,* because they point out precisely the objects to which they refer.

Rem. 5. — *Both* denotes two objects taken together. *Another* is composed of *an* and *other.* *None* is used in both numbers.

Rem. 6. — *Other* is thus declined: —

	Singular.	Plural.
Nom.	Other	others
Poss.	Other's	others'
Obj.	Other	others
Ind.	Other	others

Rem. 7. — *Another* and *one* are also declined, but *another* is used only in the singular.

4. A *participial adjective* is a word that has the form of a participle, and performs the office of an adjective; as, a *beloved* child, a *lasting* impression. See Rem. under § 81.

ARTICLES.*

§ 63. The definitive adjectives *a* or *an,* and *the,* are denominated *articles.*

1. *A* or *an* is called the *indefinite article,* because it does

---

Which demonstratives, and why? How is other *declined? What is a participial adjective? Examples.* What words are called articles? Which is called an indefinite article, and why?

---

* The most approved definition of the article is equally applicable to the words *one, that, this, these,* and other definitives; and any definition of the adjective, which is sufficiently comprehensive to include the definitives *this, that,* etc. will include also the words *a* and *the.* With what propriety, then, can the articles be separated from other definitives, and made to constitute a distinct part of speech?

"*A* or *an,* and *the,* are not a distinct part of speech in our language."— *Webster.*

"The words *a* or *an,* and *the,* are reckoned by some grammarians a separate part of speech; but, as they in all respects come under the definition of the adjective, it is unnecessary, as well as improper, to rank them as a class by themselves."—*Connon.*

"It is unnecessary, in any language, to regard the articles as a distinct part of speech."—*Buttmann's Greek Grammar.*

The articles are also ranked with adjectives by Priestley, E. Oliver, Bell, Elphinston, M'Culloch, D'Orsey, Lindsay, Joel, Greenwood, Smetham, Dalton, King, Hort, Buchanan, Crane, J. Russell, Frazee, Cutler, Perley, Swett, Day, Goodenow, Willard, Robbins, Felton, Snyder, Butler, S. Barrett, Badgley, Howe, Whiting, Davenport, Fowle, Weld, Greene, and others.

not indicate any particular object; as, *a* book; that is, *and* book.

2. *The* is called the *definite article*, because it indicates some particular object; as, *the* book; that is, some particular book.

REM. 1. — *A* is used before words beginning with a *consonant sound;* as, *a* tree, *a* house, *a* union, *a* ewe, *a* youth, *a* eulogy, *a* one, *a* world.

OBS. — The words *union*, *ewe*, and *eulogy*, commence with the consonant sound of *y;* and the word *one* commences with the consonant sound of *w*.

REM. 2. — *An* is used before words beginning with a *vowel sound;* as, *an* eagle, *an* hour, *an* outline.

REM. 3. — *An* is also employed, by most writers, before words beginning with *h* not silent, when the accent falls on the second syllable.

    Examples: — "*An* historical piece." — *Irving.* "*An* historical subject." — *Goldsmith.* "*An* hereditary government." — *E. Everett.* "*An* harmonious whole." — *Southey.*

REM. 4. — *A* or *an* is the Saxon word *ane* or *an*, signifying *one*.

COMPARISON.

§ 64. The *comparison* of adjectives is the variation by which they express different degrees of quality.

There are three degrees of comparison; — the *positive*, the *comparative*, and the *superlative*.

1. The *positive degree** is that which expresses the simple state of the quality; as, *good, wise.*

Which is called the definite article, and why? Before what words is a used? Examples. When is an used? Examples. What rule is observed respecting the form of the article before a word beginning with h not silent? Examples. What is the comparison of adjectives? What are the different degrees? What is the positive degree? Examples.

---

* It has been objected to the positive form, that, as it denotes the quality in its simple state, without increase or diminution, it cannot properly be called a *degree*. It should, however, be considered that all adjectives imply

2. The *comparative degree* denotes that one object possesses a higher or lower degree of the quality than another with which it is compared; as, *better, wiser, less wise.*

3. The *superlative degree* denotes that one of several objects possesses a higher or lower degree of the quality than any of the rest; as, *best, wisest, least wise.*

§ 65. The comparative of adjectives of one syllable, is commonly formed by adding *r* or *er* to the positive; as, *wise, wiser; great, greater;* and the superlative, by adding *st* or *est;* as, *wise, wisest; great, greatest.*

Adjectives of more than one syllable, are generally compared by prefixing *more* and *most* to the positive; as, *generous, more generous, most generous.*

Diminution of quality is expressed by *less* and *least*, whether the adjective is of one syllable or more than one; as, *bold, less bold, least bold.*

REM. 1. — Dissyllables ending in *y* or silent *e*, and those accented on the last syllable, are often compared like monosyllables, by *er* and *est;* as, *happy, happier, happiest; noble, nobler, noblest; profound, profounder, profoundest.*

REM. 2. — The foregoing principles, respecting the comparison of adjectives, are those which conform to the prevailing usage of the lan-

---

What does the comparative degree denote? Examples. The superlative? Examples. How are adjectives of one syllable generally compared? Examples. How are adjectives of more than one syllable generally compared? Examples. How is diminution of quality expressed? Examples. *What classes of dissyllables are often compared by er and est?* [*What is a dissyllable?*] *Examples of dissyllables compared by er and est.*

---

a *general* comparison of qualities. Thus, when we say that a man is discreet, we obviously mean that he has more discretion than the generality of men. So also, when we say a man is tall, it is implied that he is tall compared with other men. Hence arises the difference between the height of a tall man and that of a tall tree, each being compared with others of the same kind. In this sense, therefore, the positive is strictly and properly a *degree* of comparison guage. They are, however, in some cases, disregarded by the best writers; as, "Objects of our *tenderest* cares."—*E. Everett.* "The *commonest* material object."—*Dana.* "The *soberest* truth."—*Channing.*

REM. 3.—In all qualities capable of increase or diminution, the number of degrees from the highest to the lowest is indefinite. Whenever we wish to express any of the different shades of quality which are not denoted by the three forms of the adjective, we employ various modifying words and phrases; as, *rather, somewhat, slightly, a little, so, too, very, greatly, highly, exceedingly, in a high degree.*

Examples:— "A *very* pernicious war;"— "It is *a little* discolored;"— "*Too* strong to bend, *too* proud to learn."

REM. 4.—The termination *ish* is also joined to certain words, to denote a slight degree of quality; as, *black, blackish; salt, saltish.*

REM. 5.—When either of the words *more, most, less, least,* is prefixed to an adjective, it may be considered as forming a part of the adjective. Thus, the compound terms *more happy* and *less happy,* are regarded as adjectives in the comparative degree; but when the words are considered separately, the prefixes *more, most,* etc., are properly adverbs.

REM. 6.—The following adjectives are compared irregularly:—

Positive.	Comparative.	Superlative.
Good	better	best
Bad, evil, *or* ill	worse	worst
Far	{ farther* { further	farthest furthest
Fore	former	{ foremost *(in place)* { first *(in time or order)*
Late	later	{ latest *(referring to time)* { last *(in order)*
Little	less	least
Much *or* many	more	most
Near	nearer	{ nearest *(referring to place)* { next *(in order)*
Old	{ older { elder	oldest eldest

REM. 7.—Some adjectives in the superlative degree are formed by adding *most* to the comparative or to the word from which the comparative itself is made; as, *hind, hinder, hindermost* or *hindmost; nether, nethermost; up, upper, uppermost* or *upmost; in, inner, innermost* or *inmost.*

REM. 8.—Adjectives whose signification does not admit of increase or diminution, cannot be compared; as, *square, first, one, all, any, wooden, daily, infinite.*

What adjectives are compared irregularly? Compare them. What adjectives cannot be compared? Examples.

---

* "*Further* is the genuine Saxon word; *farther* takes precedence in modern use."—*Smart's Dict.*

ADJECTIVES.

Obs. — The word *perfect** and some others† which are not strictly comparable, are often qualified by *more* and *most*, and by *less* and *least*.
   Examples: — "A *more perfect* civilization." — *B. B. Edwards.* "The *most perfect* society." — *E. Everett.* "*Less perfect* imitations." — *Macaulay.* "The *more perfect* oneness." — *Dana.*

§ 66. Adjectives are sometimes used to perform the office of nouns, as " Providence rewards the *good;*" and nouns to perform the office of adjectives, as " An *iron* fence ; " — " *Meadow* ground."

EXERCISES.

§ 67. Good, this, seven, round, British, the, those, straight, fortieth, white, all, rich, any, Chinese, two, an, virtuous, eighteen, destructive, a, some, Alpine, first, many, boiling water, heated iron.

Which of the foregoing adjectives are descriptive and which definitive? *Which of them are proper? Which numeral? Which pronominal? Which participial?* Which are articles?

Compare the following adjectives : —

Strong, robust, sincere, low, swift, grateful, little, bad, studious.

"This site commands an extensive view of the surrounding country." — " The rapid current of a large river, the foaming cataract, the vivid flash of forked lightning, and the majestic rolling of the mighty ocean, are objects which excite in our minds emotions of grandeur and sublimity." — " Every leaf and every twig teems with life." — " Homer was the greater genius; Virgil, the better artist." — " Rhode Island is the smallest state in the Union." — " Numbers are expressed by ten Arabic characters."

Point out the adjectives in the foregoing sentences. Which of them are descriptive? Which definitive? *Which are proper? Which numeral? Which pronominal? Which participial?* Which are the articles? Which of the descriptive adjectives are in the positive degree? Compare them. Which are in the comparative? Compare them. Which in the superlative? Compare them.

---

† " Usage has given to '*more* and *most* perfect' a sanction which we dare hardly controvert." — *Crombie.*

‡ " *More complete, most complete, less complete,* are common expressions." — *Webster.*

Write sentences containing examples of descriptive and definitive adjectives; and others containing examples of adjectives in each of the three degrees of comparison.

THE PRONOUN.

§ 68. A *Pronoun** is a word used to supply the place of a noun; as, "When Cæsar had conquered Gaul, *he* turned *his* army against *his* country."

REM. — The word which is represented by a pronoun usually precedes it, and is hence called its *antecedent*.

§ 69. Pronouns may be divided into three general classes; — *personal, relative,* and *interrogative*.

PERSONAL PRONOUN.

§ 70. A *personal pronoun* is a pronoun that expresses person and number of itself.

The personal pronouns are *I, thou* or *you, he, she,* and *it*. *I* is of the first person; *thou* or *you* is of the second; and *he, she,* and *it,* are of the third.

Pronouns, like nouns, have gender, person, number, and case.

REM. 1. — Personal pronouns are varied to distinguish the numbers and cases; but variety of form to distinguish the genders, is confined to the third person singular.

What is a pronoun? Examples. *What is the antecedent of a pronoun?* Into what general classes are pronouns divided? What is a personal pronoun? Enumerate the personal pronouns, and give the person of each. What modifications have pronouns? *For what are personal pronouns varied?*

---

* The term *pronoun* is derived from two Latin words, *pro* and *nomen,* which signify *for a name*.

ADJECTIVES.

REM. 2. — As persons speaking or spoken to, are supposed to be present, and their sex sufficiently obvious, variety of form in the corresponding pronouns, to express distinction of gender, is unnecessary. But persons or things spoken of, being considered as absent, it is proper to make a distinction of gender; and the third person of the pronoun is accordingly distinguished by using *he* for the masculine, *she* for the feminine, and *it* for the neuter.

DECLENSION OF PERSONAL PRONOUNS.

§ 71. FIRST PERSON.

	Singular.	*Plural.*
Nom.	I	we*
Poss.	My *or* mine	our
Obj.	Me	us
Ind.	Me *or* I	we

REM. 1. — *Mine* and *thine* were formerly employed instead of *my* and *thy*, before words beginning with the sound of a vowel. This usage is now confined chiefly to poetry and the solemn style of prose.

Examples: — "I kept myself from *mine* iniquity." — *Ps.* 18 : 23.
"*Mine* hour is not yet come." — *John* 2 : 4.
"God stay thee in *thine* agony, my boy." — *Willis.*

REM. 2. — The first person singular is seldom used in the independent case, except by exclamation. The first person plural, when used independently, properly takes the same form as the nominative, though the objective form is sometimes employed.

Examples: — "O wretched *we!*" — *Dryden.* "O rare *we!*" — *Cowper.* "Ah! luckless *I*." — *Francis.*
"Ah *me!* neglected on the lonesome plain." — *Beattie.*
"*Me* miserable! which way shall I fly
Infinite wrath and infinite despair?" — *Milton.*

§ 72. SECOND PERSON. — Solemn Style.

	Singular.	*Plural.*
Nom.	Thou	ye *or* you
Poss.	Thy *or* thine	your
Obj.	Thee	you
Ind.	Thou	ye *or* you

Decline I. *Decline* thou.

---

* The plural of pronouns in the first and second persons, does not bear the same relation to the singular as the plural of nouns. Thus the plural *men* is equivalent to the repetition of the singular *man*. But the plural *we* is equivalent to the singular *I*, together with *others* in the second or third person, and not to the singular *I* repeated. So, also, the plural of *thou* is often equivalent to *thou*, together with *others* in the third person.

REM. 1.— The pronoun *thou* is employed in addressing the Deity, in the Sacred Scriptures, and in poetry. It also occurs in other solemn or impassioned prosaic writings, and the Society of Friends still use it in common discourse.

REM. 2.— The poets sometimes employ *ye* instead of *you* for the objective plural; as,

"Brother, sweet sister, peace around *ye* dwell "—*Hemans.*

"I told *ye* then he should prevail and speed
 On his bad errand."—*Milton.*

This usage is generally regarded as inelegant.

§ 73. SECOND PERSON.— Common Style

	Singular.	Plural.
Nom.	You	you
Poss.	Your	your
Obj.	You	you
Ind.	You	you

REM.— The word *you** was originally plural in signification;

When is thou *employed? Examples. Decline* you. *What was the original use of* you?

---

* No usage of our language is more fully established than that which recognizes *you* as the representative of nouns in the singular number.

"In the using of *you* to *one*, as well as to *more* than one (which is the Language of the Nation, not only spoke by the private persons, but extant in the both private and publick Writings of it), we do seem to imitate the French, who, as they have one word, viz. *tu* for *thou*, and one, viz. *vos* for *ye;* so they have one which they use both to *one*, and to *more* than one, indifferently; namely, *vous, you.*"—*Walker's Treatise of English Particles; London*, 1653.

Brightland, one of the earliest of our English grammarians, who wrote in 1710, classes *you* with the singular pronouns *I, thou*, and *he.* Greenwood, in his celebrated grammar, which appeared the following year, says, " *Thou* or *you* is of the second person singular." This disposition of *you* was followed by the author of the British Grammar, and by Farro, Fisher, Buchanan, Dilworth, Smetham, Menye, and several other grammatical writers of the last century.

Mr. Murray's grammar first appeared in 1795. Following the practice of the Society of Friends,—the community in which he was educated,—he restricted *you* to the plural number; and such was the influence of his example that this word was, for a time, very generally excluded from the list of singular pronouns.

There has, however, always existed a respectable class of authors, who have treated the pronoun *you* as singular, when applied to an individual; and, during the last twenty-five or thirty years, the number of this class has very rapidly increased.

"It is altogether absurd to consider *you* as exclusively a plural pronoun but it is now universally employed in popular discourse, to represent either a singular or a plural noun.

§ 74. THIRD PERSON.

	Masculine.		*Feminine.*		*Neuter.*	
	Singular.	Plural.	Singular.	Plural.	Singular.	Plural
Nom.	He	they	She	they	It	they
Poss.	His	their	Her	their	Its	their
Obj.	Him	them	Her	them	It	them
Ind.	He	they	She	they	It	they

REM. 1. — In the third person, masculine and feminine, the independent case has usually the nominative form, though the use of the objective is not wholly destitute of authority.*

Examples: — " Ah luckless *he!* " — *Shenstone.*

"God from the mount of Sinai, whose gray top
Shall tremble, *he* descending, will himself
Ordain them laws."—*Milton.*

" Miserable *they,*
Who, here entangled in the gathering ice,
Take their last look of the descending sun."—*Thomson.*

Decline he, she, and it.

---

in the modern English language. It may be a matter of *history*, that it was originally used as a plural only; and it may be a matter of *theory*, that it was first applied to individuals on a principle of flattery; but the *fact* is, that it is now our second person singular. When applied to an individual, it never excites any idea either of plurality or of adulation; but excites, precisely and exactly, the idea that was excited by the use of *thou*, in an earlier stage of the language."—*Jeffrey, in the Edinburgh Review.*

"If a word, once exclusively plural, becomes, by universal use, the sign of individuality, it must take its place in the singular number. That this is the fact with *you*, is proved by national usage."—*Webster.*

A list of additional authorities is subjoined for the gratification of the curious student. The writers here enumerated treat the pronoun *you* as singular, when applied to an individual:— Angell. C. Adams, A. Alden, Booth, Bell, Brace, Barnard, Barrie, John Barrett, D. Blair, Cochran, Cutler, Cobb, Davis, Elmore, Emmons, Felton, Fletcher, Fuller, Fowle, Gilbert, Goodenow, Goldsbury, R. W. Green, Gurney, Joel, Judson, Lewis, Morley, M'Cnlloch, Pullen, J. M. Putnam, Picket, Pinnock, Ross, W. E. Russell, Caleb Reed, Snyder, Swett, R. C. Smith, P. Smith, Stearns, Sanborn, Todd Ticken, Wilcox, Wilbur, G. Wilson, J. P. Wilson, Weld, M'Cready, Cooper Powers, Whiting, Beall, J. Ward, Fowler.

* " Of the two forms, '*him excepted*' and '*he excepted*,' the former (contrary to the sentiment of the majority of grammarians) is the correct one."—*Latham.*

" This inaccessible high strength, the seat
Of deity supreme, *us* dispossessed,
He trusted to have seized." *Milton.*

Rem. 2. — *His** was formerly employed as the possessive of both *he* and *it*.

 Examples: — " Put up again thy sword into *h's* place."—*Matt.* 26 · 52. " Learning hath *his* infancy, when it is but beginning, and almost childish."—*Bacon.*

Rem. 3. — *My, thy, his, her, its, our, your,* and *their,* are sometimes, though improperly, termed pronominal adjectives.

§ 75. *Mine, thine, his, hers, ours, yours,* and *theirs,* are *possessive pronouns,* used in construction either as nominatives or objectives;† as, " Your pleasures are past, *mine* are to come." Here the word *mine,* which is used as a substitute for *my pleasures,* is the subject of the verb *are.*

Rem. The words *hers, its, ours, yours, theirs,* are sometimes improperly written *her's, it's, our's, your's, their's* This error should be carefully avoided.

§ 76. The words *myself, thyself, yourself, himself, herself,* and *itself,* with their plurals, *ourselves, yourselves,* and *themselves,* are called *compound personal pronouns.* They are frequently joined to nouns and simple pronouns, to express emphasis; as, " You *yourselves* are the contrivers of your own ruin ; " — " The mountains *themselves* decay with years." They are also used when the subject and the object of the verb both represent the same person or thing. "I blame myself ; " — " He blames me." *I* and *myself* here denote the same person, and we use the compound pronoun.

What is said of the possessive pronouns, mine, thine, *etc.? Illustrate their use. What are the compound personal pronouns ? When are they employed ? Examples.*

---

* " The possessive *its* does not appear before the seventeenth century."— *Booth.* " *Its* is not found in the Bible, except by misprint."— *G. Brown.*

† Many grammarians parse *mine, thine,* etc., as pronouns in the possessive case, and governed by nouns understood. Thus, in the sentence, "This book is mine," the word *mine* is said to be governed by *book.* That the word *book* is not here understood, is obvious from the fact, that, when it is supplied, the phrase becomes, not " *mine* book," but " *my* book," the pronoun being changed from *mine* to *my ;* so that we are made, by this practice, to parse *mine* as governed by a word understood, before which it cannot properly be used. The word *mine* is here evidently employed as a substitute for the two words, *my* and *book.*

" That *mine, thine, yours, his, hers, theirs,* do not constitute a possessive case, is demonstrable ; for they are constantly used as the nominatives to verbs and as objectives after verbs and prepositions."— *Webster.*

See also Dr. Wilson, Smart, Jenkins, Goodenow, Jaudon, Felch, Hazen, Todd, E. Smith, Cooper, Cutler, Weld, and Davis.

REM. — The word *self*, when used alone, is a noun; as, "The love of *self* is predominant."

RELATIVE PRONOUNS.

§ 77. A *relative pronoun* is a pronoun that relates directly to some preceding word or phrase, and serves to connect sentences.

REM. 1. — When the antecedent of a relative is in the independent case, the pronoun connects a simple sentence with the independent noun or pronoun and its adjuncts; as,

"Ye undying and desperate sons of the brave,
Who so often your valor have shown."

REM. 2. — The connective office of a relative pronoun should always be pointed out in parsing. Thus, in the compound sentence, "Bless them that curse you," the pronoun *that* is the subject of the verb *curse* in one of the members; and it relates to *them*, which is the object of the verb *bless* in the other member. A relative pronoun always relates to some word out of the clause in which it stands, and thus joins the two clauses together.

§ 78. The words used as relative pronouns, are *who*, *which*, *that*, and *what*.

Who is applied to persons, and *which* to irrational animals and things without life; as, "The man *who* is accustomed to reflect, finds instruction in every thing;" — "I have found the book *which* I had lost."

That is used for *who* or *which*, and may be applied either to persons or things; as, "He *that* gathereth in summer, is a wise son;" — "A city *that* is set on a hill, cannot be hid."

What is a relative pronoun? *Illustrate the connective office of relatives.* Enumerate the relative pronouns. What are the respective applications of *who*, *which*, and *that*? Examples of each.

Who, which, and *that,* are thus declined:—

	Sing. and Plur.	Sing. and Plur.	Sing. and Plur.
Nom.	Who	Which	That
Poss.	Whose	Whose*	Whose
Obj.	Whom	Which	That
Ind.	Who	Which	

§ 79. The word *what* is often used as a *compound relative* pronoun, equivalent in signification to *that which*† or *those which;* as, "One man admires *what* [*that which*] displeases another." *What* here sustains the relation of both the *nominative* and the *objective* case. As a nominative, it is the subject of the verb *displeases;* as an objective, it is the object of *admires.*

REM. 1.— *What* sometimes performs, at once, the office of an adjective and a pronoun; as, "*What* time remained, was well employed." As an adjective, *what* here qualifies *time;* as a pronoun, it is the subject of the verb *remained.*

REM. 2.— *Whoever, whichever, whatever,* and *whosoever, whichsoever, whatsoever,* are also used as *compound* pronouns, and parsed in

---

Decline the relatives who, which, *and* that. *How is* what *often used?* Examples. *What two parts of speech does* what *sometimes represent?* Examples. *What other words are employed as compound relatives?* Examples.

---

* The possessive of *which* is, in many grammars, marked as wanting; but the use of *whose,* as the possessive of both *who* and *which,* may now be regarded as fully established by the authority of our most eminent writers and speakers.

    Examples:— "Cedar groves, *whose* gigantic branches threw a refreshing coolness over the verdure."—*Prescott.* "At such times, I am apt to seek the Hall of Justice, *whose* deep, shadowy arcades extend across the upper end of the Court."—*Irving.* "Statues, *whose* miserable and mutilated fragments are the models of modern art."—*E. Everett.* "Impressions, *whose* power can scarcely be calculated."—*Cheever.* "He wanted learning, *whose* place no splendor of genius can supply to the lawyer."—*Wirt.* "Dramas, *whose* termination is the total ruin of their heroes."—*J. G. Lockhart.* "A triangle, or three-sided figure, one of *whose* sides is perpendicular to another."—*Brougham.* Other examples from the best authorities might be multiplied at pleasure.

"I have given *whose* as the genitive of *which;* not only because this usage is sanctioned by classical authority, but likewise because the other form, *of which,* is frequently awkward and inelegant."—*Dr. Crombie.*

† Many grammarians erroneously substitute the two equivalent words, *that which,* and parse them instead of the original word *what.* This is parsing their own language, and not the author's. The word *what,* when compound, should be parsed as performing the office of two nominatives, or two objectives, or of both a nominative and an objective.

the same manner as the compound *what.* Thus, in the sentence, "Whoever disregards the laws of his being, must suffer the penalty," *whoever* is the subject of the two verbs, *disregards* and *must suffer.*

REM. 3. — *Whoso* was formerly used as a compound pronoun, in the sense of *whosoever:* as, "*Whoso*, therefore, shall swear by the altar, sweareth by it, and by all things thereon." It is now nearly obsolete.

REM. 4. — *Which* and *what* are sometimes used as adjectives; as, "For *which* reason;" — "*What tongue* can tell?"

§ 80. The distinction between personal and relative pronouns should receive special attention. Each of the *personal* pronouns is used to represent one of the three persons, and no other. Thus *I* is always of the first person, and *he* always of the third. A *relative* pronoun does not express person of itself, but always depends on its antecedent for person. Thus, we may say, "I *who* speak;" "You *who* speak;" "He *who* speaks." *Who* is here employed in each of the three persons.

INTERROGATIVE PRONOUNS.

§ 81. An *interrogative pronoun* is a pronoun that is used in asking a question; as, "*Who* is this?" The words used as interrogative pronouns, are *who, which,* and *what.*

REM. 1. — *Who*, used interrogatively, is applied only to persons; *which* and *what* are applied to both persons and things.

REM. 2. — *Whether*, signifying *which of the two*, was formerly used as an interrogative; as, "*Whether* of them twain did the will of his father?" In this sense it is now out of use.

EXERCISES.

§ 82. Give the person, number, and case of each of the following pronouns: —

His, she, its, thee, he, they, our, I, them.

Give examples of which *and* what, *used as adjectives. Explain and illustrate the distinction between personal and relative pronouns.* What is an interrogative pronoun? Enumerate the interrogatives. *To what are the interrogatives* who, which, *and* what, *respectively applied?*

What personal pronoun is in the third person singular, masculine gender, and possessive case? — in the second person singular, solemn style, and objective case? — in the third person plural, nominative case? — in the first person plural, objective case? — in the first person singular, possessive case? — in the second person plural, nominative case? — in the third person singular, neuter gender, possessive case? — in the second person singular, common style, nominative case? — in the third person singular, feminine gender, nominative case? — in the first person plural, possessive case? Give the person, number, and case of him; — me; — its; — she; — them; — us; — my; — thee.

"As he was valiant, I honor him." — "The crime which has been once committed, is committed again with less reluctance." — "I charge thee, fling away ambition." — "He that trusteth in his riches, shall fall." — "Virtue is most laudable in that state which makes it most difficult." — "Who wrote the letter?" — "You wrong yourself." — "O thou that rollest above, round as the shield of my fathers!"

Point out the pronouns in the foregoing sentences. Which of them are personal? Which relative? Which interrogative? Give the person, number, gender, and case of each, with the reasons.

MODEL. — *He* (in the first sentence above) is a pronoun, because it is a word used to supply the place of a noun; — personal, because it expresses person and number of itself; — in the third person, because it denotes a person spoken of; — in the singular number, because it denotes but one; — in the masculine gender, because it denotes a male; — and in the nominative case, because it is the subject of the verb *was*.

Write sentences containing examples of personal, relative, and interrogative pronouns.

THE VERB.

§ 83. A *Verb* * is a word that expresses an assertion or affirmation; † as, I *am;* I *teach;* I *am taught.*

What is a verb? Examples.

---

* The term *verb* is derived from the Latin *verbum,* which signifies *a word.* This part of speech is so called because the verb is the principal *word* in a sentence.

† The idea of a verb is not easily expressed in a single sentence. The

A Verb may also be used to command, exhort, request, and inquire, as "*Be* silent," "*Spare* me," "*Have* you *written* the letter?" and to express an action or state in general and abstract sense, as *doing, to obey*.

§ 84. Verbs are divided into two general classes;— *transitive* and *intransitive*.*

1. A *transitive verb* is a verb that governs an objective case; as, "Henry *has learned his lesson*."

<small>The term *transitive* signifies *passing over*.</small>

2. An *intransitive verb* is a verb that does not govern an objective case; as, "He *is;*"—"The horse *runs*."

REM.—There are some verbs which may be used either transitively or intransitively, the construction alone determining to which class they belong.

§ 85. Transitive verbs have two forms, called the *active* and the *passive voice*.†

<small>What other uses have verbs? Into what general classes are verbs divided? What is a transitive verb? Examples. What is an intransitive verb? Examples. What two forms have transitive verbs?</small>

<small>definition here adopted is based on the most distinguishing characteristic of this part of speech; and is substantially the same as that of Priestley, Blair, Harris, Beattie, Crombie, Andrews and Stoddard, the British Grammar, Rees's Encyc., Brewster's Encyc., Grant, Sutcliffe, M'Culloch, Bullions, Fletcher, Cooper, Goldsbury, Frost, Parkhurst, Butler, Hart, and others.

* "The proper division of verbs is into *transitive* and *intransitive;* for this distinction is practical, and has an effect in the formation of sentences, which is not true of the other distinctions."—*Goodenow*.

"This classification of verbs is founded on their use in the construction of sentences."—*Frazee*.

The division of words into *transitive* and *intransitive* is also adopted in the grammars of Arnold, Webster, M'Culloch, Hart, Crane, Frost, Butler, Bullions, Connon, R. W. Green, Reed, Perley, Ussher, Fuller, Staniford, Bingham, Locke, Ticknor, Lindsay, Earl, Spear, Story, Webber, Nutting, Cobb, and others.

† "Active and passive do not denote two different kinds of verb, but one kind under two different forms, denominated the *active* and *passive* voice."—*Bullions*.

"It needs no argument to prove that 'I *am struck*' is just as really a modification of *to strike*, as 'I *have struck*' is; and yet, under the old classification of active, passive, and neuter, the pupil was taught to consider these forms as two verbs belonging to different classes."—*Hart*.</small>

1. The *active voice* represents the subject or nominative as acting upon some object.

2. The *passive voice* represents the nominative as being acted upon.

Rem. 1.— In the sentence, "Cæsar conquered Pompey," the verb *conquered* represents the nominative *Cæsar* as acting upon the object *Pompey*. The verb *conquered* is therefore in the *active voice*. But in the expression, "Pompey was conquered by Cæsar," the verb *was conquered* represents the nominative *Pompey* as being acted upon. The verb *was conquered* is therefore in the *passive voice*.

[When a verb is said to be *transitive*, and no mention is made of the voice, it is understood to be in the *active voice*. The *passive voice* of a transitive verb is often denominated a *passive verb*.]

Rem. 2. — A verb in the passive voice is composed of the perfect participle of a transitive verb, and one of the forms of the verb *to be* ;* as, *are heard, were heard, am heard, to be heard*.

Rem. 3. — Most intransitive verbs do not admit of the passive form. Thus, instead of saying, "Very great abuses *are crept* into this entertainment," it would be better to say, "Very great abuses *have crept* into this entertainment." But the verbs *come* and *go*, and perhaps a few others, may, in some cases, properly assume the passive form; as, "The time *is come*." — *Channing*. "The sharp touches of the chisel *are gone* from the rich tracery of the arches." — *Irving*. Verbs of this description are usually denominated *neuter passive verbs*.

§ 86. Verbs are also divided into *regular* and *irregular*.

What does the active voice represent? The passive voice? *Illustrate. Of what is a verb in the passive voice composed? Examples. What verbs do not generally admit the passive form? Illustrate. What exceptions are there to this principle? Examples.* Into what other classes are verbs divided?

---

* Many respectable grammarians reject the passive voice of the verb altogether; parsing the participle by itself, and the verb *to be* as a principal verb. See Rees's Cyclopædia, and the Grammars of Nutting, Crombie, S. Oliver, Ash, Lewis, and Connon.

VERBS.

1. A *regular verb* is one that forms its past tense and perfect participle by adding *d* or *ed* to the present; as, present, *love;* past, *loved;* perf. part., *loved;* call, *called*, *called*.

REM. 1.— Regular verbs ending in silent *e*, form their past tense and perfect participle, by the addition of *d* only; and those ending in any other letter, by the addition of *ed*.

REM. 2. — The verbs *hear, pay, say,* and *lay*, which do not end in *e*, and which add *d* only for the past tense and perfect participle, are classed with irregular verbs.

2. An *irregular verb* is one that does not form its past tense and perfect participle by adding *d* or *ed* to the present; as, present, *see;* past, *saw;* perf. part., *seen; go, went, gone.*

EXERCISES.

§ 87. "The tree grows." — "Columbus discovered America." — "You were expected." — "Man is mortal." — "We are observed." — "He received an injury."

Point out the verbs in the foregoing sentences. Which of them are regular? Which irregular? Which are transitive? Which intransitive? Which passive?

Name three regular verbs; — three irregular.

Write sentences containing examples of transitive, intransitive, and passive verbs.

MODE.

§ 88. *Mode* is a term used to denote the *manner* in which the verb is employed.

Verbs have five modes;* — the *indicative*, the *sub-*

What is a regular verb? Examples. What is an irregular verb? Examples. What is mode? Enumerate the different modes.

---

* The recognition of *potential* mode, in so many of our popular grammars, affords a striking example of the power of custom. The expressions, "It may rain," "He may go," "I can ride," etc., are manifestly *declarative;* and the verbs *may rain, may go, can ride*, etc., are appropriately ranked in the indicative mode. "I can walk," expresses quite as distinct

junctive, the *imperative*, the *infinitive*, and the *participial.**

§ 89. The *indicative* mode is that which indicates or declares, or asks a question; as, He *can* learn; *Does* he learn? *Can* he learn?

REM. 1. — The *common form* of the indicative mode is that which *merely* expresses a declaration or an interrogation; as, "He *improves;*" — "*Will* you *go?*"

REM. 2. — The *potential form* of the indicative is that which expresses a declaration or asks a question, and also implies *possibility, liberty, power, determination, obligation, necessity,* etc.; as, "He *can walk;*" — "We *must return;*" — "What *would* they *have?*"

[In speaking of the common form of the indicative, it will generally

---

What is the indicative mode? Examples. *What is the common form of the indicative mode? Examples. The potential form? Examples.*

---

a declaration as "I walk." Thus, "I can walk," declares that I have the power to walk; while "I walk," declares the act of walking.

Most authors who recognize a potential mode, still class such expressions as "If I should go," with the subjunctive. But "I should go," *asserts* or *declares* the same thing that "If I should go," expresses under a *condition;* and hence the difference between them is precisely the distinction between the *indicative* and the subjunctive. And since the use of the conjunction *if,* produces no other effect than to change the sentence from a *declarative* to a *conditional* form, it is obvious that all of its *potential* qualities must still remain; hence the clause, "If I should go," has the same claim to be ranked with the potential, as "I should go." If, then, this form of the verb is classed with the *subjunctive* mode when it is used *conditionally,* consistency would seem to require that it should be classed with the *indicative,* when its use is *declaratory.*

Do the expressions, "He would walk," "They should learn," imply *will,* or *obligation* more clearly than "I will obey," "Thou shalt not kill," "He ought to learn"?

"The mere expressions of *will, possibility, liberty, obligation,* etc., belong to the Indicative Mode." — *Lowth.*

"As to the potential mode, it may, I think, in all cases, be resolved into either the indicative or the subjunctive." — *Beattie's Theory of Language.*

"The forms of expression, *I can go, we may ride, he must obey,* are really declaratory, and properly belong to the indicative." — *Webster.*

The potential mode is also rejected by Jamieson, H. Ward, Martin, Coote, Cobbett, Lewis, Hazlitt, Hodgson, St. Quentin, Bell, Currie, Buchanan, Coar, Trinder, Adam, Arnold, Higginson, Giles, Beall, Pe , Ross, Nutting, J. P. Wilson, Willard, Hallock, Dearborn, J. Flint, D. Adams, Judson, Pue, Cardell, Cutler, Balch, French, Spencer, and others.

* If the participle is properly regarded as a form of the verb, it is obvious that it must be employed in some *mode.* In the conjugation of verbs, it is oe found convenient to employ merely the term *indicative mode:* and in speaking of the potential form, to designate it as the *potential indicative.*]

REM. 3. — *Were* is sometimes used for *would be* or *should be;* as, "Ah! what *were* man, should Heaven refuse to hear?"

REM. 4. — *Had* is also occasionally employed for *would have,* or *should have;* as, "Had thought been all, sweet speech *had* [*would have*] been denied." — *Young.*

§ 90. The *subjunctive mode* is that which implies *condition, supposition,* or *uncertainty;* as, "If he *had* the opportunity, he would improve rapidly;" — " Take heed, lest any man *deceive* you."

REM. 1. — Every verb in the subjunctive implies two propositions; the one *principal,* and the other *subordinate.* The subordinate clause is usually preceded by a conjunction, subjoining it to the antecedent, or principal clause, on which it depends. Thus, in the sentence, "I will remain if you desire it," the dependent clause, "you desire it," is preceded by the conjunction *if,* which subjoins it to the principal clause, "I will remain."

REM. 2. — The condition of a verb in the subjunctive is sometimes expressed by transposition, without the aid of a conjunction; as, "*Had* he *taken* the counsel of friends, he would have been saved from ruin."

REM. 3. — The subjunctive mode, like the indicative, admits of the potential form; as, "He might improve, if he *would make* the necessary effort." See § 89.

What is the subjunctive mode? Examples. *What does every subjunctive clause imply? Illustrate. What modification in form does the subjunctive admit? Examples.*

uniformly introduced in connection with the other modes, and treated in every respect as a mode.

"The participle is merely a *mode* of the verb, and it might properly be termed the *participial mode.*"— *Sanborn.*

"If modes be the *manner of representing* the verb, we see no good reason why *participles* should not be reckoned a mode." — *Goodenow.*

"That the participle is a mere mode of the verb, is manifest, if our definition of a verb be admitted." — *Lowth.*

"There are four modes; the Infinitive, Indicative, Imperative, and Subjunctive, to which we may add the Participles, as necessary to be considered together with the verb." — *Higginson.*

"Mr. Murray contends strenuously for the participle, as 'a mode of the verb,' and yet has not the consistency of assigning it a place among the modes, as it must have, if it be any verb at all." — *Willard.*

The participle is also ranked as a mode of the verb by Elphinston, Allen and Cornwell, Connell, De Sacy, St. Quentin, Felch, Fletcher, Turner Day, Spencer, Pinneo, and others.

§ 91. The *imperative* mode is that which commands, exhorts, entreats, or permits; as, " *Go* thou;" — " *Study* diligently;" — " *Forgive* us our trespasses;" — " *Depart* in peace."

§ 92. The *infinitive* mode is the root or first form of the verb, used to express an action or state indefinitely; as, *to hear, to speak*. It is generally distinguished by the sign *to*.

Rem. — When the particle *to* is employed in forming the infinitive, it is to be regarded as a part of the verb.

Participles.

§ 93. The *participle* is a mode of the verb, partaking of the properties of the verb and the adjective; as, *seeing, seen, having seen, having been seen*.

Participles may be classed under two general divisions; — *imperfect** and *perfect*.

1. An *imperfect participle* denotes the continuance of an action or state; as, *calling, seeing, being seen*.

Rem. — Imperfect participles relate to present, past, or future

---

What is the imperative mode? Examples. The infinitive? Examples. How is the infinitive generally distinguished? What is the participle? Examples. Into what general classes are participles divided? What is an imperfect participle? Examples. *To what time do imperfect participles relate* ?

---

* " The *distinguishing characteristic* of this participle is, that it denotes an unfinished and progressive state of the being, action, or passion; it is therefore properly denominated the IMPERFECT participle." — *G. Brown*.

"All that is peculiar to the participles is, that the one signifies a *perfect*, and the other an *imperfect* action." — *Pickbourn's Dissertation on the English Verb*.

"The most unexceptionable distinction which grammarians make between the participles, is, that the one points to the continuation of the action, passion, or state, denoted by the verb; and the other, to the completion of it." — *Murray*.

See also Grant, Baldwin, Lewis, M'Culloch, Churchill, Connon, Butler and R. W. Green.

time, according as they are connected with verbs in the present, past, or future tense.

2. A *perfect participle* denotes the completion of an action or state; as, *called, seen, having seen.*

§ 94. Participles are also divided into two other classes, called *simple* and *compound.*

1. A *simple participle* is a participle that consists of only one word; as, *doing, done.*

2. A *compound participle* is a participle that is composed of two or more words; as, *being seen, having seen, having been seen. Being seen* is a compound imperfect participle; *having seen* and *having been seen* are compound perfect participles.

REM. 1. — Participles, like other modifications of the verb, are either transitive or intransitive. Thus, *seeing* and *having seen* are transitive; *being* and *walking,* intransitive. Transitive participles are also distinguished by voices; as, active, *seeing, having seen;* passive, *seen, having been seen.*

REM. 2. — Participles often lose their verbal character, and become adjectives; as, "A *moving* spectacle;" — "A *revised* edition." They are then called *participial adjectives.*

REM. 3. — Participles are also used to perform the office of nouns; as, "They could not avoid *submitting* to this influence." When used in this manner, they are called *participial nouns.*

§ 95. Besides the regular grammatical modes expressed by the verb, it is obvious that there must be numerous other distinctions of manner, which can be indicated only by the use of various modifying words and phrases; as, "The storm beats *violently;*" — "The horse sleeps *standing*"

TENSE.

§ 96. *Tense* is the distinction of time.

Verbs have six tenses; — the *present,* the *past,** the

What is a perfect participle? Examples. *A simple participle?* Examples. *A compound participle? Examples. Name a transitive participle; — intransitive. A participle in the active voice; — in the passive.* What is tense? Enumerate the tenses.

---

* The names of the tenses adopted in this treatise, have the sanction of Connell, Skillern, Hiley, Butler, Perley, Goodenow, Fletcher, and Farnum.

future, the *present perfect*, the *past perfect*, and the *future perfect*.

1. The *present tense* denotes present time; as, I *write;* I *am writing*.

2. The *past (imperfect) tense* denotes indefinite past time; as, I *wrote;* I *was writing*.

3. The *future tense* denotes indefinite future time; as, I *shall write;* I *shall be writing*.

4. The *present perfect (perfect) tense* denotes past time, and also conveys an allusion to the present; as, I *have written;* I *have been writing*.

5. The *past perfect (pluperfect) tense* denotes past time that precedes some other past time, to which it refers; as, "When he *had delivered* the message, he took his departure."

6. The *future perfect (second future) tense* denotes future time that precedes some other future time, to which it refers; as, "I *shall have finished* the letter before he arrives."

REM. — Besides these six grammatical tenses, there are numerous other distinctions of time, which are expressed by various modifying words and phrases; as, "I will go *immediately;*"—"I will go *soon;*"—"I will go *in an hour;*"—"I will go *to-morrow;*"—"I will go *in the course of the week*."

What is the present tense? Examples. The past tense? Examples. What is the future tense? Examples. What is the present perfect tense? Examples. The past perfect tense? Examples. The future perfect tense? Examples.

Similar terms, corresponding with the signification of the tenses, are also employed by Webster, Frazee, Day, Swett, Felton, Brace, Simmonite, Flower, Barrie, and others.

"Several of the old names either convey no idea, or an erroneous one. The imperfect tense does not, in one case of a hundred, signify an imperfect action; the perfect tense is not the only one which represents a finished action; and if we speak of first and second future tenses, we may with equal propriety have first and second present, and first and second past tenses."—*Perley*.

NUMBER AND PERSON.

§ 97. Verbs have two numbers and three persons.

The person and number of a verb are always the same as the person and number of its subject or nominative.

REM. 1.—In the simple form of the present and past indicative, the second person singular of the *solemn style* ends regularly in *st* or *est*, as Thou *seest*, Thou *hearest*, Thou *sawest*, Thou *heardest*; and the third person singular of the present, in *th* or *eth*, as He *saith*, He *loveth*.

REM. 2.—In the simple form of the present indicative, the third person singular of the *common* or *familiar style*, ends in *s* or *es*; as, He *sleeps*, He *rises*.

REM. 3.—The first person singular of the solemn style, and the first and second persons singular of the common style, have the same form as the three persons plural.

REM. 4.—In forming the compound tenses of the verb, the auxiliaries only are varied.

REM. 5.—*Be* and *ought*, and the auxiliaries *shall, will, may, can, must*, are irregular in their modifications to denote person.

REM. 6.—The verb *need* is often used in the third person singular of the indicative present, without the personal termination.

Examples:—"The truth *need* not be disguised."—*Channing.* "It *need* only be added."—*Prescott.* "It *need* not be said."—*E. Everett.* "There was one condition, which *need* not be mentioned."—*Irving.* "Nothing *need* be concealed."—*Cooper.* "Time *need* not be wasted."—*G. B. Emerson.* "No other historian of that country *need* be mentioned."—*Hallam.* "The reader *need* not be told."—*Paley.* "This is a species of inconsistency, of which no man *need* be ashamed."—*Edinburgh Review.* "It *need* not surprise us."—*J. G Lockhart.* "It *need* scarcely be said."—*N. A. Review.* "*Need* a bewildered traveller wish for more?"—*Wordsworth.*

REM. 7.—The subjunctive of all verbs, except *be*, takes the same form as the indicative. Good writers were formerly much accustomed to drop the personal termination in the subjunctive present, and write, "If he *have*," "If he *deny*," etc., for "If he *has*," "If he *denies*," etc.; but this termination is now generally retained, unless an auxiliary is understood.* Thus, "If he *hear*,"

How many persons and numbers have verbs? With what do the person and number of a verb correspond? *What is said respecting the form of verbs in the subjunctive mode? Illustrate.*

---

* "The use of the present tense of the subjunctive, without the personal terminations, was formerly very general. It was reserved for the classical

may properly be used for "If he *shall hear*" or "If he *should hear*," when the auxiliary *shall* or *should* is manifestly implied; but when no such ellipsis is obvious, the indicative form, "If he *hears*" is to be preferred. See § 107, Rem. 2.

> *Examples:* — "If the dramatist *attempts* to create a being answering to one of these descriptions, he fails."—*Macaulay.* "If he *takes* the tone of invective, it leads him to be uncharitable."—*Southey.* "If courage intrinsically *consists* in the defiance of danger and pain, the life of the Indian is a continual exhibition of it."—*Irving.* "He must feign, if he *does* not feel, the spirit and inspiration of the place."—*Story.* "If any pupil *fails* to reach this point, he is said to fall below the standard."—*N. A. Review.* Other authorities might be multiplied at pleasure.

REM. 8. — Infinitives and participles have neither number nor person.

CONJUGATION.

§ 98. The *conjugation* of a verb is the regular combination and arrangement of its several modes, tenses, numbers, and persons.

PRINCIPAL PARTS.

§ 99. The three *principal parts* of a verb are the *present tense*, the *past tense*, and the *perfect participle*. These are called the principal or radical parts, because all the other parts are formed from them.

AUXILIARIES.

§ 100. An *auxiliary verb* is one that is used to aid in the conjugation of other verbs.

What properties are wanting in infinitives and participles? What is the conjugation of a verb? What are the principal parts of a verb? Why so called? What is an auxiliary verb?

---

writers of the eighteenth century to lay aside the pedantic forms, *if he go, if it proceed, though he come,* etc., and restore the native idiom of the language."— *Webster.*

REM. — The auxiliaries are *do, be, have, shall, will, may, can,* with their variations, and *must,* which has no variation. *Do, be, have,* and *will,* are also used as principal verbs. Thus, in the sentence, "I have heard the news," *have* is used as an auxiliary to the principal verb *heard;* but in the sentence, "I have no time to devote to trifles," *have* is employed as a principal verb.

Shall *and* Will.

§ 101. In *affirmative* sentences, *shall,* in the first person, simply foretells; as, "I *shall* write." In the second and third persons, *shall* is used potentially, denoting a *promise, command,* or *determination;* as, " You *shall* be rewarded ; " — " Thou *shalt* not kill ; " — " He *shall* be punished." *Will,* in the first person, is used potentially, denoting a *promise* or *determination;* as, "I *will* go, at all hazards." In the second and third persons, *will* simply foretells; as, " You *will* soon be there ; " — " He *will* expect you."

§ 102. In *interrogative* sentences, *shall,* in the first person, may either be used potentially to inquire the will of the party addressed, as, " *Shall* I bring you another book ? " or it may simply ask whether a certain event will occur, as, " *Shall* I arrive in time for the cars ? " When *shall* is used interrogatively in the second person, it simply denotes futurity; as, " *Shall* you be in New York next week ? " *Shall,* employed interrogatively in the third person, has a potential signification, and is used to inquire the will of the party addressed ; as, " *Shall* John order the carriage ? " *Will,* used interrogatively in the second person, is potential in its signification; as, " *Will* you go ? " *Will* may be used interrogatively in the third person, to denote mere futurity, as, " *Will* the boat leave to-day ? " or it may have a potential signification, inquiring the will of the party spoken of, as. " *Will* he hazard his life for the safety of his friend ? "

§ 103. In the *subjunctive mode, shall,* in all the persons, denotes

Enumerate the auxiliaries. Which of these are also used as principal verbs ?

mere futurity; as, "If thy brother *shall* trespass against thee, go and tell him his fault." *Will*, on the contrary, is potential in its signification, having respect to the will of the agent or subject; as, "If he *will* strive to improve, he shall be duly rewarded."

§ 104. The following conjugation of *shall* and *will* is inserted to give the pupil a more distinct idea of the proper use of these auxiliaries: —

Shall *and* Will.

AFFIRMATIVE.

Simple Indicative.

Singular.		*Plural.*	
1st *Person*,	I shall	1.	We shall
2d *Person*,	{ You will { Thou wilt	2.	{ You will { Ye will
3d *Person*,	He will	3.	They will

Potential Indicative.

Singular.		*Plural.*	
1.	I will	1.	We will
2.	{ You shall { Thou shalt	2.	{ You shall { Ye shall
3.	He shall	3.	They shall

INTERROGATIVE.

Simple Indicative.

Singular.		*Plural.*	
1.	Shall I?	1.	Shall we?
2.	{ Shall you? { Shalt thou?	2.	{ Shall you? { Shall ye?
3.	Will he?	3.	Will they?

Which of the verbs in the following sentences are simple indicatives, and which have a potential signification? — "I will go;" — "I shall go;" — "He shall obey;" — "Will you go?" — "Will they go?" — "You should improve your time." [Other similar questions respecting these auxiliaries, should be added by the teacher.]

Potential Indicative.

	Singular.		Plural.
1.	Shall I?	1.	Shall we?
2.	{ Will you? { Wilt thou?	2.	{ Will you? { Will ye?
3.	Shall *or* will he?	3.	Shall *or* will they?

SUBJUNCTIVE.

Simple Subjunctive.

	Singular.		Plural.
1.	If I shall	1.	If we shall
2.	{ If you shall { If thou shalt	2.	{ If you shall { If ye shall
3.	If he shall	3.	If they shall

Potential Subjunctive.

	Singular.		Plural.
1.	If I will	1	If we will
2.	{ If you will { If thou wilt	2.	{ If you will { If ye will
3.	If he will	3.	If they will

Should *and* Would.

AFFIRMATIVE.

Simple Indicative

	Singular.		Plural.
1.	I should	1.	We should
2.	{ You would { Thou wouldst	2.	{ You would { Ye would
3.	He would	3.	They would

Potential Indicative.

	Singular.		Plural.
1.	I should *or* would	1.	We should *or* would
2.	{ You should *or* would { Thou shouldst *or* wouldst	2.	{ You should *or* would { Ye should *or* would
3.	He should *or* would	3.	They should *or* would

ETYMOLOGY.

INTERROGATIVE.

Simple Indicative.

Singular.	Plural.
1. Should I?	1. Should we?
2. { Should you? / Shouldst thou?	2. { Should you? / Should ye?
3. Would he?	3. Would they?

Potential Indicative.

Singular.	Plural.
1. Should *or* would I?	1. Should *or* would we?
2. { Should *or* would you? / Shouldst *or* wouldst thou?	2. { Should *or* would you? / Should *or* would ye?
3. Should *or* would he?	3. Should *or* would they?

SUBJUNCTIVE.

Simple Subjunctive.

Singular.	Plural.
1. If I should	1. If we should
2. { If you should / If thou shouldst	2. { If you should / If ye should
3. If he should	3. If they should

Potential Subjunctive.

Singular.	Plural.
1. If I would	1. If we would
2. { If you would / If thou wouldst	2. { If you would / If ye would
3. If he would	3. If they would

REM. — *Will*, used as a principal verb, is conjugated regularly.

§ 105. *Correct Examples.*

"Yes, my son, I *will* point out the way, and my soul *shall* guide yours in the ascent; for we *will* take our flight together." — *Goldsmith*. "The life of a solitary man *will* certainly be miserable, but not certainly devout." — *Johnson*. "The man who feels himself ignorant, *should* at least be modest." — *Ibid*. "He that *would* be superior to external influences, must first become superior to his own passions." — *Ibid*.

VERBS.

§ 106. *Incorrect Examples.*

"What we conceive clearly, and feel strongly, we will naturally express with clearness and strength." — *Blair.* "A limb shall swing upon its hinge, or play in its socket, many hundred times in an hour, for sixty years together, without diminution of its agility. — *Paley.* "We have much to say on the subject of this life, and will often find ourselves obliged to dissent from the opinions of the biographer." — *Macaulay.*

---

§ 107. CONJUGATION OF THE IRREGULAR VERB TO BE.

PRINCIPAL PARTS.

Present, Am. *Past,* Was. *Perf. Participle,* Been.

INDICATIVE MODE.

PRESENT TENSE.

	Singular.			*Plural*
1st *Person,*	I am		1.	We are
2d *Person,*	{ You are { Thou art		2.	{ You are { Ye are
3d *Person,*	He is		3.	They are

REM. 1.—In the Sacred Scriptures, and in the works of our early writers, *be* is sometimes used for *are*; as, "We *be* true men."

PAST TENSE.

	Singular.			*Plural.*
1.	I was		1.	We were
2.	{ You were { Thou wast		2.	{ You were { Ye were
3.	He was		3.	They were

Correct the erroneous examples relating to the use of shall *and* will, *and show why they are erroneous. What are the principal parts of the verb* to be? *Conjugate this verb in the indicative mode, and present tense;— past tense.*

FUTURE TENSE.

Singular.
1. I shall be
2. { You will be / Thou wilt be
3. He will be

Plural.
1. We shall be
2. { You will be / Ye will be
3. They will be

PRESENT PERFECT TENSE.

Singular.
1. I have been
2. { You have been / Thou hast been
3. He has been

Plural.
1. We have been
2. { You have been / Ye have been
3. They have been

PAST PERFECT TENSE.

Singular.
1. I had been
2. { You had been / Thou hadst been
3. He had been

Plural.
1. We had been
2. { You had been / Ye had been
3. They had been

FUTURE PERFECT TENSE.

Singular.
1. I shall have been
2. { You will have been / Thou wilt have been
3. He will have been

Plural.
1. We shall have been
2. { You will have been / Ye will have been
2. They will have been

Conjugate the verb *to be*, in the indicative mode, future tense;—present perfect tense;—past perfect tense;—future perfect tense.

SUBJUNCTIVE MODE.

PRESENT TENSE.

	Singular.		Plural.
1.	If I am	1.	If we are
2.	{ If you are / If thou art }	2.	{ If you are / If ye are }
3.	If he is	3.	If they are

PRESENT TENSE. — Ancient Style.

	Singular.		Plural.
1.	If I be	1.	If we be
2.	{ If you be / If thou be }	2.	{ If you be / If ye be }
3.	If he be	3.	If they be

PAST TENSE.

	Singular.		Plural.
1.	If I was	1.	If we were
2.	{ If you were / If thou wast }	2.	{ If you were / If ye were }
3.	If he was	3.	If they were

FUTURE TENSE.

	Singular.		Plural.
1.	If I shall be	1.	If we shall be
2.	{ If you shall be / If thou shalt be }	2.	{ If you shall be / If ye shall be }
3.	If he shall be	3.	If they shall be

PRESENT PERFECT TENSE.

	Singular.		Plural.
1.	If I have been	1.	If we have been
2.	{ If you have been / If thou hast been }	2.	{ If you have been / If ye have been }
3.	If he has been	3.	If they have been

PAST PERFECT TENSE.

	Singular.		Plural.
1.	If I had been	1.	If we had been
2.	{ If you had been / If thou hadst been }	2.	{ If you had been / If ye had been }
3.	If he had been	3.	If they had been

Conjugate the verb *to be*, in the subjunctive mode, present tense;—present tense and ancient style;—past tense;—future tense;—present perfect tense;—past perfect tense.

FUTURE PERFECT TENSE.

Singular.
1. If I shall have been
2. { If you shall have been
   { If thou shalt have been
3. If he shall have been

Plural.
1. If we shall have been
2. { If you shall have been
   { If ye shall have been
3. If they shall have been

HYPOTHETICAL FORM.*

Singular.
1. If I were
2. { If you were
   { If thou wert
3. If he were

Plural.
1. If we were
2. { If you were
   { If ye were
3. If they were

REM. 2.—This form of the verb *be* is commonly used, in the subjunctive mode, to express a supposition or hypothesis. When employed in a negative sentence, it implies an affirmation; as, "If it *were* not so, I would have told you." When used in an affirmative sentence, it implies a negation; as, "If it *were* possible, they would deceive the very elect." The time denoted by this use of the verb, is sometimes present, and sometimes indefinite. See § 97, Rem. 7.

REM. 3.—The past subjunctive of other verbs is often employed in a similar manner; as, "I would walk out, if it *did* not *rain;*"— "If I *had* the power, I would assist you cheerfully."

REM. 4.—The potential form of the subjunctive mode, is the same in most of the tenses, as the potential form of the indicative. The only difference between them is in the use of the auxiliaries, *shall* and *will.* See the conjugation of *shall* and *will*, § 104.

INFINITIVE MODE.

Present, To be *Present perfect,* To have been

Conjugate the verb *to be* in the subjunctive mode, future perfect tense. *What is the use of the hypothetical form of the verb? What peculiarity respecting the affirmative and negative use of the hypothetical form of the verb? Examples. What time is denoted by it? With what does the potential form of the subjunctive correspond? What is the infinitive present of the verb to be?*— present perfect?

---

* See Hiley, Webster, Frazee, Butler, Waldo, D'Orsey, Connon, and Crane.

IMPERATIVE MODE.

PRESENT TENSE.

Singular, Be, *or* { Be you / Be thou }   *Plural*, Be, *or* { Be you / Be ye }

REM. 7.—Though imperatives are mostly confined to the second person, they are sometimes employed in the first and third persons.*

> *Examples:*—"*Do* we all holy rites."—*Shak.* "Come, *go* we then together."—*Ibid.* "*Proceed* we to mark more particularly."—*Bp. Wilson.* "*Be* not the muse ashamed."—*Thomson.* "This *be* thy just circumference, O world."—*Milton.* "Thy kingdom *come.*"—*Matt.* 6: 10.
>
> "My soul, turn from them; *turn* we to survey
> Where rougher climes a nobler race display."—*Goldsmith.*

PARTICIPLES.

Imperfect, Being   *Perfect*, { Been / Having been }

§ 108. *Synopsis of the verb* To Be.

INDICATIVE.

Present, I am   *Present perfect*, I have been
Past, I was   *Past perfect*, I had been
Future, I shall be   *Future perfect*, I shall have been

SUBJUNCTIVE.

Present tense,   If I am
Present tense, ancient style,   If I be
Past tense,   If I was
Future tense,   If I shall be

Give the imperative;—the participles. Repeat the synopsis of the verb *to be*, in the common form of the indicative;—in the subjunctive.

---

* "In imitation of other languages which have two or three persons in the imperative mode, we occasionally meet with verbs used in a similar manner in the first, but more frequently in the third person."—*Sanborn.* See also Kirkham, Frazee, Perley, R. W. Green, Gurney, Crane, Grant, S Oliver, and Coote.

Present perfect,   If I have been
Past perfect,   If I had been
Future perfect,   If I shall have been
Hypothetical form,   If I were

INFINITIVE.

Present, To be   *Present perfect,* To have been

IMPERATIVE.

Present, Be, *or* Be you *or* thou

PARTICIPLES.

Imperfect, Being   *Perfect,* Been

---

§ 109. CONJUGATION OF THE REGULAR VERB *TO LOVE*, IN THE ACTIVE VOICE.

PRINCIPAL PARTS.

Present, Love.   *Past,* Loved.   *Perf. part.,* Loved.

INDICATIVE MODE.

PRESENT TENSE.

Singular.		*Plural.*
1. I love	1.	We love
2. You love / Thou lovest	2.	You love / Ye love
3. He loves	3.	They love

PAST TENSE.

Singular.		*Plural.*
1. I loved	1.	We loved
2. You loved / Thou lovedst	2.	You loved / Ye loved
3. He loved	3.	They loved

Repeat the synopsis of the verb *to be* in the infinitive. Give the imperative; the participles. What are the principal parts of the verb *to love?* Conjugate this verb in the indicative mode, present tense;—past tense.

FUTURE TENSE.

	Singular.		*Plural.*
1.	I shall love	1.	We shall love
2.	{ You will love / Thou wilt love }	2.	{ You will love / Ye will love }
3.	He will love	3.	They will love

PRESENT PERFECT TENSE.

	Singular.		*Plural.*
1.	I have loved	1.	We have loved
2.	{ You have loved / Thou hast loved }	2.	{ You have loved / Ye have loved }
3.	He has loved	3.	They have loved

PAST PERFECT TENSE.

	Singular.		*Plural.*
1.	I had loved	1.	We had loved
2.	{ You had loved / Thou hadst loved }	2.	{ You had loved / Ye had loved }
3.	He had loved	3.	They had loved

FUTURE PERFECT TENSE.

	Singular.		*Plural.*
1.	I shall have loved	1.	We shall have loved
2.	{ You will have loved / Thou wilt have loved }	2.	{ You will have loved / Ye will have loved }
3.	He will have loved	3.	They will have loved

REM.—The subjunctive of all verbs, except *to be*, has the same form as the indicative. See § 97, Rem. 7.

INFINITIVE MODE.

Present, To love   *Present perfect,* To have loved

IMPERATIVE MODE.

PRESENT TENSE.

Singular, Love, *or* { Love you / Love thou }   *Plural,* Love, *or* { Love you / Love ye }

PARTICIPLES.

Imperfect, Loving   *Perfect,* Having loved

Conjugate the verb *to love* in the indicative mode, future tense;—present perfect;—past perfect;—future perfect. *What is said respecting the form of the potential indicative?—of the subjunctive?* Give the infinitive present;—present perfect;—the imperative;—the participles.

§ 110. *Synopsis of* To Love.

INDICATIVE.

Present, I love *Present perfect,* I have loved
Past, I loved *Past perfect,* I had loved
Future, I shall love *Future perfect,* I shall have loved

INFINITIVE.

Present, To love *Present perfect,* To have loved

IMPERATIVE.

Present, Love, *or* love thou *or* you

PARTICIPLES.

Imperfect, Loving *Perfect,* Having loved

---

§ 111. CONJUGATION OF *TO LOVE*, IN THE PASSIVE VOICE.

INDICATIVE MODE.

PRESENT TENSE.

Singular.
1. I am loved
2. { You are loved
    { Thou art loved
3. He is loved

Plural.
1. We are loved
2. { You are loved
    { Ye are loved
3. They are loved

PAST TENSE.

Singular.
1. I was loved
2. { You were loved
    { Thou wast loved
3. He was loved

Plural.
1. We were loved
2. { You were loved
    { Ye were loved
3. They were loved

FUTURE TENSE.

Singular.
1. I shall be loved
2. { You will be loved
    { Thou wilt be loved
3. He will be loved

Plural.
1. We shall be loved
2. { You will be loved
    { Ye will be loved
3. They will be loved

Give the synopsis of the verb *to love.* Conjugate the passive voice of the verb *to love,* in the indicative mode, present tense; — past tense; — future tense.

VERBS.

PRESENT PERFECT TENSE.

Singular.
1. I have been loved
2. { You have been loved / Thou hast been loved
3. He has been loved

Plural.
1. We have been loved
2. { You have been loved / Ye have been loved
3. They have been loved

PAST PERFECT TENSE.

Singular.
1. I had been loved
2. { You had been loved / Thou hadst been loved
3. He had been loved

Plural.
1. We had been loved
2. { You had been loved / Ye had been loved
3. They had been loved

FUTURE PERFECT TENSE.

Singular.
1. I shall have been loved
2. { You will have been loved / Thou wilt have been loved
3. He will have been loved

Plural.
1. We shall have been loved
2. { You will have been loved / Ye will have been loved
3. They will have been loved

INFINITIVE MODE.

Present, To be loved   *Present perfect,* To have been loved

IMPERATIVE MODE.

PRESENT TENSE.

Singular, Be loved, *or* { Be you loved / Be thou loved
Plural, Be loved, *or* { Be you loved / Be ye loved

PARTICIPLES.

Imperfect, Being loved   *Perfect,* { Loved / Having been loved

§ 112. *Synopsis of* To be Loved.

INDICATIVE.

Present, I am loved   *Pres. perfect,* I have been loved
Past, I was loved   *Past perfect,* I had been loved
Future, I shall be loved   *Fut. perfect,* I shall have been loved

---

Conjugate this verb in the indicative mode, present perfect;—past perfect;—future perfect tense. Give the infinitive present;—present perfect;—the imperative;—the participles. Give the synopsis of *to be loved*.

INFINITIVE.

Present, To be loved   *Present perfect,* To have been loved

IMPERATIVE.

Present, Be loved, *or* Be you *or* thou loved

PARTICIPLES.

Imperfect, Being loved   *Perfect,* Loved, Having been loved

---

§ 113. CONJUGATION OF THE IRREGULAR VERB TO SEE.

PRINCIPAL PARTS.

Present, See.   *Past,* Saw.   *Perfect Participle,* Seen.

INDICATIVE MODE.

PRESENT TENSE.

	Singular.		Plural.
1.	I see	1.	We see
2.	{ You see / Thou seest	2.	{ You see / Ye see
3.	He sees	3.	They see

PAST TENSE.

	Singular.		Plural.
1.	I saw	1.	We saw
2.	{ You saw / Thou sawest	2.	{ You saw / Ye saw
3.	He saw	3.	They saw

FUTURE TENSE.

	Singular.		Plural.
1.	I shall see	1.	We shall see
2.	{ You will see / Thou wilt see	2.	{ You will see / Ye will see
3.	He will see	3.	They will see

Conjugate the verb *to see,* in the indicative mode, present tense;—past tense;—future tense;—present perfect;—past perfect;—future perfect. In the infinitive present;—present perfect. In the imperative. Give the participles.

PRESENT PERFECT TENSE.

Singular.
1. I have seen
2. { You have seen / Thou hast seen }
3. He has seen

Plural.
1. We have seen
2. { You have seen / Ye have seen }
3. They have seen

PAST PERFECT TENSE.

Singular.
1. I had seen
2. { You had seen / Thou hadst seen }
3. He had seen

Plural.
1. We had seen
2. { You had seen / Ye had seen }
3. They had seen

FUTURE PERFECT TENSE.

Singular.
1. I shall have seen
2. { You will have seen / Thou wilt have seen }
3. He will have seen

Plural.
1. We shall have seen
2. { You will have seen / Ye will have seen }
3. They will have seen

INFINITIVE MODE.

Present, To see   *Present perfect,* To have seen

IMPERATIVE MODE.

PRESENT TENSE.

Singular, See, or { See you / See thou }   *Plural,* See, or { See you / See ye }

PARTICIPLES.

Imperfect, Seeing   *Perfect,* Having seen

§ 114. *Synopsis of* To See.

INDICATIVE.

Present, I see   *Present perfect,* I have seen
Past, I saw   *Past perfect,* I had seen
Future, I shall see   *Future perfect,* I shall have seen

INFINITIVE.

Present, To see   *Present perfect,* To have seen

IMPERATIVE.

Present, See, *or* See thou *or* you

PARTICIPLES.

Imperfect, Seeing   *Perfect,* Having seen

Give the synopsis of *to see.*

PROGRESSIVE FORM OF THE VERB.

§ 115. The *progressive form* of a verb is employed to denote the continuance of an action or state. It is composed of an imperfect participle and one of the forms of the verb *to be;* as, "I am *writing* a letter;"—"He *is studying* French."

§ 116. *Synopsis of* To Write, *in the Progressive Form.*

INDICATIVE.

Pres., I am writing   *Pres. perf.*, I have been writing
Past, I was writing   *Past perf.*, I had been writing
Fut., I shall be writing   *Fut. perf.*, I shall have been writing

INFINITIVE.

Present, To be writing   *Present perfect*, To have been writing

IMPERATIVE.

Present, Be writing, *or* Be thou *or* you writing

PARTICIPLES.

Imperfect, Writing   *Perfect*, Having been writing

POTENTIAL FORM.

§ 117. *Synopsis of* To Hear *in the Potential Form.*

Present or *Future*, I may, can, *or* must hear
Present, *Past*, or *Future*, I might, could, would, *or* should hear
Present perfect or *Future perfect*, I may, can, *or* must have heard
Present perf. or *Past perf.*, I might, could, would, *or* should have heard

REM. 1.—The potential use of the auxiliaries *shall* and *will*, constitutes another form of the potential indicative and potential subjunctive. See § 104.

REM. 2.—In determining the tense of a verb used potentially, the pupil should generally be governed by the sense of the passage which contains it, without regard to the form of the verb.

THE AUXILIARY *DO*.

§ 118. In sentences which express emphasis, interrogation, or negation, the present and past tenses of the indicative and subjunctive modes, and the present imperative, are often formed by the aid of the auxiliary verb *do;* as, "I *do* know it to be true;"—"*Do* you intend to return to-morrow?"—"I *do* not understand you."

What is the progressive form of a verb? Of what is it composed? Give the synopsis of *to write*, in the progressive form. *Give a synopsis of the verb* to hear, *in the potential form. In what sentences is the auxiliary* do *employed? Examples. What tenses are often formed by the aid of the auxiliary* do?

§ 119. *Synopsis of* To Hear, *with the Auxiliary* Do

INDICATIVE.
Present, I do hear   Past, I did hear

SUBJUNCTIVE.
Present, If I do hear   Past, If I did hear

IMPERATIVE.
Present, Do hear, *or* Do thou *or* you hear.

Rem. - *Do*, as a principal verb, is conjugated like other irregular verbs.

INTERROGATIVE FORM.

§ 120. In interrogative sentences, when the verb has no auxiliary, the nominative is placed after the verb; when one auxiliary is used, the nominative is placed between the auxiliary and the principal verb; and when more auxiliaries than one are employed, the nominative is placed after the first.

§ 121. *Synopsis of* To Hear, *used Interrogatively*.

INDICATIVE.

Pres., Hear I? *or* Do I hear?   *Pres. perf.*, Have I heard?
Past, Heard I? *or* Did I hear?   *Past perf.*, Had I heard?
Fut., Shall I hear?   *Fut. perf.*, Shall I have heard?

NEGATIVE FORM.

§ 122. A verb is conjugated negatively by introducing the adverb *not* in connection with it; as, *I know not; I do not know; I shall not have known; I should not have been known.*

EXERCISES.

§ 123. "I was." — "He had been." — "They think." — "We will return." — "Strive to improve." — "It is found." — "If we shall hear." — "Thou canst see." — "If he had been." — "If he would learn." — "Shall I read?" — "Can it be understood?" — "Honor thy father and thy mother."

Give the synopsis of to hear, *with the auxiliary* do. *What is the place of the nominative, in interrogative sentences? Give the synopsis of the verb* to hear, *used interrogatively. How is a verb conjugated negatively? Examples.*

Give the mode, tense, number, and person of each of the verbs in the foregoing sentences. *Which of them are in the potential form of the indicative mode? Which in the potential form of the subjunctive?*

Mention a verb in the third person plural of the past perfect subjunctive. One in the present imperative. One in the present perfect infinitive. One in the first person singular of the future perfect indicative. *One in the third person singular of the present or future indicative, and potential form.* Mention three perfect participles. Three imperfect participles. Mention a verb in the third person singular of the present perfect indicative, and passive voice. Give the mode, tense, person, number, and voice of the following verbs: — will write; — was written; — began; — to have been seen; — had heard. [A variety of similar directions should be added by the teacher.]

Write sentences containing examples of verbs in the common form of the indicative and subjunctive modes; — *in the potential indicative and potential subjunctive;* — in the imperative and infinitive modes; — containing examples of both imperfect and perfect participles; — of verbs in the passive voice; — *containing examples of* shall *and* will, *correctly employed.*

IRREGULAR VERBS.

§ 124. An *irregular verb* is one that does not form its past tense and perfect participle by adding *d* or *ed* to the present; as, *see, saw, seen; go, went, gone.*

§ 125. The following list comprises nearly all the simple irregular verbs in our language.

REM. 1. — When more forms than one are used in the past tense or perfect participle, that which stands first is to be preferred.

LIST OF IRREGULAR VERBS.

Present.	*Past*	*Perf. Part.*
Abide	abode, abided	abode, abided
Am *or* be	was	been

What is an irregular verb? Examples. *Give the past tenses and perfect participle of the verb* abide; — *of the verb* am; — *of the verb* awake. [The teacher should proceed in this manner through the list, and repeat the exercise till the pupils are able to name with readiness the past tense and perfect participle of all the irregular verbs.]

Present.	Past.	Perf. part.
Awake	awoke, awaked	awaked, awoke
Bear (to bring forth)	bore, bare*	born
Bear (to sustain) *for*-	bore, bare*	borne
Beat	beat	beaten, beat
Begin	began	begun
Bend, *un*-	bent, bended	bent
Bereave	bereft, bereaved	bereft, bereaved
Beseech	besought	besought
Bid, *for*-	bid, bade	bidden, bid
Bind, *un*-, *re*-	bound	bound
Bite	bit	bitten, bit
Bleed	bled	bled
Blow	blew	blown
Break	broke, brake*	broken
Breed	bred	bred
Bring	brought	brought
Build, *re*-, *up*	built, builded	built, builded
Burn	burned, burnt	burned, burnt
Burst	burst	burst
Buy	bought	bought
Cast	cast	cast
Catch	caught, catched†	caught, catched†
Chide	chid	chidden, chid
Choose	chose	chosen
Cleave (to adhere)	cleaved, clave*	cleaved
Cleave (to split)	clove, cleft, clave*	cloven, cleft
Cling	clung	clung
Clothe	clothed, clad	clothed, clad
Come, *be*-, *over*-	came	come
Cost	cost	cost
Creep	crept	crept
Crow	crowed, crew	crowed
Cut	cut	cut
Dare‡ (to venture)	dared, durst	dared
Deal	dealt, dealed	dealt, dealed
Dig	dug, digged	dug, digged
Do, *un*,- *mis*-, *over*-	did	done
Draw, *with*-	drew	drawn
Dream	dreamed, dreamt	dreamed, dreamt
Drink	drank	drank,§ drunk
Drive	drove, drave*	driven

---

* Obsolete. † Obsolescent. ‡ *Dare,* to challenge, is regular.

§ "From the disagreeable idea excited by the participle *drunk, drank* has been long in polite usage adopted instead of it."— *Walker, the Lexicographer.*
"If we mistake not, *drank* is oftener used by good writers than *drunk* or *drunken.*"— *Fowle.*

Drank is also given as a perfect participle of *drink* by Sanborn, Webster Goldsbury, Jenkins, Kirkham, Powers, Fletcher, R. W. Green, Frazee, Parkhurst, Badgley, Jones, Davis, Weld, Day, Whiting, Beall, and others.

Examples: — "Bats and hideous birds had *drank* up the oil which nourished the perpetual lamp in the temple of Odin."—*Johnson.* "The cold

Present.	Past.	Perf. Part.
Dwell	dwelt, dwelled	dwelt, dwelled
Eat	ate, eat	eaten
Fall, be-	fell	fallen
Feed	fed	fed
Feel	felt	felt
Fight	fought	fought
Find	found	found
Flee	fled	fled
Fling	flung	flung
Fly	flew	flown
Forsake	forsook	forsaken
Freeze	froze	frozen
Freight	freighted	fraught, freighted
Get, be-, for-	got, gat*	got, gotten
Gild	gilded, gilt	gilded, gilt
Gird, be-, un-, en	girt, girded	girt, girded
Give, for-, mis-	gave	given
Go, fore-, under	went	gone
Grave, en-	graved	graven, graved
Grind	ground	ground
Grow	grew	grown
Hang‡	hung	hung
Have	had	had
Hear, over-	heard	heard
Heave	heaved, hove	heaved, hoven*
Hew	hewed	hewn, hewed
Hide	hid	hidden, hid
Hit	hit	hit
Hold, be-, with, up-	held	held, holden†
Hurt	hurt	hurt
Keep	kept	kept
Kneel	kneeled, knelt	kneeled, knelt
Knit	knit, knitted	knit, knitted
Know, fore-	knew	known
Lade§ (to load)	laded	laden
Lay (to place), in-	laid	laid
Lend, mis-	lent	lent
Leave	left	left
Lend	lent	lent
Let	let	let
Lie ‖ (to recline)	lay	lain

water that was *drank*."—*Pres. Hopkins*. "The man hath *drank*."—*Southey*. "Such a discourse could have emanated only from a mind which had *drank* deeply from the fountains of experience, observation, and reflection."—*Horace Mann*.

"It is a sultry day; the sun has *drank*
The dew that lay upon the morning grass."—*Bryant*.

* Obsolete. † Obsolescent.

‡ *Hang*, to take away life by hanging, is regular; as, "Judas departed, and went and hanged himself."

§ *Lade*, to dip, is regular. ‖ *Lie*, to deceive, is regular.

Present.	Past.	Perf. Part.
Light	lighted, lit	lighted, lit
Load, *un-*, *over-*	loaded	loaded, loaden*
Lose	lost	lost
Make	made	made
Mean	meant	meant
Meet	met	met
Mow	mowed	mown, mowed
Pay, *re-*	paid	paid
Pent (to enclose)	penned, pent	pent, penned
Put	put	put
Quit	quit, quitted	quitted, quit
Read	read	read
Rend	rent	rent
Rid	rid	rid
Ride	rode, rid*	rode, ridden, rid*
Ring	rang, rung	rung
Rise, *a-*	rose	risen
Rive	rived	riven
Run, *out-*	ran	run
Saw	sawed	sawn, sawed
Say, *un-*, *gain*	said	said
See, *fore-*	saw	seen
Seek	sought	sought
Seethe	seethed, sod	seethed, sodden
Sell	sold	sold
Send	sent	sent
Set, *be-*	set	set
Sit (to rest)	sat	sat
Shake	shook	shaken
Shape, *mis-*	shaped	shaped, shapen
Shave	shaved	shaved, shaven
Shear	sheared	shorn, sheared
Shed	shed	shed
Shine	shone, shined	shone, shined
Shoe	shod	shod
Shoot, *over-*	shot	shot
Show *or* shew	showed *or* shewed	shown *or* shewn
Shred	shred	shred
Shrink	shrunk, shrank	shrunk
Shut	shut	shut
Sing	sang, sung	sung
Sink	sunk, sank	sunk
Slay	slew	slain
Sleep	slept	slept
Slide	slid	slidden, slid
Sling	slung, slang*	slung
Slink	slunk	slunk
Slit	slit, slitted	slit, slitted
Smite	smote	smitten, smit
Sow‡ (to scatter)	sowed	sown, sowed

* Obsolete.   † *Pen*, to write, is regular.   ‡ *Sew*, to stitch, is regular.

Present.	Past.	Perf. Part.
Speak, *be-*	spoke, spake*	spoken, spoke
Speed	sped	sped
Spell, *mis-*	spelled, spelt	spelled, spelt
Spend, *mis-*	spent	spent
Spill	spilt, spilled	spilt, spilled
Spin	spun, span*	spun
Spit‡	spit, spat*	spit, spitten*
Split	split	split
Spread, *over-, be-*	spread	spread
Spring	sprang, sprung	sprung
Stand, *with-, under-*	stood	stood
Steal	stole	stolen
Stick	stuck	stuck
Sting	stung	stung
Stride, *be-*	strode, strid	stridden, strid
Strike	struck	struck, stricken*
String	strung	strung
Strive	strove	striven
Strow *or* Strew, *bs*	strowed *or* strewed	strown, strowed strewn, strewed
Swear, *for-*	swore, sware*	sworn
Sweat	sweat, sweated	sweat, sweated
Sweep	swept	swept
Swell	swelled	swollen, swelled
Swim	swam, swum	swum
Swing [*re-, over-*	swung	swung
Take, *mis-, under-, be-,*	took	taken
Teach, *un,- mis-*	taught	taught
Tear	tore, tare*	torn
Tell, *fore-*	told	told
Think, *be-*	thought	thought
Thrive	throve, thrived	thriven, thrived
Throw, *over-*	threw	thrown
Thrust	thrust	thrust
Tread, *re-*	trod	trodden, trod
Wax	waxed	waxed, waxen
Wear	wore	worn
Weave, *un-*	wove	woven, wove
Weep	wept	wept
Wet	wet, wetted	wet, wetted
Whet	whetted, whet	whetted, whet
Win	won	won
Wind, *un-*	wound	wound
Work	worked, wrought	worked, wrought
Wring	wrung, wringed	wrung, wringed
Write	wrote, writ*	written, writ

REM. 2. — When the past tense is a monosyllable not ending in a single vowel, the second person singular of the solemn style is generally

---

* Obsolete. ‡ *Spit*, to put on a spit, is regular.

formed by the addition of *est*; as, *heardest, fleddest, tookest*. *Hadst, wast, saidst*, and *didst*, are exceptions; and instances frequently occur in which good writers prefer the shorter form of other words; as, *fledst* for *fleddest*, *heardst* for *heardest*.

REM. 3.—Compound verbs (except *welcome* and *behave*, which are regular), are conjugated like the simple verbs from which they are formed; as, *see, saw, seen; foresee, foresaw, foreseen*.

DEFECTIVE VERBS.

§ 126. A *defective verb* is one that cannot be used in all the modes and tenses. Thus, we cannot say, "I had could," "I shall can," etc.

The defective verbs are *can, could, may, might, shall, should, will, would, must, ought, quoth*, and *beware*.

UNIPERSONAL VERBS.

§ 127. A *unipersonal** verb is one that is used only in the third person singular; as, It *hails;* It *snows;* It *behoves*.

REM.— *Methinks* is an anomalous word, compounded of *me* and *thinks*. It is generally ranked with unipersonal verbs.

EXERCISES.

§ 128. Write sentences containing examples of irregular verbs; — of defective verbs; — of unipersonal verbs.

How are compound verbs conjugated? What is a defective verb? *Enumerate the defective verbs.* What is a unipersonal verb? Examples.

---

* The term *impersonal* is commonly applied to this class of verbs; but a word which is always employed in one of the three grammatical persons, cannot, with any degree of propriety, be said to be *without* person.

"As to the verbs which some grammarians have called *impersonal*, there are, in fact, no such things in the English language." — *Cobbett.*

"This form is commonly called *impersonal;* but this denomination is incorrect and inadmissible, since these verbs are really in the third person." — *De Sacy.*

Hiley denominates these verbs *monopersonal;* and De Sacy, Sutcliffe, and Morgan, call them *verbs of the third person*. The term *unipersonal* is adopted in the English grammars of Crane, Clark, Pinneo, and Fowle, in Bachi's Italian Grammar, and in the French grammars of Bolmar and Bugard.

THE ADVERB.

§ 129. An *Adverb** is a word used to modify the sense of a verb, an adjective, or another adverb; as, "He is *not* understood;"—"He speaks *very* fluently;"—"A *remarkably* diligent boy."

REM. 1.—Adverbs generally express in one word what would otherwise require two or more. Thus, *now* is used for *at this time; there*, for *in that place*.

REM. 2.—Many adverbs are formed by the union of two or more words. Thus, *indeed* is composed of *in* and *deed; sometimes*, of *some* and *times; herein*, of *here* and *in*.

§ 130. Adverbs may be divided into several classes, of which the following are the most important:—

1. Adverbs of Manner; as, *justly, rapidly*.
2. Of Place; as, *here, there*.
3. Of Time; as, *now, soon, lately*.
4. Of Degree; as, *more, less, hardly*.
5. Of Affirmation; as, *yes, certainly, doubtless*.
6. Of Negation; as, *not, no*.

REM. 1.—Other classes might be enumerated, but they are less distinctly marked; and the different uses of adverbs are so numerous that a perfect classification is impracticable.

REM. 2.—The words *to-day, to-night, to-morrow*, and *yesterday*, though sometimes classed with adverbs, are properly nouns.

CONJUNCTIVE ADVERBS.

§ 131. A *conjunctive adverb* is one that performs the office of a modifier and also of a connective; as, "*When* Crusoe saw the savages, he became greatly alarmed."

COMPARISON OF ADVERBS.

§ 132. Many adverbs, like adjectives, admit of comparison.

What is an adverb? Examples. Name the principal classes of adverbs, and give examples of each. What is a conjunctive adverb? Examples.

---

* The term *adverb* is derived from the two Latin words, *ad* and *verbum*, which signify *to a verb*.

Most of those ending in *ly* are compared by *more* and *most;* as, wisely, more wisely, most wisely.

A few are compared by adding *er* and *est;* as, soon, sooner soonest.

The following are compared irregularly: —

Far, { farther, farthest
{ further, furthest
Well, better, best

Little, less, least
Much, more, most
Ill *or* badly, worse, worst.

EXERCISES.

§ 133. "The tree grows very rapidly." — "Iron is much harder than copper." — "Fortune sometimes favors those whom she afterwards destroys." — "Diligence is seldom unrewarded." — "Truth never fears examination, however rigid it may be." — "Whatever is done willingly is done well."

Point out the adverbs in the foregoing sentences. *Give the class of each.*

Name three adverbs ending in *ly;* — three that do not end in *ly.*

Write sentences containing examples of adverbs which modify verbs, adjectives, and other adverbs.

Write sentences containing adverbs of manner, place, time, degree, affirmation, and negation.

THE PREPOSITION.

§ 134. A *Preposition** is a word used to express the relation of a noun or pronoun depending upon it, to some other word in the sentence; as, "He went *from* Boston *to* Albany;" — "Washington was the father *of* his country."

How are adverbs ending in ly *generally compared? Examples. Give examples of adverbs compared by* er *and* est; *— of adverbs compared irregularly.* What is a preposition? Examples.

---

* The term *preposition* is derived from the Latin word *præpositus*, which signifies *placed before.*

REM.— In the foregoing examples, *from* expresses the relation between *went* and *Boston*; *to*, the relation between *went* and *Albany*; and, *of*, the relation between *father* and *country*.

§ 135. The following list of prepositions embraces most of those in common use:—

About	at	by	on	under
above	athwart	concerning	over	underneath
across	before	down	respecting	until
after	behind	during	round	unto
against	below	except	since	up
along	beneath	excepting	through	upon
amid *or*	beside *or*	for	throughout	with
amidst	besides	from	till	within
among *or*	between	in	to	without
amongst	betwixt	into	towards	worth*
around	beyond	of		

THE CONJUNCTION.

§ 136. A *Conjunction*† is a word that is used to connect words or sentences; as, "Seven *and* five are twelve;"—"Straws swim on the surface; *but* pearls lie at the bottom."

REM. — The words belonging to this part of speech do not admit of a satisfactory division into classes.‡

What is a conjunction? Examples.

* "*Worth* has the construction of a preposition, as it admits of the objective case after it, without an intervening preposition."—*Worcester's Dict.*

"The word *worth* is often followed by an objective, or a participle which it appears to *govern*; as, 'If your arguments produce no conviction, they are *worth* nothing to me.'—'This is life indeed, life *worth* preserving.' It is not easy to determine to what part of speech *worth* here belongs. Dr. Johnson calls it an *adjective*, but says nothing of the *objective* after it, which some suppose to be governed by *of* understood. In this supposition, it is gratuitously assumed, that *worth* is equivalent to *worthy*, after which *of* should be expressed; as, 'Whatsoever is *worthy of* their love, is *worth* their anger.' But, as *worth* appears to have no *certain* characteristic of an *adjective*, some call it a *noun*, and suppose a double ellipsis; as, 'The book is [of the] worth [of] a dollar.' This is still less satisfactory; and, as the whole appears to be mere guess-work, we see no good reason why *worth* is not a preposition, governing the noun or participle."—*G. Brown.*

Worth is also classed with prepositions by Davis, Everest, Jenkins, Todd, Badgley, and others.

† The term *conjunction* is derived from the Latin word *conjungo*, which signifies *to join together.*

‡ "The old distinction of conjunctions into *copulative* and *disjunctive*,

§ 137. The following is a list of the words most frequently employed as conjunctions:—

And	but	neither	than	though
although	either	nor	that	unless
as	for	notwithstanding	then	wherefore
because	if	or	therefore	yet
both	lest	since		

THE INTERJECTION.

§ 138. An *Interjection*[*] is an exclamatory word, used merely to express some passion or emotion.

The following list of interjections includes most of those which are in general use:—

Ah! alas! fie! ha! hallo! indeed! lo! O! oh! pshaw! ho! welcome!

REM.—Other parts of speech are frequently used to perform the office of interjections; as, hark! surprising! mercy!

EXERCISES.

§ 139. "Of what use are riches without happiness?"—"Whatsoever ye would that men should do to you, do ye even so to them."—"The sun, moon, and stars, admonish us of a superior and superintending power."—"Righteousness exalteth a nation; but sin is a reproach to any people."—"Whence are thy beams, O sun!"

What is an interjection? Examples.

---

was founded in error, and is, happily, going into disuse in our grammars."—*Frazee.*

"Conjunctions are generally divided into *copulative* and *disjunctive;* but more confusion than practical advantage seems to be derived from the division."—*Goodenow.*

"I shall not take up time, and confuse the understanding of the learner, by dividing the words considered as conjunctions, into *copulative, disjunctive, concessive,* etc."—*Lewis.*

"The common division of the words termed conjunctions, into *copulative,* as *and; disjunctive,* as *either, or, neither, nor,* etc.; *concessive,* as *though, although, yet; adversative,* as *but, however; causal,* as *for, because, since; illative,* as *therefore, wherefore, then; conditional,* as *if; exceptive,* as *unless;* deserves little consideration."—*Grant.*

[*] The term *interjection* is derived from the Latin word *interjectus,* which signifies *thrown between.*

Point out the prepositions, conjunctions, and interjections, in the foregoing sentences.

Write sentences containing examples of prepositions, conjunctions, and interjections.

DERIVATION.*

§ 140. *Derivation* is that part of Etymology which treats of the origin and primary signification of words.

REM. — The words of every cultivated language may be reduced to groups or families, each of which is composed of words related to each other by identity of origin and similarity of signification. Thus, the words *justice, justify, justification, justly, adjust, readjust, unjust, injustice*, etc., are all kindred words, connected with the common parent *just.* So also, the words *terrace, terraqueous, terrene, terrestrial, terrier, territory, inter, interment, disinter, Mediterranean, subterranean*, etc., are all connected with their parent *terra*, the earth.

§ 141. Words are divided into two general classes: — *primitive* and *derivative*.

A *primitive* word is one that is not derived from any other word or words in the language; as, *man, obey*.

A *derivative* word is one that is formed from some primitive word or words; as, *manly, disobey*.

ORIGIN OF ENGLISH WORDS.

§ 142. The basis of the English language is the Anglo-Saxon, which was introduced into England from Germany about the middle of the fifth century.

REM. — This original stock, besides being greatly modified by use, has received large additions from other languages. The inva

---

What is derivation? *To what may the words of every cultivated language be reduced?* *Examples.* Into what two general classes are words divided? What is a primitive word? Examples. A derivative word? Examples What is the basis of our language?

---

* For a full and well-digested system of Derivation, the learner is referred to McElligott's "Analytical Manual."

sion of the Danes and Normans introduced many Danish and Norman-French words; and a great number of Latin and Greek words have been since incorporated. We are also indebted for some of our words to the French, Italian, Spanish, German, and other languages.

PREFIXES AND SUFFIXES.

§ 143. Most of the derivative words of our language, are formed by the aid of *prefixes* and *suffixes*.

A *prefix* is a letter, syllable, or word, joined to the beginning of a word; as, *a*loft, *re*build, *over*come.

A *suffix* is a letter or syllable, joined to the end of a word; as, storm*y*, proud*ly*, law*less*.

REM. 1.—Most of the suffixes do not admit of precise and accurate definitions.

REM. 2.—Two or more prefixes or suffixes are sometimes employed in the same word; as, *rediscover*, *powerfully*. *Rediscover* contains two prefixes, *re* and *dis*; and *powerfully*, two suffixes, *ful* and *ly*.

REM. 3.—Many of the roots or essential parts of the words before which prefixes are placed, are not used as distinct words in our language.

REM. 4.—When a prefix ends in a sound that will not readily unite with the sound of the word before which it is placed, the final letter of the prefix is oftened changed or omitted; as, *ignoble*, for *innoble*; *coexist*, for *conexist*.

English or Saxon Prefixes.

§ 144. The following are the prefixes of English or Saxon origin, with their significations:—

1. *A* signifies *on*, *in*, or *at*; as, *a*shore, on shore; *a*sleep, in sleep.
2. *Be* signifies *upon*, *over*, *about*, etc.; as, *be*speak, *be*dew, *be*sprinkle.
3. *For* signifies *from* or *against*; as, *for*bear, *for*bid.
4. *Fore* signifies *before*; as, *fore*see, *fore*tell.

What changes has our language undergone since the period of the Anglo Saxons? How are most English derivatives formed? What is a prefix? Examples. What is a suffix? Examples. What is sometimes done with the final letter of a prefix?

5*

5. *Mis* signifies *wrong, erroneous, or defective;* as, *mis*conduct, *mis*rule.

6. *Out* signifies *beyond, more,* or *exterior;* as, *out*run, *out*live, *out*side.

7. *Over* implies *excess* or *superiority;* as, *over*do, *over*come.

8. *Un* denotes *negation* or *privation;* as, *un*certain, *un*bind.

9. *Under* generally signifies *beneath, inferior,* or *subordinate;* as, *under*lay, *under*mine.

10. *Up* denotes *elevation* or *subversion;* as, *up*land, *up*set.

11. *With* generally denotes *opposition* or *separation;* as, *with*stand, *with*draw.

Latin Prefixes.

§ 145. The following are the principal prefixes derived from the Latin, with their significations: —

1. *A, ab,* or *abs,* signifies *from;* as, *a*vert, to turn from; *ab*solve, to release from; *abs*tract, to draw from.

2. *Ad* signifies *to* or *at;* as, *ad*join, to join to. In composition this prefix may become *a, ac, af, ag, al, an, ap, ar, as,* or *at;* as, *a*scend, *ac*cede, *af*fix, *ag*grandize, *al*lot, *an*nex, *ap*peal, *ar*rest, *as*sume, *at*tract.

3. *Ante* signifies *before;* as, *ante*cedent, going before; *ante*diluvian, before the Flood.

4. *Circum* signifies *round* or *about;* as, *circum*navigate, to sail round.

5. *Con* signifies *with* or *together;* as, *con*voke, to call together. This prefix takes also the forms *co, cog, col, com,* and *cor;* as, *co*here, *cog*nate, *col*lect, *com*press, *cor*relative.

6. *Contra* signifies *against;* as, *contra*dict, to speak against. This prefix is sometimes changed to *counter;* as, *counter*act.

7. *De* generally signifies *from* or *down;* as, *de*duce, to draw from; *de*base, to bring down.

8. *Dis* generally implies *separation* or *disunion;* as, *dis*solve. It has sometimes a negative use; as, *dis*approve. *Dis* takes also the forms *di* and *dif;* as, *di*verge, *dif*fuse.

9. *E* or *ex* signifies *out, out of,* or *from;* as, *e*ject, to cast out; *e*vade, to escape from. This prefix takes also the forms *ec* and *ef;* as, *ec*centric, *ef*face.

10. *Extra* signifies *beyond,* or *more than;* as, *extra*ordinary.

11. *In*, before an adjective, has a negative signification, nearly equivalent to *not;* as, *in*active, not active; *in*secure, not secure. Before a verb, *in* signifies *in*, *into*, or *against;* as, *in*sert, to place in; *in*dict, to speak against. This prefix takes also the forms *en*, *im*, *ig*, *il*, *ir*, and *em;* as, *en*grave, *im*placable, *ig*noble, *il*legal, *ir*radiate, *em*boss.

12. *Inter* signifies *between* or *among;* as, *inter*vene, to come between; *inter*sperse, to scatter among.

13. *Ob* generally signifies *against;* as, *ob*struct, to build against *Ob* takes also the forms *oc*, *of*, and *op;* as, *oc*cur, *of*fend, *op*pose.

14. *Per* generally signifies *through* or *by;* as, *per*vade, to pass through; *per*chance, by chance.

15. *Pre* or *præ* signifies *before;* as, *pre*cede, to go before.

16. *Pro* signifies *for*, *forth*, or *forward;* as, *pro*noun, for a noun, *pro*voke, to call forth; *pro*mote, to move forward.

17. *Re* signifies *again* or *back;* as, *re*ënter, to enter again; *re*call, to call back.

18. *Se* denotes *departure* or *separation;* as, *se*cede, to withdraw from.

19. *Sub* signifies *under;* as, *sub*scribe, to write under. *Sub* has also the forms *suc*, *suf*, *sug*, *sup*, and *sus;* as, *suc*ceed, *suf*fuse, *sug*gest, *sup*port, *sus*pend.

20. *Super* generally signifies *beyond*, *above*, or *over;* as, *super*natural, beyond nature; *super*vise, to oversee. This prefix often becomes *sur;* as, *sur*charge.

21. *Trans* signifies *over* or *beyond;* as, *trans*fer, to carry over; *trans*atlantic, beyond the Atlantic.

Greek Prefixes.

§ 146. The following are some of the principal prefixes derived from the Greek, with their significations: —

1. *A* or *an* denotes *privation*, and is generally equivalent to *without;* as, *a*theist, without a God; *an*archy, without government.

2. *Anti* signifies *against;* as, *anti*christian, against Christianity.

3. *Mono* signifies *single;* as, *mono*syllable, one syllable.

4. *Poly* signifies *many;* as, *poly*syllable, a word of many syllables.

5. *Syn* signifies *with* or *together;* as, *syn*thesis, putting together. *Syn* takes also the forms *sy*, *syl*, and *sym;* as, *sy*stem, *syl*logism, *sym*pathy.

PART III.

SYNTAX.

§ 147. SYNTAX treats of the construction of sentences according to the established laws of speech.

§ 148. A *sentence* is an assemblage of words making complete sense.

Sentences are of two kinds;—simple and compound.

A *simple sentence* is a sentence that contains only one finite verb; as, "The sun *rises* in the east."

REM.—The subject of a simple sentence may itself be compound; as, "*Five and three* are eight."

A *compound sentence* is one that contains two or more simple sentences; as, "Industry procures competence, and frugality preserves it;"—"He fills, he bounds, connects, and equals all."

§ 149. The simple sentences which unite to form a compound sentence, are called *members* or *clauses*.

§ 150. The principal parts of a simple sentence are the subject or nominative, the verb, and the object. Thus, in the sentence, "Temperance promotes health," *temperance* is the subject, *promotes* the verb, and *health* the object.

Of what does syntax treat? What is a sentence? Into what two general classes are sentences divided? What is a simple sentence? Examples. A compound sentence? Examples. What are the simple sentences embraced in a compound sentence called? What are the principal parts of a simple sentence? Illustrate.

REM.—A sentence in which the verb is intransitive, has only two principal parts, the subject and the verb; as, "He runs."

§ 151. A *Phrase* is a combination of words forming a part of a sentence, but not containing a finite verb; as, "At length;"—"Hand in hand;"—"The hour having arrived;"—"To confess the truth."

§ 152. Words used to explain or modify other words, are called *adjuncts*. This term embraces all the words of a simple sentence, except the *principal parts*. Many adjuncts are composed of two or more words; as, "Printing was invented *in the fifteenth century*." The whole phrase, "in the fifteenth century," is here an adjunct of *was invented*. *The* and *fifteenth* are also adjuncts of *century*.

§ 153. An *Idiom* is a form of expression peculiar to a language; as, "*Bear with me;*"—"They came forward, *to a man*."

REM.—The idioms of a language are not governed by the ordinary rules of syntax. A knowledge of them is therefore best acquired by observing carefully the phraseology of the best speakers and writers.

§ 154. *Agreement* is the correspondence of one word with another, in gender, number, person, case, or form.

§ 155. *Government* is the power which one word has over another, in determining its state.

EXERCISES.

§ 156. "Philosophers have often mistaken the true source of happiness."—"Pride goeth before destruction and a haughty spirit before a fall."—"Children are supported by their parents."—"Phocion was always poor, though he might have been very rich."—"Dryden knew more of man in his general nature; Pope in his local manners."—"He will go by and by."—"In a word, the time for action has come."

What are the principal parts of a sentence in which the verb is intransitive? Examples. What is a phrase? Examples. What is an adjunct? Examples. What is an idiom? Examples. What is agreement? What is government?

Which of the foregoing sentences are simple? Which compound? Point out the principal parts of each simple sentence. *Which of the simple sentences have three principal parts? Which have only two? Point out one or more phrases. Point out the adjuncts in each simple sentence. What idioms occur?*

Write a simple sentence;—a compound sentence;—a simple sentence having three principal parts;—one having only two. *Write a sentence having a phrase connected with it;—one containing an idiom.*

ANALYSIS.*

§ 157. The *analysis* of a sentence consists in resolving it into its constituent parts, and pointing out their several relations, connections, and dependences.

Every simple sentence consists essentially of two parts;—a *subject* and a *predicate*. The *subject* is that of which something is affirmed; and the *predicate* is that which is affirmed of the subject.

§ 158. The subject and predicate may be distinguished as either *grammatical* or *logical*.

The *grammatical subject* is a noun, or some word, phrase, or sentence, used as a noun.

Examples:—"No man was ever great by imitation."—*Johnson.* "To tell our own secrets, is generally folly."—*Ibid.* "Who can understand his errors."—*Ps.* 19: 12. "That you have wronged me, doth appear in this."—*Shak.*

The *logical subject* includes all the words that are employed to express the whole idea of the subject.

Examples:—"No man was ever great by imitation."—"To tell our own secrets, is generally folly."—"The desire of being pleased, is universal."

In what does the analysis of a sentence consist? Of what does every simple sentence consist? Define the subject and the predicate. What is the grammatical subject? Examples. What is the logical subject? Examples.

---

* Andrews and Stoddard's Latin Grammar, Kühner's Latin and Greek Grammars, Crosby's Greek Grammar, De Sacy's General Grammar, Crane's English Grammar, and Mulligan's Grammatical Structure of the English Language.

The *grammatical predicate* is a finite verb.*

Examples:—"No genius *was* ever *blasted* by the breath of critics."—*Johnson.* "Malice often *bears* down truth."—*Ibid.* "We *dwell* with pious fondness on the characters and virtues of the departed."—*Story.*

The *logical predicate* includes all the words that are employed to express the whole idea of the predicate.

Examples:—"No genius *was ever blasted by the breath of critics.*"—"Malice *often bears down truth.*"—"The discriminating power of conscience *is improved by reflecting upon the moral character of our actions.*"—*Wayland.*

REM. 1.—The grammatical subject and predicate are often the same as the logical. Thus, in the sentence, "Time flies," the whole idea of the subject is expressed by the noun *Time*, and the whole idea of the predicate, by the verb *flies*. *Time* is therefore both the grammatical and the logical subject, and *flies* both the grammatical and the logical predicate.

REM. 2.—When the grammatical subject or predicate is modified by other words, it is said to be *complex*.† The *complex* subject or

---

What is the grammatical predicate? Examples. The logical predicate? Examples.

---

* Some grammarians still adhere to the principle, that the grammatical predicate may consist of a noun or adjective, in connection with the verb *to be*. Thus, in the sentence, "Snow is white," it is said that *is* does not express what is asserted of *snow*, and therefore the grammatical predicate is not properly *is*, but *is white*. In the sentence, "He has friends," we might, with equal propriety, say that the word *has* does not express what is asserted of *he*, and therefore the grammatical predicate is not properly *has*, but *has friends*. This mode of reasoning proves too much. It would destroy all distinction between the grammatical and the logical predicate.

Since the above note was written, similar views have been expressed in an able and elaborate treatise on the Structure of the English Language, by J. Mulligan. The following is an extract from his remarks on this subject:—"Another difficulty which presented itself, was to ascertain the distinction between the grammatical functions performed by *is*, for example, in the proposition, 'The man *is* old,' and the function performed by *becomes* in the proposition, 'The man *becomes* old,' or by *grows* in the proposition, 'The man *grows* old,' or by *seems* in the proposition, 'The man *seems* old.' The difference of *meaning* of all these verbs is abundantly clear, but we could not discover or assign any *grammatical* distinction. Till this was done, we felt bound, if we called *is* the copula, to call *becomes, grows, seems*, etc., copulas. In this case, copulas would be numerous enough, since every verb which can take an adjective after it as a modification might claim this name. This was the difficulty which actually arrested our progress, and the attempt to solve it has led to the conclusion, that between *is* and the other verbs mentioned above, there is no *grammatical*, no *functional difference whatever;* that both it and they alike express a predicate, whilst, in common with all verbs, they *indicate predication*, that is, serve as *copula;* consequently, that there is no word in our language which expresses a mere naked copula." † De Sacy.

predicate is also called the *modified* subject or predicate. The *logical subject* may be either a complex subject or a grammatical subject unmodified; and the *logical predicate* may be either a complex predicate or an unmodified grammatical predicate.

EXERCISES.
Model.

§ 159. "His agreeable manners have made him a universal favorite."—"We often remember things without any voluntary effort."

In the first of these sentences, the grammatical subject is *manners;* the logical subject, *his agreeable manners.* The grammatical predicate is *have made;* the logical predicate, *have made him a universal favorite.*

In the second sentence, *we* is both the grammatical and the logical subject. The grammatical predicate is *remember;* the logical predicate, *often remember things without any voluntary effort.*

"The island of Borneo is traversed by the equator."—"True hope is based on energy of character."—"The day dawns."—"To seek to govern men by their fears and their wants, is an unworthy purpose."—"Anger is a short madness."—"The vice of covetousness enters deepest into the soul."—"Nature is unlimited in her operations."—"The meaning of many English words has changed during the last century."—"Extreme selfishness is often the cause of its own disappointment."—"The love of life is deeply implanted in the human heart."—"Solon gave laws to the Athenians."—"Valuable knowledge always leads to some practical results."—"Heaven from all creatures hides the book of fate."

Point out the grammatical and the logical subject in each of the foregoing sentences;—the grammatical and the logical predicate.

Explain the use of the terms complex *and* modified, *as applied to the subject or predicate.*

Simple and Compound Subjects and Predicates.

§ 160. The subject and the predicate may be either *simple* or *compound*.

A *simple subject* is a single noun, or a word or phrase used as a noun, either standing by itself or accompanied by modifying adjuncts; as, " *The pride of wit* has kept ages busy in the discussion of useless questions."—*Johnson*. In this sentence, the simple grammatical subject is *pride*, and the simple logical subject is *the pride of wit*.

A *compound subject* consists of two or more simple subjects; as, "*Wild beasts* and *savage Indians* lurked in the ravines." The compound *grammatical* subject, in this sentence, consists of the words *beasts* and *Indians*. The compound *logical* subject embraces the phrases *wild beasts* and *savage Indians*.

A *simple predicate* is a single verb, either standing alone or accompanied by modifying adjuncts; as, " No genius *was ever blasted by the breath of critics.*" The simple *grammatical* predicate, in this sentence, is *was blasted*, and the simple *logical* predicate is *was ever blasted by the breath of critics*.

A *compound predicate* consists of two or more simple predicates; as, " Men overpowered by distress, *eagerly listen to the first offers of relief, close with every scheme, and believe every promise.*"—*Johnson*. In this sentence, the compound *grammatical* predicate embraces the words *listen, close,* and *believe*. The compound *logical* predicate embraces all the words that are expressed in Italics.

What is a simple subject? Examples. A compound subject? Examples. A simple predicate? Examples. A compound predicate? Examples.

EXERCISES.

§ 161. "Anger and haste hinder good counsel."—"Pharaoh and his host were drowned in the Red Sea."—"The Roman empire fell by its own corruptions."—"The city was besieged and taken."—"The violence of the storm and the darkness of the night, prevented all approach to the ship, and rendered our situation truly alarming."—"Few things are impracticable in themselves."—"Temperance and exercise are the best means of preserving health."—"Friendship eases and unloads the mind, clears and improves the understanding, animates virtue and good resolutions, and finds employment for our most vacant hours."

Point out the simple subjects in the foregoing sentences;—the compound subjects;—the simple predicates;—the compound predicates.

Write a sentence containing a simple subject;—one containing a compound subject;—a simple predicate;—a compound predicate.

§ 162. The principal words employed to modify the grammatical subject and predicate, may themselves be modified by other words, and these again by others still. Thus, in the sentence, "The discriminating power of conscience is improved by reflecting upon the moral character of our actions," *by reflecting* is an adjunct of *is improved;* *upon character* is an adjunct of *reflecting;* *character* is modified by *the moral,* and *of actions;* and *our* modifies *actions.*

§ 163. The adjuncts of the subject and predicate are distinguished as either grammatical or logical.

Those words which refer directly to the grammatical subject, are called *grammatical adjuncts* of the subject. The grammatical adjuncts and their various modifiers form the *logical adjuncts* of the subject. In the sentence, "The members of a period connected by proper copulatives, glide smoothly and gently along," the grammat-

---

How may the principal words used to modify the grammatical subject and predicate be themselves affected? Illustrate. Explain the application of the terms grammatical *and* logical *to the adjuncts of the subject and predicate. Examples.*

ical subject *members* is modified *directly* by *the, of period,* and *connected.* These words are, therefore, called the *direct* or *grammatical* adjuncts of the subject. The *logical* adjuncts are *the, of a period,* and *connected by proper copulatives.*

Those words in the predicate which refer directly to the verb, are called *grammatical adjuncts* of the predicate. The grammatical adjuncts and their various modifiers form the *logical adjuncts* of the predicate. In the sentence, "Endeavor always to have noble sentiments," the *direct* or *grammatical* adjuncts of the predicate are *always* and *to have.* The *logical* adjuncts are *always* and *to have noble sentiments.*

§ 164. All the different adjuncts of a sentence admit of *grammatical* and *logical* distinctions. Thus in the sentence, "We are inclined to believe those who have never deceived us," the grammatical object of *to believe* is *those,* and the logical object is *those who have never deceived us.* So also, in the sentence, "Neither ⸺ nor practice will always supply a hasty writer with the most proper diction," the grammatical object of *with* is *diction,* and the logical object is *the most proper diction.*

REM.—In the *analysis* of sentences, the predicate sometimes embraces a word, which in common *parsing* belongs properly to the subject or nominative. Thus, in *analyzing* the sentence, "The fields are green," the word *green* is considered a part of the *predicate;* but in *parsing* the same sentence, the word *green* is said to belong to the nominative *fields.* *Green* is here a quality predicated of the nominative *fields.* See Rule 8, Rem. 13.

EXERCISES.
Model.

§ 165. "Some of Milton's most pathetic passages are due to his loss of sight."

The grammatical subject, in this sentence, is *some.* The grammatical adjunct of *some* is *of passages;* the logical adjunct, *of Milton's most pathetic passages.* The grammatical object of the preposition *of* is *passages;* the logical object, *Milton's most pathetic passages.* The grammatical adjuncts of *passages* are *Milton's* and *pathetic;* its logical adjuncts are *Milton's* and *most pathetic.*

The grammatical predicate is *are.* The grammatical adjunct of *are* is *due;* the logical adjunct, *due to his loss of sight.* The grammatical object of *to* is *loss;* the logical object, *his loss of sight.* *His* and *of sight* are both grammatical and logical adjuncts of *loss.*

"Habits formed in youth, accompany us through life."—"Men

in the highest stations have the least liberty."—" True greatenss consists in the exercise of the benevolent virtues."—" The honors due to learning, have been justly distributed by posterity."—" The different passions of the mind must be expressed by different tones of the voice."—" The principles of true philosophic taste are unchangeable."—" Men tear themselves from their families in search of things rare and new."—" The habit of using words accurately begets the habit of thinking accurately."

In the foregoing sentences, point out the grammatical and the logical adjuncts of the grammatical subjects; of the grammatical predicates. Point out the grammatical and logical distinctions in all the different adjuncts, as in the model above.

Modifications of the Grammatical Subject.

6. A grammatical subject may be modified in the following different ways:—

1. By an apposition noun, either alone or in connection with its modifying adjuncts; as, "Romulus, *the founder of Rome*, slew his brother."

REM.—As the grammatical subject and predicate may be used either with or without modifying adjuncts, so also a word employed to modify the grammatical subject or predicate may itself be used either with or without modification by other words. Thus, in the sentence, "Romulus, the founder of Rome, slew his brother," the word *founder*, which is in apposition with *Romulus*, is itself modified by the adjuncts *the* and *of Rome*. But in the sentence, "Good men are esteemed," the word *good*, which modifies *men*, is itself unmodified.

2. By a preposition and its object, taken by themselves or with modifying adjuncts; as, "One *of us* must remain;"—"The report *of this unfortunate occurrence* soon reached our ears."

OBS.—In the above example, *of us* is both the grammatical and the logical modifier of the subject, *one*. The grammatical modifier of *report* is *of occurrence;* and the logical modifier is *of this unfortunate occurrence.*

3. By a noun or pronoun in the possessive; as, "*His* departure was delayed."

4. By an adjective or participle, taken alone or with its adjuncts; as, "*Wise* men lay up knowledge;"—"*Retiring from public life*, he devoted the remainder of his days to study and meditation."

What are the different ways in which a grammatical subject may be modified? Give an example of each class.

OBS.—In the above examples, *wise* is both the grammatical and the logical modifier of the subject, *men;* the grammatical adjunct of *he* is *retiring;* the logical adjunct, *retiring from public life.*

5. By a verb in the infinitive, taken alone or with its adjuncts; as, " His desire *to improve* was greatly strengthened ;"—" His efforts *to acquire knowledge* were not unrewarded."

6. By an entire clause ; as, " The man *who feels himself ignorant,* should at least be modest."

Modifications of the Grammatical Predicate.

§ 167. A grammatical predicate may be modified in the following different ways:—

1. By a noun or pronoun in the same case as the subject, taken either alone or with its adjuncts; as, " She walks *a queen.*"

2. By the object of the verb, taken alone or with its adjuncts; as, " No man forgets *his original trade.*"

3. By an adverb, taken alone or with its adjuncts; as, " He is *very seldom* seen."

4. By a verb in the infinitive, taken alone or with its adjuncts; as, " He desires *to study* French."

5. By an adjective or participle referring to the subject, taken alone or with its adjuncts; as, " He was *faithful to his employers ;*" —" The ball was left *suspended by a thread.*"

6. By a preposition and its object, taken by themselves or with modifying adjuncts; as, " He has returned *to his friends.*"

7. By an entire clause; as, " I am informed *that he is about to leave us.*"

EXERCISES.

§ 168. " Every person's safety requires that he should submit to be governed."—" The desire to see and hear what is new is universal."—" The relations between man and man cease not with life." —" He that getteth wisdom, loveth his own soul."—" Every blade of grass is a representative of nature."—" How easily are men diverted from a good object."—" Richard lost no time in giving the sanction of a coronation to his title."—" The finest hair casts a shadow."—

" Full many a flower is born to blush unseen."—

In what ways may a grammatical predicate be modified? Give an example of each class.

"But he, our gracious Master, kind and just,
Knowing our frame, remembers we are dust."

Let the pupil point out the grammatical subjects and the grammatical predicates, in the foregoing sentences, and tell how each is modified.

Write a sentence containing a grammatical subject modified by an apposition noun;—one containing a grammatical subject modified by a preposition and its object;—modified by a noun or pronoun in the possessive;—modified by an adjective;—by a participle;—by a verb in the infinitive;—by an entire clause.

Write a sentence containing a grammatical predicate modified by a noun in the same case as the subject;—one containing a grammatical predicate modified by the object of the verb;—by an adverb;—by a verb in the infinitive;—by an adjective referring to the subject;—by a preposition and its object;—by an entire clause.

Classification of Sentences.

§ 169. The clauses of a compound sentence are either dependent or independent.

An *independent clause* is one that makes complete sense of itself; as, "The trees wave, the birds sing, and all is life." Each of the three clauses in this sentence is independent.

A *dependent clause* is one that makes complete sense only in connection with another clause; as, "He will fall a victim to his habits, *unless he reforms.*" In this sentence, the first clause is independent and the second is dependent.

§ 170. A *coördinate compound sentence* consists of two or more clauses so combined that each of them is complete and independent of itself; as, "It was night and the moon shone brightly;"—"A prince may grant titles, or wealth may purchase them; but virtue alone ennobles man."

The members of a coördinate sentence are called coördinate clauses.*

Into what two classes are clauses divided? What is an independent clause? Examples. A dependent clause. Examples. Define a coördinate sentence. Example. What are the members of a coördinate sentence called?

---

* The following subdivision of coördinate sentences is introduced by Kühner in both his Latin and his Greek Grammar; and it has also been employed, with some modifications, by other authors. It embraces distinc-

§ 171. A *complex sentence** consists of two or more clauses so combined that one of them is dependent upon another; as, "He will be pardoned, if he repents."

That member of a complex sentence on which the others depend, is called the *principal* or *leading clause*, and dependent members are called *subordinate clauses*. In the following examples of complex sentences, the principal clauses are printed in Roman letters, and the subordinate clauses in Italics:—" It cannot be questioned, *that knowledge confers power;*"—" The Britons, *with whom Cæsar contended*, defended their country bravely;"—" *Where your treasure is*, there will your heart be also."

REMARK.—*Subordinate* members of a complex sentence are often *coördinate* in respect to each other; as, "He has gone *where friends are never false and disappointment is unknown.*" The last two clauses in this sentence are *subordinate* to the first clause, and *coördinate* to each other.

NOTE.—While most compound sentences may be readily distinguished as either coördinate or complex, there are others in which this distinction is not well marked. They seem to occupy middle ground between these two classes. The following is an example:—" Employ the present wisely, *for the future is uncertain.*" Sentences of this description are usually regarded as *coördinate;* but the clause in Italics is obviously as distinct from clauses strictly *independent* and *coördinate*, as it is from many clauses that are called *subordinate*.† In analyzing a sentence in which the subjoined clause sustains a relation that is not strictly either coördinate or subordinate, it is sufficient to explain the relation of the clauses to each other, without attempting to make a distinction that does not properly exist. In the example cited above, the clause, *for the future is uncertain*, is subjoined to the leading clause to assign a *reason* why the present should be wisely improved.

What is a complex sentence? Example. How are the members of a complex sentence divided? Examples.

---

tions which are often difficult to decide, and which are in many cases of little practical utility.

The relation of coördinate clauses is,—
1. *Copulative*, which is expressed by *and, both and, also, first, second*, etc.
2. *Adversative*, which is expressed by *but, yet, nevertheless, but yet*, etc.
3. *Disjunctive*, which is expressed by *or, either or, else*, etc.
4. *Causal*, which is expressed by *for, namely, to wit, surely*, etc.

* See De Sacy, Greene, Fowler, and Clark.
† See Mulligan, p. 440.

EXERCISES.

§ 172. "There are many peculiarities in plants, which excite the greatest interest."—"Hear instruction and be wise."—"The shrill whistle again sounded, when a blast from a bugle roused every soul in an instant."—"The night was dark, the storm raged furiously, and the shipwrecked mariners were in despair."—"If the world were to see our real motives, we should be ashamed of some of our best actions."—"Many of the young Athenians, who observed the confusion and difficulty of the old man, made signs that they would accommodate him, if he came where they sat."

Which of the foregoing compound sentences are coördinate? Which are complex? Point out all the independent clauses;—all the dependent clauses. Point out the leading clause in each of the complex sentences.

Write a compound sentence containing two coördinate clauses;—one containing three coördinate clauses;—a complex sentence containing one principal and one subordinate clause;—a complex sentence containing one principal and two subordinate clauses.

Classification of Subordinate Clauses.

§ 173. Most of the clauses that are regarded as subordinate may be reduced to three general classes:—*substantive*, *adjective*, and *adverbial*.*

A *substantive clause* is one that performs the office of a noun; as, "He knows *that you were the cause of his defeat.*" The clause in Italics is here used as the object of the transitive verb *knows*.

An *adjective clause* is one that performs the office of an adjective; as, "He *that hath knowledge*, spareth his words." The clause, *that hath knowledge*, is used as an adjective, limiting *he*.

An *adverbial clause* is one that performs the office of an adverb; as, "An honest man speaks *as he thinks*." The clause, *as he thinks*, is employed in the sense of an adverb, modifying the verb *speaks*.

How are subordinate clauses divided? What is a substantive clause? Example. An adjective clause? Example. An adverbial clause? Example. What other application is made of the terms substantive, adjective, *and* adverbial?

---

* This division of subordinate clauses is borrowed from the German grammarians, and was first introduced into the grammar of our own language by George Crane, of London. The most thorough and elaborate expansion of this system of classification is contained in Mulligan's Grammatical Structure of the English Language.

§ 174. Phrases, like clauses, may be distinguished as *substantive*, *adjective*, or *adverbial*.

In the sentence *"Doing nothing is laborious," doing nothing* is a *substantive phrase*, used as the subject of *is*.

In the sentence, "This is a scheme *of his own devising*," the phrase in Italics limits *scheme*, and is called an *adjective phrase*.

In the sentence, "*By attending to these directions*, we shall save ourselves much trouble," the phrase in Italics modifies the predicate, and is called an *adverbial phrase*.

EXERCISES.

§ 175. "We cannot reap, where we have not sown."—"The man who instructs me, is my friend."—"That we should love our enemies, is a divine command."—"By these means, he was enabled to escape."—"To write well, is difficult."—"A man of cultivated intellect possesses the power of innumerable enjoyments, of which the rude and illiterate are wholly deprived."

Point out the substantive clauses in the foregoing sentences;—the adjective clauses;—the adverbial clauses. Point out one or more substantive phrases; —one or more adjective phrases;—one or more adverbial phrases.

Write a sentence containing a substantive clause;—one containing an adjective clause;—one containing an adverbial clause. Write a sentence containing a substantive phrase;—one containing an adjective phrase;—one containing an adverbial phrase.

§ 176. ILLUSTRATIVE EXAMPLES OF COMPLEX SENTENCES.

[The most abstruse and difficult principles in the science of grammar are involved in the disposition of subordinate clauses. The following examples embrace a considerable number of the practical difficulties that arise in analyzing complex sentences; and the explanations accompanying them will be more useful to the learner than a series of abstract rules. Beginners should not attempt to point out any but the plainer and more obvious distinctions of clauses: obscure and intricate examples will require the best efforts of the most disciplined minds.]

Subordinate Substantive Clauses.

§ 177. "*That the earth is spherical*, may be clearly demonstrated." —" He heard *that the* enemy had fled." The subordinate clause, *that the earth is spherical*, is here employed as the subject of the principal verb, *may be demonstrated;* and the subordinate clause, *that the enemy had fled*, is the object of the verb *heard*. These are

---

Give an example of each class.

examples of a large class of *nominative* and *objective clauses* introduced by *that*.

§ 178. "It may be clearly demonstrated, *that the earth is spherical.*" This is a different form of the sentence given above. The word *it* is here used as an *inceptive substitute* for the clause, *that the earth is spherical*, which is still to be regarded as the subject of the principal verb. This idiom presents an example of *pleonasm*, but not of *apposition*.*

§ 179. "*Who plotted the conspiracy*, has never been discovered."—"I have forgotten *whose portrait it was.*" The first example contains a nominative clause, and the second an objective clause. Sentences like these must not be confounded with those in which the antecedent of the pronoun is understood. *Who* and *whose* are here used absolutely, and have properly no antecedents, either expressed or implied. But in the example, "*Who steals my purse*, steals trash," the pronoun *who* relates to *he* understood.

§ 180. "His decision was, *that the garrison should be surrendered.*" The subordinate clause in this sentence is used as a predicate nominative.

§ 181. "The plea, *that he was ignorant of the law*, did not vindicate his conduct." *That he was ignorant of the law*, is a substantive clause, in apposition with *plea*.

Subordinate Adjective Clauses.

§ 182. "The time *when Homer lived*, is not certainly known."—"He enrolled such *as presented themselves.*"—"The consciousness *that we are responsible agents*, should govern all our actions." In the foregoing sentences, the adjective clauses qualify respectively the words *time*, *such*, and *consciousness*. In the last example, the subordinate clause is in apposition with *consciousness;* but words in apposition are always used to limit the meaning of nouns or pronouns. In the analysis of sentences, both nouns in apposition and apposition clauses are regarded as performing the office of adjectives.

§ 183. "The dread of censure ought not to prevail over *what is*

---

* See Rule V., Rem. 1, Obs.

"It is not, as we think, perfectly correct to say, that either a proposition or a word is in apposition with that which really serves as its representative. Such extension of the term *apposition* is not to be defended."—*Mulligan*.

right." The word *what* here performs the office of both antecedent and relative. As relative it is used in connection with *is right* to form the adjective clause, *what is right;* and this clause qualifies *what,* used as antecedent. See § 79.

§ 184. "The colonist leaves a garden *where he found a wilderness.*" The adverbial clause in this sentence denotes *place,* and modifies the predicate, *leaves a garden.*

§ 185. "You write so illegibly, *that no one can read your letters.*" The adverbial clause here denotes *manner.* It is employed to give *intensity* to the meaning of *illegibly.*

§ 186. "We must spare in youth, *that we may not want in age.*' —"Reprove not a scorner, *lest he hate thee.*"· In each of these sentences, the adverbial clause expresses a *motive* or *end,* and indicates the *origin* or *source* of the assertion in the principal clause.

NOTE.—Examples frequently occur in which a subjoined clause does not properly modify any particular word or phrase in the leading clause.*
In such cases, the proper mode of analyzing the sentence is to point out the true relation and office of the clause, without attempting to distinguish it as either *substantive, adjective,* or *adverbial.*

Change of Construction.—Equivalent Expressions.†

§ 187. A single word or a phrase is often employed as an equivalent for an entire clause.

Examples:—"A man *devoid of gratitude,* is unworthy of pity;" "A man *who is devoid of gratitude,* is unworthy of pity."—"The fear *of offending,* prevented a renewal of his application;" "The fear *that he might offend,* prevented a renewal of his application."— "The *faithful* steward deserves commendation;" "The steward *who is faithful* deserves commendation."‡—"The work being fin-

---

What different forms of speech are often employed to express the same idea? Give several examples.

---

* See Mulligan, p. 474.
† See Crane, *passim,* De Sacy, Kühner, and Mulligan.
"Sentences in every language must consist of the same members, though often differently expressed: it is in a great measure upon the mode of their expression that the genius of a language depends, and it is the faculty of appreciating these peculiarities promptly and accurately that constitutes the grammarian."—*Crane.*
‡ "We suspect that the *adjective* modification is a refinement on the *adjective accessory* modification—a mere abbreviation of the accessory, always implying a suppressed predication."—*Mulligan.*

ished, we all returned home;" "When the work was finished, we all returned home."—"The king, *extending his hand*, smiled graciously, and raised the suppliant;" "The king *extended his hand*, smiled graciously, and raised the suppliant."—"I know *him to be wise*;" "I know *that he is wise*."—"This discovery was made by Newton, *the greatest philosopher of his age*;" "This discovery was made by Newton, *who was the greatest philosopher of his age*."

REM.—The learner will find it a useful employment to select different examples, and exercise his judgment and taste in deciding whether the abridged or the expanded form of expression is to be preferred. When both are equally elegant, it is generally better to employ the abridged form.*

EXERCISES.

§ 188. "The clouds having dispersed, the travellers departed."—"I know thee to be expert."—"A man who is honest, can be safely trusted."—"Wolsey, the son of a butcher at Ipswich, became a cardinal."—"And Barnabas determined to take with them John, whose surname was Mark."—"When different forms of expression are equally elegant, it is generally best to employ the shortest."—"The object is so high that it is invisible."

Change the form of each of the foregoing sentences, substituting a clause for an abridged expression, or an abridged expression for a clause, and explain the change.

Write three sentences containing abridged expressions, and three equivalent sentences in which these abridged forms are expanded into clauses.

§ 189. Besides the examples that occur of clauses equivalent to words or phrases, or of words or phrases equivalent to clauses, there are numerous other instances in which a word, phrase, or sentence may be modified in form without materially affecting the sense; as, "James heard the sound;" "The sound was heard by James;"—"The stranger was *without a penny*;" "The stranger was *penniless*."

Two or more simple sentences, standing disconnected from one another, may often be united in one compound sentence; or a com-

Name other examples in which equivalent forms of expression may be used. What equivalent may we employ for two or more simple sentences, standing disconnected from one another?

* "In defining a substantive, the genius of our language leans to the brevity of the verbal substantive or the infinitive, rather than to the more formal method of an entire sentence."—*Crane.*

pound sentence may be resolved into two or more simple and disconnected sentences.

> *Example:*—"Man is a rational being. He is endowed with the highest capacity for happiness. He sometimes mistakes his best interests. He sometimes pursues trifles with all his energies. He sometimes considers them the principal objects of desire in this fleeting world."—"Man, who is a rational being, endowed with the highest capacity for happiness, sometimes mistakes his best interests, and pursues trifles with all his energies, considering them the principal object of desire in this fleeting world."

Five simple sentences are here united in one compound sentence, which contains only three clauses. *Who* and *and* are introduced as connectives, and participial phrases are employed instead of the second and fifth of the simple sentences.

NOTE.—We cannot write a single paragraph without being required to choose between different forms of expression that are nearly equivalent in meaning. One of the last sentences above was first written, "Five simple sentences are here united in one compound sentence, *containing* only three clauses," and afterwards changed to the form in which it now stands. The success of the learner in choosing the best words and the best forms that may be given them when combined in sentences and phrases, is the measure of his attainment in the art of speaking and writing. This power must be acquired mainly by familiarity with good speakers and writers, and by frequent practice of the art itself.

EXERCISES.

§ 190. "This piece was written in 1820, at which time Southey was poet laureate."—"The wolf was devoured by the lamb."—"The danger could not be avoided."—"In his manners he was free from affectation."—"When do you intend to leave?"

Change the form of each of the foregoing sentences, preserving the meaning unaltered.

"A bear was pained by the sting of a bee. The bear ran quite mad into the bee garden. The bear overturned all the hives."

"We are come to a very important period in our course. The strength of our political system is beginning to be tried. The tendencies of our institutions are becoming apparent."—*B. B. Edwards.*

Change each of the two foregoing series of simple sentences into a single compound sentence.

"Alexandria, one of the most celebrated cities of antiquity, and formerly the residence of the kings of Egypt, is situated on the shores of the Mediterranean."—"The art of writing, which contributes much to the convenience and necessity of mankind, was not invented all at once."—"Sugar, which is a nutritious article of food, and is obtained in Europe from the beet-root, is a staple production of the West Indies, where it is produced from the sugar-cane, which is extensively cultivated."

Resolve each of the foregoing compound sentences into simple disconnected sentences.

ORDER OF ANALYSIS.

§ 191. In analyzing a simple sentence, the pupil should first resolve it into its logical subject and logical predicate.

In analyzing the logical subject, the grammatical subject should first be pointed out, and then its various modifying adjuncts. These adjuncts themselves should also be analyzed, and the office of each word particularly explained. The logical predicate should be disposed of in a similar manner.

If the sentence to be analyzed is compound, the pupil should first distinguish the different clauses, point out the connectives, tell which of the clauses are independent and which dependent, and explain their relation to one another. Members that are used as *substantive, adjective,* or *adverbial clauses,* should also be pointed out. The different clauses or simple sentences may then be analyzed in the manner already described.

NOTE.—It is not always easy to decide whether a clause is independent or dependent. In doubtful cases, it is generally sufficient to explain the sense of the passage and the relation of the clauses to one another.

Pupils should frequently be required to change words or phrases to equivalent clauses, and clauses to equivalent words or phrases; and to point out other changes in forms and modes of expression that may be made without materially affecting the sense.

MODELS OF ANALYSIS.

[The Models here given illustrate very fully the foregoing principles, and should receive the special attention of the learner.]

§ 192. "To avenge an injury, places us on a level with our enemy."

This is a simple sentence. The logical subject is *to avenge an injury;* and *places us on a level with our enemy* is the logical predicate. The grammatical subject is *to avenge*, which here performs the office of both noun and verb. *An injury* is the logical object of *to avenge*, and *injury* is the grammatical object. *Injury* is modified by the article *an.* The grammatical predicate is *places.* The adjuncts of places are *us* and *on a level with our enemy.* *Us* is the object of *places;* *level* is the object of *on*, which relates it to *places;* and *a* modifies *level.* *With our enemy* is the logical adjunct of *level.* *Enemy* is the object of *with*, which relates it to *level;* and *our* modifies *enemy.*

The form of this sentence may be changed by converting the infinitive phrase into a participial phrase:—"By avenging an injury, we place ourselves on a level with our enemy."

§ 193. "Established custom is not easily broken, till some great event shakes the whole system of things."—*Johnson.*

This is a compound sentence, embracing two clauses, which are connected by the conjunction *till.* First clause:—*Established custom is not easily broken.* Second clause:—*Some great event shakes the whole system of things.*

The first clause is independent. The second is an *adverbial clause*, modifying the first and depending upon it.

Analysis of the first clause:—The logical subject is *established custom:* and *is not easily broken* is the logical predicate. The grammatical subject is *custom*, which is modified by the participial adjective *established.* The grammatical predicate is *is broken*, which is modified by the adverbs *not* and *easily.*

Analysis of the second clause:—The logical subject is *some great event*, and the logical predicate is *shakes the whole system of things.* The grammatical subject is *event*, which is modified by the adjectives *some* and *great.* The grammatical predicate is *shakes*, which is modified by its logical object, *the whole system of things.* The grammatical object of *shakes* is *system*, which is modified by the adjuncts *the*, *whole*, and *of things.* *Of* shows the relation between *system* and *things.*

The form of this sentence may be changed by converting the word *established* into a relative clause:—"Custom that is established is not easily broken," etc. This change is not an improvement.

§ 194. "Reverence for our own moral nature, on which we have now insisted, needs earnest and perpetual inculcation."

This is a compound sentence, embracing two clauses. The principal clause is *reverence for our own moral nature needs earnest and perpetual inculcation.* The dependent or subordinate clause is *on which we have now insisted.*

The subordinate clause is connected to the principal clause by the relative *which.* *Which* is the object of *on,* which relates it to *have insisted* in the subordinate clause; and it relates to *reverence,* which is the subject of the verb in the leading clause.

The logical subject of the principal sentence is *reverence for our own moral nature;* and the logical predicate is *needs earnest and perpetual inculcation.*

The grammatical subject is *reverence.* This is modified by the phrase, *for our own moral nature.* *Our, own,* and *moral* modify *nature,* and *nature* is the object of *for,* which relates it to *reverence.*

The grammatical predicate is *needs,* which is modified by its logical object, *earnest and perpetual inculcation.* The grammatical object of *needs* is *inculcation,* which is modified by the adjectives *earnest* and *perpetual.* The conjunction *and* connects the two adjectives.

In the subordinate clause, *on which we have now insisted, we* is both the grammatical and the logical subject. The logical predicate embraces *have now insisted* and *on which.* The grammatical predicate is *have insisted,* which is modified by *now* and *on which.* *On* and *which* have already been disposed of.

§ 195. "He that is faithful will be rewarded."

This is a compound sentence, in which the subordinate clause, *that is faithful,* is used to modify *he,* which is the subject in the principal sentence, *he will be rewarded.*

The relative pronoun *that* is the connective. *That* is the subject of *is* in the subordinate clause, and it relates to *he,* which is the subject of the principal verb, *will be rewarded.*

The logical subject of the principal sentence is *he that is faithful;* and *will be rewarded* is both the grammatical and the logical predicate. The grammatical subject is *he,* which is modified by the clause, *that is faithful.*

That is faithful is an *adjective clause,* qualifying *he.* *That* is both the grammatical and the logical subject. The logical predicate is *is faithful.* The grammatical predicate is *is,* which is modified by *faithful.*

NOTE.—The learner will observe a marked distinction between the relative clause in this section and that in § 194. In this example, the relative clause is essential to the completeness of the principal subject. It is not *he,* but *he that is faithful,* who will be rewarded.

In the previous example, *on which we have now insisted* is not a restrictive clause, but a clause added incidentally; and the sentence would be complete without it:—*Reverence for our own moral nature needs earnest and perpetual inculcation.* Or, we might change the construction and convert the relative clause into an independent clause:—*We have now insisted on reverence for our own moral nature, and this reverence needs earnest and perpetual inculcation.*

So also in the sentence, "The consciousness *that we are responsible agents,* should govern all our actions," the subordinate clause is restrictive, and must be taken in connection with the logical subject of the principal sentence. But in the sentence, "The boy had neglected his lesson, *for which he was severely censured,*" the subordinate clause is not restrictive, and should not be taken with the logical subject of the principal sentence.*

When a subordinate clause is employed as an essential modifier of the principal sentence, it is called an *incorporated clause.*

§ 196. "Praise, said the sage, with a sigh, is to an old man an empty sound."

The relation of the two clauses in this compound sentence is peculiar

---

* "Subordinate propositions may be divided into two classes—*determinative* and *explanatory.*

"A *determinative subordinate* is added to another proposition, to determine or limit the sense of the term which it qualifies, or to express some indispensable quality respecting it; so that the determinative subordinate cannot be removed from the sentence without affecting or destroying the sense of the proposition which it qualifies.

"'The messengers who brought the news of the army's defeat were immediately seized and imprisoned by order of the magistrates.'

"In this sentence, the proposition, *who brought the news of the army's defeat,* is a determinative subordinate, the removal of which would entirely alter the meaning of the sentence.

"The office of the *explanatory subordinate* proposition in a sentence is merely to explain more fully, or express some circumstance belonging to the term to which it relates; so that it is very possible to suppress the explanatory subordinate proposition without destroying, or even in the least degree injuring the sense of the sentence.

"'Shakspeare, who lived in the reign of Queen Elizabeth, was the greatest of all the English poets.'

"Here, the proposition, *who lived in the reign of Queen Elizabeth,* is an explanatory subordinate; and it is evident that its removal will not in the slightest degree affect the sense of the remaining proposition, which will then stand, *Shakspeare was the greatest of all the English poets.*"—*Graham on English Composition.*

The principal clause is *said the sage, with a sigh*. The subordinate clause, *praise is to an old man an empty sound*, is connected to the principal clause by standing as the object of the principal verb *said*. The subordinate clause here performs the office of a noun, and is hence called a *substantive clause*. The simple sentences are analyzed as in previous examples.

§ 197. "Whatever is done willingly is done well."

This is a compound sentence in which the subordinate clause is restrictive. The connective is *whatever*, a compound pronoun, including both antecedent and relative. The subordinate clause is *whatever* (used as relative) *is done willingly*.

The logical subject of the principal sentence is *whatever is done willingly*. The logical predicate is *is done well*. The grammatical subject is *whatever (that,)* used as antecedent. It is modified by the adjective clause, *whatever (which) is done willingly*. The grammatical predicate is *is done*, which is modified by *well*.

In the subordinate clause, *whatever (which)* is both the grammatical and the logical subject. The logical predicate is *is done willingly*. The grammatical predicate is *is done*, which is modified by *willinglg*. See § 195, Note.

§ 198. "We heard that the foe had retreated."

In this sentence, the subordinate clause, *that the foe had retreated*, is the logical object of the principal verb *heard*. This is another example of an *incorporated clause*. See § 195, Note. The connective is *that*.

We is both the grammatical and the logical subject in the principal sentence. The logical predicate is *heard that the foe had retreated*. The grammatical predicate is *heard*, which is modified by the substantive clause, *that the foe had retreated*.

The subordinate clause is analyzed as in previous examples.

NOTE.—The most difficult and important part of Analysis consists in resolving compound sentences into simple ones, and explaining the connections and dependences of the different members. As soon as pupils become familiar with the analysis of simple sentences, they should have frequent exercises in resolving compound sentences into clauses, and pointing out the connectives and explaining the relation of the clauses to one another. By attending to the office of the several clauses in general discourse, and omitting for the time the analysis of simple sentences, the learner will secure most of the substantial benefits of analyzing a page in the time that would otherwise be consumed on half a dozen lines.* In the Models that follow, attention is directed chiefly to the resolution of compound sentences.

§ 199. "Rowing is a healthful exercise, but it is not always free from danger."

This is a compound sentence, containing two independent clauses, which are connected by *but*.

§ 200. "As your fathers did, so do ye."

The principal clause in this compound sentence is *so do ye*, and the subordinate clause is *as your fathers did*. The connective is *as*, which corresponds with *so*. The subordinate clause is *adverbial*, and the whole sentence expresses a comparison of equality.

§ 201. "The Romans and Albans being on the eve of a battle, an agreement was made between them, that three champions should be chosen on each side, by whom the victory should be determined."

This is a compound sentence, consisting of one independent phrase, *the Romans and Albans being on the eve of a battle*, and three clauses:—

1. *An agreement was made between them.*
2. *That three champions should be chosen on each side.*
3. *By whom the victory should be determined.*

The connectives are *that* and *whom*. The first clause is independent; the second is subordinate to the first; and the third is subordinate to the second. The second is an *adjective clause*, modifying *agreement* in the first; and the third clause is explanatory of the second.

Analysis of the independent phrase:—*Romans* and *Albans* are used absolutely, with the participle *being*. They are connected by *and* and limited by *the*. *Being* is modified by the phrase, *on the eve of a battle*. The logical object of *on* is *the eve of a battle*. The grammatical object is *eve*, which is modified by *the* and *of a battle*. The logical object of *of* is *a battle*, and the grammatical object is *battle*. *Battle* is limited by *a*.

This independent phrase may be expanded into a clause:—" *When the Romans and Albans were on the eve of a battle*, an agreement was made." etc.

§ 202. " My sentence is for open war: of wiles,
More unexpert, I boast not: them let those
Contrive who need, or when they need, not now:

---

* See Mulligan, p. 499.

For while they sit contriving, shall the rest,
Millions that stand in arms and longing wait
The signal to ascend, sit lingering here,
Heaven's fugitives, and for their dwelling-place
Accept this dark opprobrious den of shame,
The prison of his tyranny who reigns
By our delay?" MILTON.

This passage embraces twelve clauses:—

1. *My sentence is for open war.*
2. *Of wiles, more unexpert, I boast not.*
3. *Them let those contrive.*
4. *Who need.*
5. *Or* [let them contrive them] *not now.*
6. *When they need.*
7. *For, shall the rest, millions, sit lingering here, Heaven's fugitives.*
8. *That stand in arms.*
9. *And longing wait the signal to ascend.*
10. *While they sit contriving.*
11. *And for their dwelling-place accept this dark opprobrious den of shame, the prison of his tyranny.*
12. *Who reigns by our delay.*

The first, second, third, fifth, seventh, and eleventh clauses are independent; and the fourth, sixth, eighth, ninth, tenth, and twelfth, are dependent.

The first, second, and third clauses have no grammatical connection.

The fourth is an adjective clause, qualifying *those* in the third clause. It is to be taken as a part of the logical object of the principal verb *let*. The connective is *who*.

Or connects the fifth clause to the third.

The sixth is an adverbial clause, subordinate to the fifth, and modifying the verb *contrive*, understood. The connective is *when*.

The third and fifth clauses, with their subordinates, are connected to the seventh by *for*.

The eighth and ninth are adjective clauses, qualifying *millions*. They are connected to the seventh clause by *that*, and to each other by *and*.

The tenth clause is adverbial, modifying the predicate of the seventh. The connective is *while*.

The eleventh clause is connected to the seventh by *and*.

The twelfth is an adjective clause, subordinate to the eleventh, and modifying the word *his*. The connective is *who*.

[Let the pupil analyze each of the following extracts, according to the directions and illustrations already given.]

§ 203. Leonidas and his three hundred Spartans fought bravely at Thermopylæ, against the whole Persian army."—" In ancient times, the benefactors of mankind were deemed worthy of immortal honors."—" Misfortunes make men more thoughtful."—" Numa Pompilius, the most fortunate of the Roman kings, is said to have lived above eighty years."—" Industry and application will make amends for the want of a quick and ready wit."—" A new order of cultivated intellect is greatly needed." —" Those who attain any excellence, commonly spend life in one pursuit."—" Neither genius nor practice will always supply a hasty writer with the most proper diction."

" The consciousness that we have done our duty, will console us, even if our efforts are unsuccessful."*—" He who assists us when we are in need, is a true friend."—" What thou bidd'st, unargued, I obey."—" That the government of our desires is essential to the enjoyment of true liberty, is a truth never to be forgotten by the citizens of a free state."

" Men of great and stirring powers, who are destined to mould the age in which they are born, must first mould themselves upon it.—*Coleridge.*

" War will never cease, while the field of battle is the field of glory, and the most luxuriant laurels grow from a root nourished with blood."—*Channing.*

> " The earth was made so various, that the mind
> Of desultory man, studious of change,
> And pleased with novelty, might be indulged.
> Prospects, however lovely, may be seen
> Till half their beauties fade; the weary sight,
> Too well acquainted with their smile, slides off
> Fastidious, seeking less familiar scenes."—*Cowper.*

---

* One independent clause and two subordinate clauses.

§ 204. GRAMMATICAL CONNECTION OF WORDS.

[Of the various exercises that have been employed as collateral aids to syntactical analysis and parsing, no one has proved more useful or important than that of tracing the grammatical connections and relations of the different words in a sentence. The method here presented relieves entirely the monotony of common parsing, and carries the pupil at once to the true nature and office of the different words. It has the advantage of combining the essential principles of both analysis and parsing, and of presenting them in a condensed and synoptical form. If this method was generally adopted in schools, it would render the study of Grammar more intellectual, and save much valuable time. It should never take the place of either parsing or analysis, but be employed as an auxiliary to both. It will be found specially useful in conducting reviews.*]

EXERCISES.
Models.

§ 205. "There is one Being to whom we can look, with a perfect conviction of finding that security which nothing about us can give, and which nothing about us can take away."—*Greenwood.*

Point out the simple sentences or clauses in the foregoing passage, and their connection with one another.—The period embraces four clauses:—*There is one being; to whom we can look with a perfect conviction of finding that security; which nothing about us can give; which nothing about us can take away.* The second clause is connected to the first by the relative *whom;* and the third and fourth are connected to the second by the relatives *which* and *which.* The third and fourth clauses are also connected to each other by *and.*

Trace the chain of connection between the words *away* and *is:*—*Away* modifies *can take;* which is governed by *can take,* and relates to *security; security* is the object of *finding,* which is related by *of* to *conviction; conviction* is the object of *with,* which relates it to *can look; to* expresses the relation between *whom* and *can look,* and *whom* relates to *Being,* which is the subject of *is.*

Trace the connection between *that* and *we:*—*That* defines *security,* which is the object of *finding; finding* is related by *of* to *conviction; conviction* is related by *with* to *can look,* which agrees with *we.*

---

* For the principal features of this system, the author takes pleasure in acknowledging himself indebted to his first instructor in English Grammar, T. L. Wright, Esq., of Beloit, Wis., formerly Principal of the Hartford Grammar School, Hartford, Conn., and one of the ablest teachers that our country has produced.

§ 206. But hoary Winter, unadorned and bare,
Dwells in the dire retreat, and freezes there;
There he assembles all his blackest storms,
And the rude hail in rattling tempests forms."

Addison.

Point out the clauses in the foregoing passage, and their connection with one another.—The number of clauses is four. The first commences with *hoary* and ends with *retreat;* the second is *freezes there;* the third embraces all the words in the third line; the fourth, all the words in the last line, except *and.* The first and second clauses are connected to each other by *and*, in the second line; and the third and fourth are connected by *and*, in the last line. Between the first two clauses and the last two, there is no direct grammatical connection.

Trace the chain of connection between *dire* and *bare.*—*Dire* qualifies *retreat; retreat* is the object of *in*, which relates it to *dwells; dwells* agrees with *Winter*, and *Winter* is qualified by *bare.*

Trace the grammatical connection between *there*, in the second line, and *dwells.*—*There* modifies *freezes; and* connects the two clauses, of which *freezes* and *dwells* are the verbs.

Trace the connection between *his* and *assembles.*—*His* possesses *storms,* and *storms* is the object of *assembles.*

Trace the connection from *rattling* to *blackest.*—*Rattling* qualifies *tempests; tempests* is the object of *in*, which relates it to *forms; and* connects the clauses, of which *forms* and *assembles* are the verbs; *assembles* governs *storms*, and *blackest* qualifies *storms.*

§ 207. "Our cemeteries, rightly selected and properly arranged, may be made subservient to some of the highest purposes of religion and human duty."—*Story.*

In the foregoing sentence, let the pupil trace the grammatical connection from *selected* to the verb;—from *properly* to the verb;—from *highest* to *subservient;*—from *duty* to *subservient.*

§ 208. "He who would advance in any department of knowledge, must know what others have done before him."—*B. B. Edwards.*

Trace the connection, in the foregoing sentence, from the verb *would advance* to the verb *must know;*—from *must know* to *have done;*—from *knowledge* to *would advance;*—from *him* to *others.*

§ 209. "The faults of a writer of acknowledged excellence are more dangerous, because the influence of his example is more extensive; and the interest of learning requires that they should be discovered and stigmatized, before they have the sanction of antiquity bestowed upon them, and become precedents of indisputable authority."—*Johnson.*

Point out the clauses in this sentence, and their connection with one another. Trace the grammatical connection between *acknowledged* and *are;*—between *his* and *is;*—*more extensive* and *are;*—*stigmatized* and *learning;*—*them* and *have;*—*indisputable* and *become.* Trace the chain of grammatical connection from *authority* to *faults.*

§ 210.
"There is a power
Unseen that rules th' illimitable world,
That guides its motions, from the brightest star
To the least dust of this sin-tainted mould;
While man, who madly deems himself the lord
Of all, is nought but weakness and dependence.
This sacred truth, by sure experience taught,
Thou must have learnt, when wandering all alone,
Each bird, each insect, flitting through the sky,
Has more sufficient for itself than thou."—*Thomson.*

Point out the clauses in the foregoing extract, and their connection with one another. Trace the connection between *unseen* and *rules;*—between *guides,* in the third line, and *is* in the first;—*sin-tainted* and *guides;*—*all* and *deems;*—*dependence,* in the sixth line, and *power,* in the first;—*sure,* in the seventh line, and *learnt;*—*wandering* and *learnt;*—*sky* and *has;*—*itself* and *has;*—*thou,* in the last line, and *truth,* in the seventh.

§ 211. RULES OF SYNTAX.

Rule I.—Nominatives.

The subject of a finite verb must be in the nominative case; as, "The *moon* shines with borrowed light;"—"*Thou* shalt not steal."

What is the rule respecting nominatives? Examples.

Rule II.—Apposition.

A noun or pronoun used to identify or explain another noun or pronoun, is put, by apposition, in the same case; as, "The salutation of me, *Paul;*"—"Xenophon, the *soldier* and *historian,* was a disciple of Socrates."

Rule III.—Possessives.

The possessive case is governed by the noun which denotes the thing possessed; as, "The *sun's* rays;"—"*My* native land."

Rule IV.—Independent Case.

When a noun or pronoun is used absolutely, having no dependence on any other word, it is put in the independent case; as, "These are thy glorious works, *Parent* of good;"—"*He* that hath ears to hear, let him hear."

Rule V.—Pronouns.

Pronouns must agree with their antecedents, in gender, number, and person; as, "On the seventh day, God ended *his* work *which he* had made;"—"Every tree is known by *its* fruit."

Rule VI.—Pronouns.

When two or more words denoting different objects are taken conjointly, forming one common antecedent, the pronoun agreeing with them must be in the plural number; as, "Virtue and good breeding render *their* possessors truly amiable."

Rule VII.—Pronouns.

When two or more antecedents in the singular, are so

What is the rule respecting apposition? Examples. Respecting possessives? Examples. Respecting the independent case? Examples. Respecting the agreement of pronouns? Examples. Respecting the agreement of a pronoun with two or more words denoting different objects, taken conjointly? Examples.

connected that the pronoun agrees with each term separately, or with one of them exclusively, the pronoun should be in the singular number.

> *Examples:*—"Man is not such a machine as a clock or a watch, *which* moves merely as *it* is moved;"—"He, and no one else, was allowed to follow *his* inclinations;"—"Every good act and every good purpose will receive *its* reward."

Rule VIII.—Adjectives.

Adjectives belong to the nouns or pronouns which they qualify or define; as, "*A good* man;"—"*These* things."

Rule IX.—Verbs.—Agreement.

A verb must agree with its nominative, in number and person; as, "I *go;*"—"Thou *seest;*"—"He *hears.*"

Rule X.—Verbs.—Agreement.

When two or more nominatives denoting different objects are taken conjointly, forming one common subject, the verb agreeing with them should be in the plural number; as, "Socrates and Plato *were* eminent philosophers;"—"The air, the earth, the water, *teem* with delighted existence."

Rule XI.—Verbs.—Agreement.

When two or more singular nominatives are so connected that the verb agrees with each subject separately, or with one of them to the exclusion of the others, the verb should be in the singular number.

What is the rule respecting the agreement of a pronoun with each of two or more antecedents taken separately, or with one of them exclusively? Examples. What is the general rule for adjectives? Examples. The rule respecting the agreement of verbs? Examples. Respecting the agreement of a verb with two or more nominatives denoting different objects taken conjointly? Examples. What is the rule respecting two or more singular nominatives so connected that the verb agrees with each separately, or with one to the exclusion of the others?

Examples:—"Duty, and not interest, *was* his constant rule of action;"—"Nor cloud, nor speck, nor stain, *breaks* the serene of heaven;"—"Neither astrology, nor alchemy, *deserves* the name of a science;"—"In every tribe, superstition, or gratitude, or fortune, *has exalted* a particular family;"—"Cæsar, as well as Cicero, *was* remarkable for his eloquence;"—"Thine *is* the kingdom, and the power, and the glory."

" Every tongue and every eye
 Does homage to the passer-by."

Rule XII.—Verbs.—Government.

Transitive verbs, in the active voice, govern the objective case; as, "I *have heard him;*"—"*Honor* thy *father* and thy *mother.*"

Rule XIII.—Predicate Nominative.

Intransitive and passive verbs have the same case after them as before them, when both words refer to the same person or thing: as, "*Society* is the true *sphere* of human virtue;"—"They wished *him* to be their *king;*"—"*He* soon became the *leader* of his party;"—"*He* was chosen *librarian;*"—"*Homer* has been styled the *prince* of poets."

Rule XIV.—Government of the Infinitive.

The infinitive mode may be governed by a verb, a noun, or an adjective; as, "*Strive to improve;*"—"I am in *haste to return;*"—"The ship was *ready to sail.*"

Rule XV.—Tenses.

In the use of verbs, those tenses should be employed which express correctly the sense intended.

Examples. What is the rule respecting transitive verbs? Examples. Respecting the same case? Examples. What is the rule respecting the government of infinitives? Examples. What is the rule respecting tenses?

Rule XVI.—Participles.

Participles relate to nouns or pronouns; as, "He stood *leaning* on his spade, and *gazing* at the brightness in the west."

Rule XVII.—Adverbs.

Adverbs modify verbs, adjectives, and other adverbs; as, "Men *frequently* contend for trifles;"—"It was *very thankfully* received."

Rule XVIII.—Conjunctions.

Conjunctions connect words or sentences; as, "Idleness *and* ignorance are the parents of many vices;"—"He fled *because* he was afraid."

Rule XIX.—Prepositions.—Relation.

Prepositions connect words, and show the relation between them.

Examples:—"He *travelled* FOR *pleasure;*"—"They were *destitute* OF *food;*"—"This is an *age* OF *improvement;*"—"Ambassadors were sent *previously* TO *the declaration.*"

Rule XX.—Prepositions.—Government.

Prepositions govern the objective case; as, "They came *to us in* the *spirit of kindness;*"—"*From him* that is needy, turn not away."

Rule XXI.—Interjections.

Interjections have no grammatical relation to the other words of a sentence; as, "These were delightful days, but, *alas!* they are no more."

What is the rule respecting participles? Examples. What is the rule respecting adverbs? Examples. Respecting conjunctions? Examples. Respecting the relation expressed by prepositions? Examples. What do prepositions govern. Examples. What is the rule respecting interjections? Examples.

Rule XXII.—General Rule.

The different parts of a sentence should be made to harmonize with one another: and the several clauses should be so constructed and arranged as to express clearly the various relations, connections, and dependences intended, according to the best usages of the language.

§ 212. PARSING.

[It will often be found expedient, in parsing, to omit the *etymological* modifications of a word, and give only its *syntax* or *constructive office* in the sentence. Advanced classes should attend less to the common *Order of Parsing*, and more to the *Analysis* of language; but learners should be required to parse many of the more difficult and important words, at all stages of their progress. It is hoped that teachers will take special pains to render the exercises in parsing as *intellectual* as possible. Pupils should be taught that correct *parsing* always requires correct *thinking*; and that it is indispensably necessary for them to understand thoroughly *the sense* of any piece of writing before they attempt to parse it. They should be required to explain the more difficult passages, by transposing the order of the words, or by expressing the sense in their own language; but the words employed by the author should be preserved unaltered in parsing.]

§ 213. *Parsing* is an explanation of the properties and offices of words, according to the principles of grammar.

ORDER OF PARSING.

A *Noun*, and why?—Common or Proper, and why?—Gender, and why?—Person, and why?—Number, and why?—Case, and why?—Disposal, and Rule.

An *Adjective*, and why?—Class, and why?—If a descriptive adjective, give the Degree of Comparison, with the reason.—Compare it.—Disposal, and Rule.

In parsing an *Article*, the pupil should tell whether it is Definite or Indefinite, and why; to what it belongs; and assign the Rule. See *Models for Parsing*, under Rule VIII.

A *Pronoun*, and why?—Class, and why?—Gender, Number, and Person, and why?—[If a Relative Pronoun, point out its antecedent, and tell what clauses are connected by it.]—Case, and why?—Decline it, if declinable.—Disposal, and Rule.

What is the general rule of syntax? What is parsing? Give the order of parsing the different parts of speech.

A *Verb*, and why?—Regular, or Irregular, and why?—Principal parts.—Transitive or Intransitive, and why?—[If transitive, tell whether it is in the Active or Passive Voice.]—Mode, and why?—Tense, and why?—Person and Number, and why?—Disposal, and Rule.

In parsing a *Participle*, the following order should be observed:—A Participle, and why?—Principal Parts of the verb.—Perfect or Imperfect, and why?—Transitive or Intransitive, and why?—[If Transitive, tell whether it is in the Active or Passive Voice.]—Disposal, and Rule.

An *Adverb*, and why?—Class, and why?—Disposal, and Rule.

A *Preposition*, and why?—Relation expressed, and Rule.

A *Conjunction*, and why?—Connection, and Rule.

An *Interjection*, and why?—Rule.

NOUNS AND PRONOUNS.
Rule I.—Nominatives.

§ 214. The subject of a finite verb must be in the nominative case; as, "The *moon* shines with borrowed light;"—"*Thou* shalt not steal."

REMARK 1.—A verb in the infinitive mode, a sentence, or a phrase, sometimes performs the office of a noun or pronoun in the nominative; as, "*To err* is human;"—"*That one man should be punished for the crimes of another*, is unjust."

REM. 2.—In poetry, the nominative is sometimes omitted; as, "Lives there who loves his pain?" When the verb is in the imperative mode, the nominative is frequently omitted, both in prose and poetry; as, "*Take care of the minutes, and the hours will take care of themselves.*"

REM. 3.—In declaratory and conditional sentences, the nominative usually precedes the verb; but in interrogative and imperative sentences, the nominative most commonly follows either the principal verb or an auxiliary.

What is the rule respecting nominatives? Examples. What is sometimes used to supply the place of a noun or pronoun in the nominative? Examples. What position does the nominative usually take in declaratory and conditional sentences? In interrogative and imperative sentences?

OBSERVATION 1.— The nominative is also placed after the verb:— 1. When a sentence is introduced by the expletive adverb *there;* as, " There are many good *pieces* in this collection." 2. When a supposition is expressed without the use of the conjunction *if;* as, " Were there no *difference*, there would be no choice." 3. When a sentence is introduced by *neither* or *nor*, not used as a correspondent to another conjunction; as, "The eye which saw him shall see him no more, neither shall his *place* any more behold him."

OBS. 2.— When *who, which,* or *what,* is used as the subject of the verb in an interrogative sentence, and also when *which* or *what* is used as an adjective belonging to the subject, the nominative precedes the verb; as, " *Who* is there to oppose him?"—" What object will be accomplished?"

OBS. 3. — Besides the cases here enumerated, there are many others in which the nominative may either precede or follow the verb, and for which no definite rules can be given.

RULE II.— APPOSITION.

§ 215. A noun or pronoun used to identify or explain another noun or pronoun, is put, by apposition, in the same case; as, " The salutation of me, *Paul;* "— " Xenophon, the *soldier* and *historian*, was a disciple of Socrates."

REM. 1.— *Apposition* signifies *adding to*, and denotes that another name is added for the same person or thing.

REM. 2. — A noun is sometimes put in apposition with a sentence or phrase; as, " He permitted me to make free use of his valuable library;— a *kindness* which I shall always remember with gratitude."

REM. 3. — A noun denoting a whole is sometimes followed by two or more words in apposition with it, denoting the parts of which it is composed; as, " They travelled in company, *some* on horseback, *some* in carriages, and *others* on foot."

REM. 4. — A distributive term in the singular number, or a word in the singular modified by a distributive, is often put in apposition with a noun or pronoun in the plural; as, " They have fallen, *each* in his field of glory."— *Cowper.* " They fled, every *man* into his tent."— 1 *Sam.* 4 : 10.

What is the rule respecting apposition? **Examples.** *With what besides a noun or pronoun is a noun sometimes in apposition? Examples. What remark is made respecting words denoting the several parts of a whole? Examples. What is the remark respecting a distributive term in the singular number, or a word in the singular modified by a distributive? Examples*

REM. 5. — In the phrases *one another* and *each other*, the words *one* and *each* have a construction similar to that described in the last Remark; as, "They confide in *each other;*" — "Bear ye *one another's* burdens." In the former of these sentences, *each* is in apposition with *they*, and *other* is governed by the preposition *in*. In the latter, *one* is in apposition with *ye*, and *another's* is governed by *burdens*.

REM. 6. — Two or more proper names, applied to the same individual, may be regarded as forming one complex noun; as, "*Thomas Jefferson* was the third president of the United States."

REM. 7. — Anomalous expressions sometimes occur, in which a noun used without the sign of possession, is put in apposition with a noun or pronoun in the possessive case;* as, "This did not prevent *John's* being acknowledged and solemnly inaugurated *Duke* of Normandy." — *Henry's Hist. of Brit.* "*His* eminence as a *judge* was great and undeniable." — *Brougham.* See Rule 18, Rem. 10.

RULE III. — POSSESSIVES.

§ 216. The possessive case is governed by the noun which denotes the thing possessed; as, "The *sun's* rays;" — "*My* native land." See § 55, Rem. 5.

REM. 1. — When the governing word is rendered obvious by the use of the possessive, it is frequently omitted; as, "I called at the *bookseller's;*" that is, "at the bookseller's store."

REM. 2. — When the thing possessed belongs to two or more possessors conjointly, the sign is annexed to the last only of the possessive nouns; as, "Mason and *Dixon's* line;" — "Andrews and *Stoddard's* Grammar;" — "Allen, Morrill, and *Wardwell's* store." But when different things of the same name belong severally to

---

Explain and illustrate the construction of the phrases, each other *and* one another? *What is said of two or more proper names, applied to the same individual? Examples.* What is the rule respecting possessives? Examples. *What use is made of the sign when the thing possessed belongs to two or more possessors conjointly? Examples. What, when different things of the same name belong severally to two or more possessors? Examples.*

---

* Grammarians differ widely in opinion respecting the proper mode of parsing words of this class. In the sentence quoted from Henry's History G. Brown and Goldsbury would make the word *Duke* a *possessive*, in apposition with *John's*. Sanborn would make it *independent*. Butler would call it a *predicate nominative*. Hart would say that *Duke* is used in the *nominative indefinite*. Bullions would make it an *objective*.

two or more possessors, the sign should be annexed to each possessive; as, "*Webster's, Worcester's,* and *Smart's* Dictionary;" that is, Webster's Dictionary, Worcester's Dictionary, and Smart's Dictionary.

REM. 3. — Two or more words closely united, and forming essentially one complex noun, have the sign annexed to the last only; as, "*Henry the Eighth's* reign;" — "*Thomas Jefferson's* administration;" — "*John the Baptist's* head."

REM. 4. — When two or more possessive nouns in apposition are governed by a noun *expressed*, the governing word is usually placed after the others, and the sign annexed to the last only of the possessives; as, "For David my *servant's* sake."

REM. 5. — When an explanatory term consisting of several words, or a number of explanatory terms, are subjoined to a noun in the possessive, and the governing word is understood, the sign is generally annexed to the first possessive only; as, " I left the book at Johnson's, a respectable bookseller, and a worthy man."

REM. 6. — Other cases sometimes occur for which no certain rule can be given. Thus, we may say, "I called at Mr. Brown, the jeweller's," or "I called at Mr. Brown's the jeweller;" since both these forms are authorized by usage.

REM. 7. — When a noun or pronoun, preceding a participle used as a noun, is properly in the possessive case, the sign of possession should not be omitted.

Correct Examples: — " A great public, as well as private advantage, arises from every *one's* devoting himself to that occupation which he prefers, and for which he is specially fitted." — *Wayland.* " This is known by the *moon's* always keeping nearly the same face towards us." — *Olmsted.*

False Syntax: — " Such is the advantage we receive from the chain being composed of so many links, the spine of so many bones." — *Paley.* " There was a chance of him recovering his senses." — *Macaulay.* " A contemporary scholar speaks of the author being unknown." — *Thomas Campbell.*

What, when two or more words closely united, form one complex noun? Examples. What is said respecting two or more possessives in apposition, governed by a noun expressed? Examples. What care should be observed respecting possessives before participial nouns? Examples. Correct the false syntax, and show why it is false

7

Rem. 8. — When we wish to mention a *part* only of the objects possessed, we should employ both the preposition *of* and the possessive case, as, "An anecdote of Dr. Franklin's;" — "These poems are as good as some of Dana's."

Rem. 9. — An explanatory clause should never be inserted between a possessive noun and the word by which it is governed. The following sentence is faulty in this respect: — "She began to extol the farmer's, as she called him, excellent understanding." It should be, "She began to extol the excellent understanding of the farmer, as she called him."

RULE IV. — INDEPENDENT CASE.

§ 217. When a noun or pronoun is used absolutely, having no dependence on any other word, it is put in the independent case; as, "These are thy glorious works, *Parent* of good;" — "*He* that hath ears to hear, let him hear."

Rem. 1. — This rule applies, —

(1) When a direct address is made, and the noun or pronoun has no dependence on the rest of the sentence; as, "The fault, dear *Brutus*, is not in our stars, but in ourselves." This is the case independent *by address*.

(2) When a noun or pronoun is joined with a participle having no dependence on any other word; as, "The *sun having risen*, we departed on our journey." This is the case independent *with a participle*.

(3) When a noun is used to introduce the subject of remark, and then left independent of the rest of the sentence; as, "The Pilgrim *fathers*, where are they?" This is the case independent *by pleonasm.**

Obs. 1. — This redundant use of the noun or pronoun is generally inelegant, but in poetry and animated prose it is sometimes employed with happy effect.

Obs. 2. — A plural term is sometimes used emphatically after a series

---

What is the rule respecting the independent case? Examples. *Name the several circumstances under which nouns and pronouns are used independently, and give examples of each kind.*

---

* For several of the divisions embraced in this classification of words in the independent case, the author is indebted to the excellent treatise of Mr. G. Brown.

of words or phrases comprehended under it; as, "*Ease, fortune, life,* ALL were squandered." — *Bancroft.* In this sentence, the words *ease, fortune,* and *life,* may be regarded as independent *by pleonasm.* So also, in the following sentence, the infinitive verbs may be regarded as independent or absolute *by pleonasm:* — " *To be murdered, to be tortured, to be robbed, to be sold* into slavery, *to be exposed* to the outrages of gangs of foreign banditti calling themselves patriots, — these are evidently evils from which men of every religion and men of no religion wish to be protected." — *Macaulay.*

(4) When a noun or pronoun is used to express an exclamation; as, "Oh, the *miseries* of war!" This is the case independent *by exclamation.*

(5) When a noun, having no dependence on any other word, is used to express a name or title, as, "The Sketch Book," "Day's Algebra;" or to denote *time, measure, distance, direction,* or *place,* as, "He left the country ten *years* ago," "The tree was found to be eighty *feet* in height," "He walked twelve *miles.*" This is the case independent *by ellipsis.*

OBS. — This class of words in the independent case is not intended to include those nouns before which a preposition is properly understood. In all such examples the preposition should be supplied in parsing, and the noun made to depend upon it in the objective case. There are, however, instances in which the noun is not properly dependent on a preposition either expressed or implied; and examples of this class should be put in the independent case.*

REM. 2. — A noun is sometimes used *indefinitely* after an infinitive or participle; as, "To be the *slave* of passion is of all slavery the most wretched." The word *slave,* in this sentence, may be parsed by Rule 4, in the *independent case.* See Rule 8, Rem. 14.

§ 218. EXERCISES IN COMPOSITION.

[It is hoped that teachers will not fail to insist on a thorough performance of these exercises. Rules may be recited very fluently without being understood; but an application of them in the construction of sen-

---

* "In expressing *distance* or *duration,* either in *time* or *space,* we use the noun absolutely; as, 'He walked ten *miles;*' — 'He stood three *hours.*'" — *Latham.*

"Nouns signifying the *time when,* and *time how long, weight, measure,* and *distance,* are put in the objective case absolute." — *Ainsworth.*

"Lowth, followed by the whole tribe of writers on this subject, alleges some prepositions to be understood before these expressions of time; but this is a palpable error, arising from preconceived notions of the necessity of such words. The fact is otherwise. All these peculiar phrases are idiomatic; and the remains of the early state of our language." — *Webster.*

See also Smart, J. M. Putnam, Frazee, Goldsbury, Webber, Flower Allen and Cornwell, Cooper, Davenport, and Nutting.

tences, requires a careful attention to principles, while it also aids the learner in forming an accurate style of writing. See Oral Instruction.]

Write sentences containing nouns and pronouns in the nominative; — *containing a verb in the infinitive, a sentence, or a phrase, used as the subject of a verb;* — nouns and pronouns in apposition with other words; — nouns and pronouns in the possessive case; — *two or more possessives, governed by a noun denoting joint possession;* — *two or more possessives, governed by nouns denoting different objects of the same name;* — *two or more words, forming essentially one complex noun in the possessive;* — *two or more possessives in apposition, governed by a noun expressed;* — *a noun or pronoun in the possessive, preceding a participial noun;* — *a noun or pronoun in the case independent by address;* — *in the case independent with a participle;* — *in the case independent by pleonasm;* — *in the case independent by exclamation;* — *in the case independent by ellipsis.*

Rule V. — Pronouns.

§ 219. Pronouns must agree with their antecedents in gender, number, and person; as, "On the seventh day, God ended *his* work *which he* had made;" — "Every tree is known by *its* fruit."

Rem. 1. — The neuter pronoun *it* is one of the most general terms in the language. It may be used, —

(1) To represent a noun in the plural number; as, "*It* was the heretics that first began to rail."

(2) To represent a noun in the masculine or feminine gender; as, "*It* is a brother of the prince;" — "*It* is the queen."

(3) To represent a noun in the first or second person; as, "*It* is I;" — "Is *it* you?"

(4) To represent a sentence or phrase; as, "*It* is impossible *to please all men*;" — "*It* is observed by Seneca, *that prosperity greatly obstructs the knowledge of ourselves.*"

(5) To denote some state or condition; as, "*It* rains;" — "Has *it* come to this?"

What is the rule respecting the agreement of pronouns? Examples. Enumerate the peculiar uses of the pronoun it, and give examples of each.

(6) *It* is sometimes employed in a vague or indefinite sense; as, "During this time, they had lorded *it* over the land with absolute sway." — *Prescott.*

OBS. — In most of the cases here enumerated, *it* is an *inceptive pronoun*, used to form an easy and agreeable introduction to a sentence.

REM. 2. — The personal pronoun *them* should never be employed as an adjective. We should say, "Bring me *those* books;" — not "*them* books."

REM. 3. — When two or more personal pronouns in the second person, are employed in the same connection, they should be made to correspond in style. (§§ 72, 73.) The following passage is therefore inaccurate: —

"Enjoy *your* dear wit, and gay rhetoric
That hath so well been taught her dazzling fence;
Thou art not fit to hear *thyself* convinced." — *Milton.*

Your should be *thy*, to correspond with *thou* and *thyself*.

False Syntax.

"Ere you remark another's sin,
Bid thy own conscience look within." — *Gay.*

"What strange events can strike with more surprise
Than those which lately struck thy wondering eyes?
Yet, taught by these, confess th' Almighty just,
And where you can't unriddle, learn to trust." — *Parnell.*

REM. 4. — The use of different relatives in the same sentence referring to the same antecedent, should generally be avoided. The following sentence is faulty in this respect: — "I have amused myself with remarking some of the motley characters *that* have thus usurped the ancient abode of royalty, and *who* seem as if placed here to give a farcical termination to the drama of human pride." — *Irving. Who* should be changed to *that*, to correspond with *that* in the preceding clause.

REM. 5. — Monarchs and editors of periodical publications often employ the plural form of a pronoun in the first-person, instead of the singular; as, "*We*, taking into *our* royal consideration the various disorders and abuses," etc. — "*We* charge you, on allegiance to *ourself*;" — "*We* cheerfully admit the following communication

---

What improper use is sometimes made of the pronoun them? *Illustrate. What rule should be observed, when two or more personal pronouns in the second person are employed in the same connection? Correct the false syntax, and show why it is false. What form of expression is peculiar to sovereigns and editors of periodical publications? Examples.*

into our columns, but do not hold *ourself* responsible for the sentiments which it embodies."

REM. 6. — The relative *who* is applied to persons, and *which* to irrational animals and inanimate things; as, "Homer, *who* wrote the Iliad;" — "The man *whom* we saw;" — "The horse *which* Alexander rode;" — "The rain *which* fell."

OBS. — The pronoun *who* should not be used to represent a name which is taken as a word merely. Thus, "The court of queen Elizabeth, *who* was but another name for prudence and economy," should be, "The court of queen Elizabeth, *whose* name was but another word for prudence and economy."

REM. 7. — The pronoun *that* is applied either to persons or things; as, "He *that* hath knowledge, spareth his words;" — "The bird *that* sung so sweetly;" — "The house *that* was built last year."

OBS. 1. — *That* should be employed in preference to *who* or *which*, —

(1) When its use will prevent an unpleasant repetition of either of these pronouns; as, "Who *that* is not blinded by prejudice will believe this report?"

(2) When persons form a part only of the antecedent; as, "The men and things *that* he saw."

(3) After a collective noun denoting a body of persons; as, "The army *that* was defeated was composed of veteran soldiers."

OBS. 2. — There are other cases in which *that* may be employed or not, according to the taste of the writer; as, "He *that* formed the eye, shall he not see?" — *Ps.* 94 : 9. "He *who* plants an oak, looks forward to future ages, and plants for posterity." — *Irving*. "There is a serene and settled majesty in woodland scenery, *that* enters into the soul, and dilates and elevates it, and fills it with noble inclinations." — *Ibid*.

REM. 8. — The possessive *whose* is applied to both persons and things; as, "Franklin, *whose* name will ever be remembered;" — "Virtue, *whose* reward is lasting;" — "Frowning rocks, *whose* lofty summits." See § 78, Note.

What distinction is observed in the use of *who* and *which?* Select several examples of each from other works. *To what is the pronoun* that *applied? Examples. When is that employed in preference to* who *or* which? *Examples of each class. To what is the possessive* whose *applied? Examples.*

Rem. 9. — When two or more pronouns, or nouns and pronouns, of different persons, are closely united in the same construction, the word which is in the second person should generally be placed first, and that in the first person, last; as, "You and Charles, and I, were engaged in the same transaction;" — "You and your friend were absent;" — "My brother and I were detained."

Rem. 10. — The word *what* should not be used for the conjunction *that*, nor *that* for the compound relative *what*. The following sentences are faulty in this respect: — "They would not believe but *what* he was guilty;" — "We speak *that* we do know, and testify *that* we have seen."

Rem. 11. — Relatives should be so placed as to prevent all ambiguity in regard to the words which they are intended to represent. The following sentence is therefore objectionable: — "He is unworthy the confidence of a fellow-being *that* disregards the laws of his Maker." Corrected: — "He *that* disregards the laws of his Maker, is unworthy of the confidence of a fellow-being."

Obs. — "I am the man who command you." This sentence is ambiguous, and may be corrected in two different ways. If *who* is intended to refer to *I*, we should say, 'I who command you, am the man." But if *who* is intended to refer to *man*, then we should say, "I am the man who commands you."

Rem. 12. — In familiar language, the relative is sometimes improperly omitted. Thus, "He is a man I greatly esteem," should be, "He is a man *whom* I greatly esteem." So also, "I am dissatisfied with the manner I have spent my time," should be, "I am dissatisfied with the manner *in which* I have spent my time."

Rem. 13. — *Whatever* is sometimes employed merely for the purpose of rendering a word or phrase emphatic; as, "No condition *whatever*."

Rem. 14. — *What* is sometimes used adverbially, in the sense of *partly*, or *in part;* as, "*What* with 'wooding' at two or three places, and *what* with the excitement of the day, we were too fatigued to give more than a glance and a passing note of admiration to the beauty of the scene." - - *Willis*.

Rem. 15. — A pronoun is frequently employed to represent a sentence or phrase; as, "Josephus received a liberal education among the Pharisees, after *which* he went to Rome, where he cultivated his talents to great advantage." *Which* here represents the whole clause, "received a liberal education among the Pharisees."

What is the rule respecting two or more pronouns, or nouns and pronouns, of different persons? Examples. What is the rule respecting the position of relatives? Illustrate. What besides nouns are often employed as the antecedents of pronouns? Examples.

Rem. 16. — A pronoun sometimes relates to an adjective for its antecedent; but this usage is inelegant, and should generally be avoided.*

Rem. 17. — A pronoun sometimes relates to a verb for its antecedent but this usage is also objectionable.†

Rule VI. — Pronouns.

§ 220. When two or more words, denoting different objects, are taken conjointly, forming one common antecedent, the pronoun agreeing with them must be in the plural number; as, "Virtue and good breeding render *their* possessor truly amiable."

Rem. — When the antecedents are of different persons, the plural pronoun referring to them should be of the first person, if either of the antecedents is of the first; but if neither of the antecedents is of the first person, the pronoun should be of the second person; as, "James and I have finished *our* lessons;" — "You and Henry shared it between *you*."

Rule VII. — Pronouns.

§ 221. When two or more antecedents in the singular are so connected that the pronoun agrees with each term separately, or with one of them exclusively, the pronoun should be in the singular number; as, "Man is not such a machine as a clock or a watch, which moves merely as *it* is moved;" — "He, and no one else, was allowed to follow *his* inclinations;" — "Every good act and every good purpose will receive *its* reward."

What is the rule respecting the agreement of a pronoun with two or more words denoting different objects taken conjointly? Examples. *What is the rule respecting the agreement of a plural pronoun with antecedents of different persons? Examples.* What is the rule respecting the agreement of a pronoun with each of two or more antecedents taken separately, or with one of them exclusively? Examples.

---

* "If this enumeration is *complete, which*, of course, we would not affirm it to be." — *N. A. Review.*

† "Nor is it less pleased with its first successful endeavors to walk, or rather *to run, which* precedes walking." — *Paley.*

REM.—When a singular and plural antecedent are joined by the connective *or* or *nor*, the pronoun agreeing with them should be in the plural number; as, "Neither he nor his friends have interested *themselves* in this subject."

EXERCISES IN COMPOSITION.

§ 222. Write sentences containing examples which illustrate the agreement of pronouns with their antecedents; — *one or more examples of* it, *used to represent a word in the plural;* — *of* it, *representing a noun in the masculine or feminine;* — containing examples of *who, which,* and *that,* correctly employed; — *of* whose, *referring to persons;* — *of* whose, *referring to irrational animals, and things without life;* — *two or more pronouns, or nouns and pronouns, of different persons, joined in the same construction;* — examples illustrating Rule 6th; — *a plural pronoun referring to antecedents of different persons;* — examples illustrating Rule 7th; — *a pronoun agreeing with a singular and a plural antecedent connected by* or *or* nor.

§ 223. EXERCISES IN PARSING.

[The words which are designed to be parsed, are printed in Italics. The sentences following the dividing line, require an application of the *Remarks* and *Observations,* and may be omitted by beginners.]

Model.

"*His* task is accomplished."

His is a pronoun, because it is a word used to supply the place of a noun; — personal, because it expresses person and number of itself; — in the masculine gender, because it denotes a male: — in the third person, because it represents a person spoken of; — in the singular number, because it implies but one object; — in the possessive case, because it denotes possession. Nom. *he;* Poss. *his;* Obj. *him;* Ind. *he.*—It is governed by *task.* The possessive case is governed by the noun which denotes the thing possessed.

Task is a noun, because it is used to express the name of an object; — common, because it may be applied to any one of a whole class; — in the neuter gender, because it denotes an object which is neither male nor female; — in the third person, because it denotes an object spoken of; — in the singular number, because it implies but one; and in the nominative case, because it is the subject of the verb *is accomplished.* The subject of a finite verb must be in the nominative case.

What is the rule respecting a pronoun agreeing with a singular and a plural antecedent, connected by or *or* nor*? Examples.*

7*

"The *cars* have arrived." — "*He who* overcomes *his* passions conquers *his* greatest *enemies*." — " Venerable *men!* you have come down to *us* from a former *generation*." — " *Alexander* and Napoleon were destroyers of *their* race." — " *Gibbon* the *historian*, was an infidel." — " *It* was neither he nor his brother, *that* brought the intelligence." — " *Our country* is ruined, if *it* becomes too prosperous."—*B. B. Edwards*. " There is no *service which* a *man* of commanding *intellect* can render *his* fellow-creatures, better than that of leaving behind *him* an unspotted example."—*Andrews Norton*.

§ 224. " Whether *teachers* are to continue in the *brighter* ages *which prophecy* announces, *is rendered* doubtful by a very striking prediction of the times of the *Messiah*."—*Channing*.

" *Scenes* must be beautiful, *which*, daily *viewed*,
Please daily, and *whose novelty* survives
Long knowledge and the scrutiny of years;—
Praise justly due to those *that I* describe."—*Cowper*.

" *Edward* the *Confessor's* tomb." — " *It* would be fruitless, *to investigate* the peculiarities of their respective institutions, *which* bear a *very* close affinity to *one another*."—*Prescott*. " *John Marshall* was an illustrious *judge*." — " *Marsh, Capen*, and *Lyon's* publications." — " These *points* being known, his *ignorance* of *other* points, his doubts concerning other points, *affect not* the certainty of his reasoning."—*Paley*. " These are different *questions* from the question of the *artist's* existence ; or, *which* is the same, whether the *thing* before us be a *work* of art or not."—*Ibid*. " They had heard of the arrival of *two* independent *companies* twenty *days* before."— *Sparks*. " No *member* or *members* could arrogate to *themselves* the exclusive merit."—*N. Y. Review*. " It is we *who* are *Hamlet*."— *Hazlitt*.

" My *friends*, do *they* now and then send
A *wish* or a thought after *me?* "—*Cowper*.

RULE VIII. — ADJECTIVES.

§ 225. Adj~~ectiv~~es belong to the nouns or pronouns

What is the general rule for adjectives. Examples.

which they qualify or define; as, "*A good* man;"— "*These* things."

REM. 1.—The adjectives *this* and *that*, *these* and *those*, must agree in number with the nouns which they define; as, *this book, these books; that man, those men.*

REM. 2.—When *this* and *that* are used in the sense of *former* and *latter*, *this* and *these* correspond with *latter*, *that* and *those* with *former*.

> *Examples:*—"Religion raises men above themselves; irreligion sinks them beneath the brutes;—*this* [irreligion] binds them down to a pitiable speck of earth, *that* [religion] opens for them a prospect to the skies."
> "Then palaces and lofty domes arose;—
> *These* for devotion, and for pleasure *those*."—*Pope.*

REM. 3.—Adjectives which imply unity, must be joined to singular nouns, and those which imply plurality, to nouns in the plural; as, *one hour; three days; both houses; all men.*

OBS. 1.—The adjective *every* is frequently joined to a plural noun used collectively to denote one aggregate; as, "*Every* ten years."

OBS. 2.—The word *all* is connected with singular nouns denoting quantity, and with plural nouns denoting number; as, "*All* the corn was consumed;"—"*All* things pass away."

OBS. 3.—The adjective *many* is sometimes placed before a singular noun, the article *a* or *an* being inserted between them; as, "Full *many a gem* of purest ray serene."

REM. 4.—An adjective is sometimes used to qualify a phrase or sentence; as, "To be blind is *calamitous;*"—"That he should have refused the appointment, is *extraordinary*."

REM. 5.—An adjective is often used to qualify a noun and another adjective, taken as one compound term; as, "A *venerable* old man;"—"The *best* upland cotton."

REM. 6.—An adjective is sometimes used to modify the sense of another adjective; as, "*Red* hot iron;"—"*Five* hundred men."

REM. 7.—*Either* is occasionally employed by good writers in the sense of *each*.

> *Examples:*—"This merciless devastation extended more than two leagues on *either side* of the line of march."—*Prescott.* "The Sabine hills and the Albanian mountains stretch on *either* hand."—*Irving.*
> "On *either* side the giant guards divide."—*Southey.*

What rule is observed respecting the number of the adjectives this, that, these, *and* those? *Examples. What of adjectives which imply unity and plurality? Examples. What besides nouns and pronouns, do adjectives sometimes qualify? Examples of each class.*

Rem. 8. — When an adjective is employed to express a comparison between two objects only, or objects of two different classes, it should generally take the form of the comparative; as, "Homer was the *greater* genius; Virgil the *better* artist."—*Pope.* "Our brig was the *faster* sailer of the two."—*Willis.* "William is *taller* than James;"—"William is the *taller* of the two;"—"George and John are *more studious* than James and Charles."

Obs. — Sometimes, however, the superlative form is employed when only two objects are compared;* as, "Of the two, the English system is the *safest.*"—*Humphrey.* "The *largest* boat of the two was cut loose."—*Cooper.* "Both of these opinions have the sanction of high authority, and it may be worth while to examine which of them be *wisest.*"—*N. A. Review.* "I think the English one rather the *best* of the two."—*Lockhart.*

Rem. 9. — When a comparison is expressed between more than two objects of the same class, the superlative degree is employed; as, "The *last* of the Roman tribunes;"—"The *most ancient* poet;"—"The *noblest* of the Greeks."

Rem. 10. — In the use of comparative and superlative adjectives, care should be taken not to include a noun or pronoun in a class to which it does not belong, nor exclude it from a class to which it does belong. Thus, it would be improper to say, "Socrates was wiser than any Athenian," because Socrates was himself an Athenian, and could not be wiser than himself. The correct form would be, "Socrates was wiser than any *other* Athenian," or "Socrates was the wisest of the Athenians." The following sentence is also erroneous:—"The vice of covetousness, *of all others*, enters deepest into the soul." Covetousness is not one of the *other* vices, as the construction of the sentence would imply. Corrected:—"Of all the vices, covetousness enters deepest into the soul."

What is the general rule respecting an adjective used to express a comparison between two objects, or two classes of objects? Examples. What is the general rule respecting an adjective, used to express a comparison between more than two objects of the same class. Examples. What care should be observed in the use of comparatives and superlatives?

---

* "The strict rule laid down by grammarians, that the comparative is to be used when two things are spoken of, and the superlative when more than two are the subject of discourse, has not been observed, even by the best writers, and still less by the best speakers, and need not now be insisted on."—*Connon.*

"The superlative is often more agreeable to the ear; nor is the sense injured. In many cases a strict adherence to the comparative form renders the language too stiff and formal."—*Lennie.*

See also Angus's Grammar and Campbell's Philosophy of Rhetoric.

Correct Examples. — "An aristocracy is, of all forms of government, the most tenacious of life, and the least flexible in its purposes." — *Bancroft.* "Time ought, above all other kinds of property, to be free from invasion." — *Johnson.* "Transcribing was, of all occupations, that which Cowper disliked the most." — *Southey.*

False Syntax: — "The high reputation which he afterwards obtained, came too late to gladden the heart which, of all others, would have most rejoiced in it." — *Southey.* "This kind of wit is that which abounds in Cowley, more than in any author that ever wrote." — *Addison.* "Breathing with ease, is a blessing of every moment; yet, of all others, it is that which we possess with the least consciousness." — *Paley.* "In the age of Elizabeth, England was more distinguished for patriotism than any nation in civilized Europe." — *N. A. Review.*

REM. 11. — Double comparatives and superlatives, as *worser, most straitest*, should be carefully avoided.

OBS. — The word *lesser* is, however, sometimes employed by good writers; as, "The *lesser* incidents." — *N. Y. Review.* "*Lesser* sympathies." — *Dana.* "Of *lesser* note." — *Goldsmith.* "Fifty *lesser* angels." — *Prof Wilson.* "*Lesser* graces." — *Blair.* "Like *lesser* streams." — *Coleridge.*

REM. 12. — An adjective is sometimes used to perform the office of an adverb; as, "*Soft* sighed the flute." — *Thomson.* This usage is mostly confined to the poets.

REM. 13. — An adjective may be used to express an attribute or quality which results from the action of the verb with which it is connected. Adjectives of this description relate both to the verb and the noun or pronoun, and may be called *adverbial adjectives.*

Examples: — "The door was painted *green.*" — "Heaven opened *wide* her ever-during gates." — *Milton.* "The exiles of a year had grown *familiar* with the favorite amusement of the Indians." — *Bancroft.* "Children just let *loose* from school." — *Goldsmith.*

REM. 14. — An adjective is sometimes used *absolutely*, having no direct reference to any noun or pronoun expressed or implied; as, "The desire of being *happy* reigns in all hearts;" — "To be *wise* and *good* is to be *great* and *noble.*" See Rule 4, Rem. 2.

REM. 15. — Nouns are sometimes used to perform the office of adjectives, as, "A *stone* cistern," "A *gold* watch;" and adjectives to perform the office of nouns, as "The *great* and *good* of all ages."

Correct the false syntax, and show why it is false. What of double comparatives and superlatives? What is an adverbial adjective? Examples Give examples of nouns used to supply the place of adjectives and adjectives used to supply the place of nouns.

ARTICLES.

REM. 16.—The article *a* or *an* belongs to nouns of the singular number only, or to nouns denoting a plurality of objects in one aggregate; as, "*A* house;"—"*An* eagle;"—"*A* million."

REM. 17.—The article *the* belongs to nouns either in the singular or plural number; as, "*The* President;"—"*The* Europeans."

REM. 18.—Articles are sometimes used to modify the sense of other adjectives; as, "*A few* days;"—"*A thousand* years;"—"So much *the stronger* proved he."

REM. 19.—The article *the* is sometimes used to modify the sense of an adverb; as, "*The longer* you delay, *the more* your difficulties will increase."

REM. 20.—When the article *a* or *an* is placed before the words *few* and *little*, it generally changes their meaning from negative to positive Thus, when we say, "There were *few* persons present," the word *few* is used in a *negative* sense, in distinction from *many*, to denote the smallness of the number. But when we say, "There were *a few* persons present," the word *few* is used in a *positive* sense, in distinction from *none*, to denote that there were some persons present. The expressions, "He needs *little* aid," and "He needs *a little* aid," serve also to illustrate this remark.

REM. 21.—When two nouns following a comparative refer to different persons or things, the article should be repeated before the second noun; but when the two nouns refer to the same person or thing, the article should not be repeated. Thus, in the sentence, "He is a better soldier than a scholar," the terms *soldier* and *scholar* relate properly to different individuals, and it is implied that he is a better soldier than a scholar would be. But, in the sentence, "He is a better soldier than scholar," the terms *soldier* and *scholar* are limited to one individual, and it is implied that he is better in the capacity of a soldier than in that of a scholar.

REM. 22.—When two or more adjectives standing in connection are used to describe different objects of the same name, the article should generally be placed before each of them; as, "*A* red and *a* white flag;" that is, two flags, one red and the other white.

What is the rule for the agreement of the article *a* or *an*? Examples. Of the article *the*? Examples. *What besides nouns, do articles sometimes modify? Examples of each class What is the general rule respecting the article, when two or more adjectives standing in connection describe different objects of the same name? Examples.*

But when no ambiguity is likely to arise from the omission of the article, its repetition is not essential. Thus we may say with equal propriety, "The fourteenth and the fifteenth century," or "The fourteenth and fifteenth centuries."

REM. 23. — When two or more adjectives are used to describe the same object, the article should generally be employed before the first only; as, "*A* red and white flag;" that is, one flag, both red and white. But when we wish to give particular prominence to each adjective, the article may be inserted before each, if no ambiguity would arise; as, "*The* learned, *the* eloquent, *the* patriotic Chatham."

REM. 24. — A noun taken in its widest and most general sense, is commonly used without an article; as, "*Man* is mortal;" — "*Vice* is odious;" — "*Iron* is the most useful of the metals;" — "He was called *Master.*"

OBS. — Sometimes, however, the article *the* is used with a singular noun to denote the whole species, or an indefinite portion of the species; as, "*The horse* is a noble animal."

REM. 25. — The article is generally omitted before proper names, and such other nouns as are of themselves sufficiently definite in their signification; as, "George Washington was born in the year 1732." — "To-day is yesterday returned." — *Young.* There are, however, some cases, in which the use of the article before proper names, is admissible; as, "*The* Pyrenees;" — "*The* French;" — "*The* Earth;" — "*The* illustrious Franklin;" — "*A* Mr. William Jones addressed the meeting."

REM. 26. — The letter *a* is sometimes employed by mercantile men in the sense of the preposition *to;** as, "Baltimore flour sold at $4.50 *a* $4.58;" that is, "Baltimore flour sold at prices varying from $4.50 *to* $4.58."

OBS. — *A* appears also to have the force of a preposition in the following and other similar examples: — "He set the public *a* reading." — *Blackwood's Magazine.* "There is some ill *a* brewing." — *Shakspeare.* In such expressions as, "Thomas *a* Becket," "Thomas *a* Kempis," *a* is employed in the sense of the preposition *of.*

REM. 27. — *A* is sometimes employed as a mere expletive prefix; as, "I begin to be *a-weary* of thee." — *Shakspeare.* "Poor Tom's *a-cold.*" — *Ibid.*

What exception to this rule? Examples. What is the general rule when two or more adjectives describe the same object? Examples. What exception? Examples. What of a noun taken in its widest sense? Examples.

---

* "This I take to be a relic of the Norman French, which was once the law and mercantile language of England; for, in French, *a,* with an accent, means *to* or *at.*" — *Cobbett.*

REM. 28.— *An* was formerly used as a conjunction, in the sense of *if* as, "Fortune is to be honored and respected, *an* it be but for her daughters, Confidence and Reputation."— *Bacon.*

POSITION OF ADJECTIVES.

REM. 29.— Adjectives should be so placed as to show clearly which nouns they are intended to qualify. Thus, instead of saying, "This *disconsolate* soldier's widow," we should say, "This soldier's *disconsolate* widow."

OBS. 1.— When an adjective is used to qualify another adjective and a noun, taken jointly, it should not be placed between the other adjective and the noun. Thus, in the expression, "An amiable young man," the word *amiable* qualifies the phrase *young man*; it would therefore be improper to say, "A *young amiable* man."

OBS. 2.— The adjective generally precedes the noun to which it belongs; as, "A *patriotic* citizen." But in the following cases the adjective most commonly follows the noun:— 1. When some word or phrase is dependent on the adjective; as, "The knowledge *requisite* for a statesman;"— "A river twenty yards *wide.*" 2. When the adjective is used as a title; as, "Alfred the *Great:*"— "George the *Fourth.*" 3. When the quality expressed by the adjective is dependent on the action of a transitive verb; as, "Vanity often renders man *contemptible.*"

OBS. 3.— When an adjective is qualified by an adverb it is sometimes placed before the noun, and sometimes after it; as, "A very *good* man;" — "A man conscientiously *exact.*"

OBS. 4.— When a verb comes between an adjective and its noun, the adjective may either precede or follow the noun; as, "*Great* is our God;" — "Gaming is *ruinous.*"

"How *vain* the ardor of the crowd,
How *low*, how *little* are the proud,
How *indigent* the great."— *Gray.*

OBS. 5.— When several adjectives belong to one noun, they may either precede or follow the noun; as, "A *learned, wise,* and *amiable* man." or "A man *learned, wise,* and *amiable.*" The longest adjective is usually placed last.

OBS. 6.— An adjective relating to a pronoun is generally placed after the pronoun; as, "He is *faithful* and *kind.*"

OBS. 7.— When a noun is preceded by an article in connection with one or more other adjectives, the article is generally placed first: as, "*A* great and good man." But when the words *many, such, both, all,* and *what,* are employed, they generally precede the article; as, "*Many a*

What rule is to be observed respecting the position of adjectives? Illustrate. What rule is to be observed respecting an adjective used to qualify another adjective and a noun? Illustrate.

day;"—"*Such a favor;*"—"*Both the trees.*" The article is also placed after adjectives which are modified by *as, so, how,* and *however*; as, "*How great a work.*"

OBS. 8.—Some grammarians object to the use of the numerals, *two, three, four,* etc., before the adjectives *first* and *last*. There seems, however, to be no good reason for the objection,* and the expressions *two first, three last,* etc., are fully sanctioned by good usage.

Examples:—"My *two last* letters."—*Addison.* "The *two first* lines are uncommonly beautiful."—*Blair.* "At the *two last* schools."—*Johnson.* "The *three first* generations."—*E. Everett.* "The *two first* years."—*Bancroft.* "The *two first* days."—*Irving* "The *two first* cantos."—*A. H. Everett.* "The *four first* centuries."—*Prescott.* "The *two last* productions."—*N. A. Review.* "The *four first* are altogether and unequivocally poetical."—*Cheever.* "The *three first* of his longer poems."—*Southey.*

OBS. 9.—The expressions *first three, last two,* etc., are also in good use, and, in some cases, are to be preferred.

Examples:—"The *first eighteen* years."—*N. A. Review.* "The history of the world for the *last fifty* years."—*E. Everett.* "During the *last seven* or *eight* years."—*Brougham.*

What is said of the use of numerals before the adjectives first and last? Examples. What other form is also employed? Examples.

---

* "It has been fashionable of late to write the *first three,* and so on, instead of the *three first.* People write in this way to avoid the seeming absurdity of implying that more than *one* thing can be the *first;* but it is, *at least,* equally absurd to talk about the *first four,* when (as often happens) there is no *second four.*"—*Arnold.*

"Surely, if there can be only '*one* last,' '*one* first,' there can be only 'a *last* one,' 'a *first* one.' I need only observe, that usage is decidedly in favor of the former phraseology."—*Grant.*

The following remarks respecting this question, are extracted from a paper read by Dr. Murdock before the New Haven Academy of Sciences:—

"The only argument against the use of *two first,* and in favor of substituting *first two,* so far as I can recollect, is this. In the nature of things, there can be only *one first* and *one last,* in any series of things. But is it true that there can never be more than *one first* and *one last?* If it be so, then the adjectives *first* and *last* must always be of the *singular* number, and can never agree with nouns in the plural. We are told that the *first years* of a lawyer's practice are seldom very lucrative. The poet tells us, that his *first essays* were severely handled by the critics, but his *last efforts* have been well received. Examples like these might be produced without number. They occur everywhere in all our standard writers. * * When a numeral adjective and a qualifying epithet both refer to the same noun, the *general rule* of the English language is to place the numeral first, then the qualifying epithet, and afterwards the noun. Thus we say, 'the *two wise* men,' 'the *two tall* men;' and not, 'the *wise two* men,' 'the *tall two* men.' And the same rule holds in *superlatives.* We say, 'the *two wisest* men,' 'the *two tallest* men;' and not 'the *wisest two* men,' 'the *tallest two* men.' Now if this be admitted to be the general rule of the English lan-

EXERCISES IN COMPOSITION.

§ 226. Write sentences containing examples of descriptive and definitive adjectives; — *containing an adjective that qualifies a sentence or phrase; — an adjective that qualifies a noun and another adjective, taken as one compound term; — an adjective expressing a comparison between two objects only; — one expressing a comparison between more than two objects; — an adverbial adjective; — a noun used to perform the office of an adjective, and an adjective used to perform the office of a noun;* — examples of the articles; — *one or more examples illustrating* Rem. 22nd; — Rem. 23rd; — Rem. 24th.

EXERCISES IN PARSING.

Model.

§ 227. "*The* country abounds in *excellent* fruit."

The is an article. This title is applied to the definite adjectives *a* or *an*, and *the*. — It is definite, because it indicates some particular object; — and belongs to *country*. Adjectives belong to the nouns or pronouns which they qualify or define.

Excellent is an adjective, because it is joined to a noun to qualify or define its meaning; — descriptive, because it expresses some quality of the noun *fruit;* — in the positive degree, because it expresses the simple state of the quality. Positive, *excellent;* comparative, *more excellent;* superlative, *most excellent*. — It belongs to *fruit*. Adjectives belong to the nouns or pronouns which they qualify or define.

"*Wise* men." — "A *virtuous* life." — "*Rural scenery* is always interesting." — "Are *these things* so?" — "The *noblest spirits* sometimes grow up in the *obscurest* spheres." — "*More agreeable* conversation." — "*An able* statesman." — "The rose is *sweet.*" — "Our *highest* interests." — "*All hope* was lost." — "*Time* is so *swift* of foot that none can overtake *it.*" — "*Modesty* is one of the *greatest* ornaments of youth." — "*Our good* or *bad fortune* depends greatly on the choice *we* make of our friends."

---

§ 228. "*Men* grew *old* in camps, and acquired the *highest* renown by *their warlike* achievements, without being once required to face *serious danger.*" — *Macaulay*. "Any one can conquer *his passions*

---

guage, then it follows, that generally we should say, 'the *two first*,' 'the *two last*,' etc., rather than 'the *first two*,' the '*last two*,' etc. This I say should *generally* be the order of the words. Yet there are some cases in which it seems preferable to say, 'the *first two*,' 'the *first three*,' etc."

who calls in the *aid* of religion." — *Crabb.* " *Every nine* days must have *its wonder*, no matter of *what* kind." — *Irving.* " We have *the* rather availed *ourselves* of *this* testimony of a *foreign* critic in behalf of *Shakspeare, because* our own countryman, *Dr. Johnson*, has not been *so favorable* to *him.*" — *Hazlitt.* " I made *the greater* progress." — *Franklin.* " A century is a *period* of *a hundred* years." — " Rectitude in *all its* branches, is the *supreme good.*" — *Channing.* " The *purest* clay is *that which* burns *white.*" — " The door was *red hot.*" — *Dickens.* " That mind and body often *sympathize, is plain.*" — *Jenyns.* " The *two last* qualities are *indeed* so *common* in *all* the poetry of his nation, *that we* need scarcely *enlarge* upon the phrase as *belonging* peculiarly *to* him." — *J. G. Lockhart.* " Without frugality *none* can be *rich;* and with *it, very few* would be *poor.*" — *Johnson.*

" *Man often* clouds with *vain or fancied* ills,
His narrow *span, when Nature's* stainless light
Dispenses only *happiness,* and fills
The world *with* things *so* beautiful and *bright.*
Her plains, her mountains, and her valleys *teem*
With *living* verdure in the *fairest* dress;
And *ocean, river, lake, and singing stream,*
Combine *to harmonize* her loveliness." — *W. C. Lodge*

Rule IX. — Verbs. — Agreement.

§ 229. A verb must agree with its nominative in number and person; as, " I *go;*" — " Thou *seest;*" — " He *hears.*"

False Syntax: — " The singular admixture of serious faults which call for severe criticism, with great merits which excite our warmest admiration, render our task one of unusual perplexity." — *Westminster Review.* " He was forced to account for it by one of the most absurd, unphilosophical notions that was ever started." — *Addison.* " They dwelt with a contented fondness on the scenes amidst which they had been born and nurtured with a purity and exulta-

---

What is the rule respecting the agreement of verbs? Examples Correct the false syntax, and show why it is false.

tion of feeling which powerfully captivates the heart." — *N. A. Review.*

"A few brief summer days, and thou
No more amid these haunts shall glide." — *Bernard Barton.*
"What art thou, speak, that on designs unknown,
While others sleep, thus range the camp alone?" — *Pope.*

REM. 1. — When a verb is placed between two nominatives of different numbers or persons, it should generally be made to agree with that which precedes it; as, "His *meat was* locusts and wild honey;" — "Thou *art* the man." But when the verb is followed by the direct and principal subject, it should be made to agree with the latter nominative; as, "Who *art* thou?" — "What *are* we?"

COLLECTIVE NOUNS.

REM. 2. — The singular form of a collective noun, may have a verb agreeing with it either in the singular or plural number; as, "The nation *is* powerful;" — "The assembly *were divided* in their opinions."

OBS. — No definite rule can be given to decide, in all cases, which number should be employed to agree with a collective noun. When the noun most naturally suggests the idea of *unity*, the verb should be singular; but when the noun conveys the idea of *plurality*, the verb should be plural. In modern usage, the plural form is most frequently employed.

REM. 3. — The transitive verbs *need* and *want* are sometimes employed in a general sense, without a nominative expressed or implied.*

Examples: — "There *needed* a new dispensation of religion for the moral reform of society." — *Caleb Cushing.* "There *needs* no better picture of his destitute and piteous situation, than that furnished by the homely pen of the chronicler." — *Irving.* "Wheresoever the case of the opinions came in agitation, there *wanted* not patrons to stand up to plead for them." — *Sparks's Am. Biog.*
"Nor did there *want*,
Cornice or frieze, with bossy sculptures graven." — *Milton.*

REM. 4. — A verb in the imperative is sometimes used *absolutely*,

---

What of a verb placed between two nominatives of different numbers or persons? Examples. What is said respecting the agreement of a verb with a collective noun? Examples. How are we to be governed in deciding which number should be employed to agree with a collective noun?

---

* See Webster, Perley, and Ingersoll.

having no direct reference to any particular subject expressed or implied.*

Examples: — "And God said, '*Let* there be light;' and there was light." — *Gen.* 1 : 3.

"'I've lost a day,'—the prince who nobly cried,
Had been an emperor without his crown, —
Of Rome? —*say*, rather, lord of human race." — *Young.*

RULE X. — VERBS. — AGREEMENT.

§ 230. When two or more nominatives denoting different objects are taken conjointly, forming one common subject, the verb agreeing with them should be in the plural number; as, "Socrates and Plato *were* eminent philosophers;" — "The air, the earth, the water, *teem* with delighted existence."

False Syntax: — "When the desire of pleasing and willingness to be pleased is silently diminished, the renovation of friendship is hopeless."—*Johnson.* " The stamp and denomination still continues, but the intrinsic value is frequently lost."—*Addison.*

REM. 1. — When two or more nominatives are thus employed, they are generally connected by the conjunction *and*, expressed or understood.

REM. 2. — A singular nominative and an objective after *with*, are sometimes made to form the joint subject of a plural verb; as, "Pharaoh with all his host, *were* drowned in the Red Sea." This copulative use of *with* is occasionally adopted by good writers; but it would be better, in most cases, either to put *and* in the place of *with* or to employ the singular form of the verb.† Thus, instead of saying, "This noble ship *with* her gallant crew were buried beneath the waves," it would be more correct to say, "This noble ship *and* her gallant crew were buried beneath the waves." So also, "This brave officer with a company of only fifty

---

What is the rule respecting the agreement of a verb with two or more nominatives denoting different objects, taken conjointly? Examples. *Correct the false syntax, and show why it is false.*

---

* See Frazee, Allen and Cornwell, Nutting, Lynde, and Chapin.

† The use of a plural verb to agree with a singular nominative and an objective after *with*, is sanctioned by Priestley, Grant, Milligan, Cobbett, Lewis, Hendrick, Lennie, Hort, Del Mar, and Simmonite; and condemned by G. Brown, Murray, Sanborn, Kirkham, Picket, Hiley, Meilan, Higginson, Hazlitt, and Latham.

"This phraseology, though not strictly consonant with the rules of concord, frequently obtains, both in ancient and modern languages. In some cases indeed it seems preferable to the syntactical form of expression.'— *Dr. Crombie.*

men, *have* succeeded in quelling the insurrection," would be better expressed by saying, "This brave officer, with a company of only fifty men, *has* succeeded in quelling the insurrection."

Examples: — "This principle, with others of the same kind, *supposes* man to act from a brute impulse."—*Johnson.* "He himself, with others, *was taken.*"—*Bancroft.* "A body of two thousand men succeeded in surprising the quarters of the marquis of Cadiz, who, with his followers, *was exhausted* by fatigue and watching."—*Prescott.*

Rem. 3. — When two or more singular nominatives denoting the *same* object are taken conjointly, the verb agreeing with them must be singular; as, "This renowned patriot and statesman *has retired* to private life."

Rule XI. — Verbs. — Agreement.

§ 231. When two or more singular nominatives are so connected that the verb agrees with each subject separately, or with one of them to the exclusion of the others, the verb should be in the singular number.

Examples: — "Duty, and not interest, *was* his constant rule of action;" — "Nor cloud, nor speck, nor stain, *breaks* the serene of heaven;" — "Neither Astrology, nor Alchemy *deserves* the name of a science," — "In every tribe, superstition, or gratitude, or fortune, *has exalted* a particular family;" — "Cæsar, as well as Cicero, *was* remarkable for his eloquence;" — "Thine *is* the kingdom, and the power, and the glory."
"Every tongue and every eye
Does homage to the passer by."

False Syntax: — "Neither romantic fancy, nor extreme pathos, nor sublimity of the very first order, are discoverable in Pope."—*Edinburgh Review.* "The most trifling occasion, a transient scarcity of flesh or lentils, the neglect of an accustomed salutation, a mistake of precedency in the public baths, or even a religious dispute, were at any time sufficient to kindle a sedition."—*Gibbon.*

"Danger, long travel, want, or woe,
Soon change the form that best we know."—*Scott.*

When two or more singular nominatives denoting the same object, are taken conjointly, in what number must the verb be? Examples. What is the rule respecting two or more singular nominatives so connected that the verb agrees with each separately, or with one to the exclusion of the others? Examples. Correct the false syntax, and show why it is false.

REM. 1. — When a singular and a plural nominative are connected by *or* or *nor*, the verb should generally be in the plural; and, when the harmony of the sentence admits of it, the plural nominative should be placed next to the verb; as, "Neither poverty nor riches *were* injurious to him."

REM. 2. — When two or more nominatives of different persons are connected by *or* or *nor*, the verb is often made to agree with the nearest nominative; as, "Either you or I *am* in fault." But it would generally be better to express the verb in connection with each nominative, unless the different persons of the verb agree in form; as, "Either you *are* in fault, or I *am*."

EXERCISES IN COMPOSITION.

§ 232. Write exercises containing a verb that agrees with a singular nominative; — a plural nominative; — a nominative in the first person; — one in the second; — one in the third; — a verb agreeing with a collective noun; — a verb agreeing with two or more nominatives denoting different objects taken conjointly; — several different examples, illustrating Rule 11th; — *a verb agreeing with a singular and a plural nominative, connected by* or or nor; — *a verb agreeing with two or more nominatives of different persons*.

EXERCISES IN PARSING.

Model.

§ 233. "I *saw* the sun *sinking* behind the hills."

Saw is a verb, because it expresses an assertion or affirmation; — irregular, because it does not form its past tense and perfect participle by adding *d* or *ed* to the present; — *see, saw, seen;* — it is a transitive verb, in the active voice, because it governs the object *sun;* — in the indicative mode, because it expresses a declaration; — in the past tense, because it denotes indefinite past time; — in the first person singular, to agree with its nominative *I*. A verb must agree with its nominative in number and person.

Sinking is a participle, because it is a mode of the verb which partakes of the properties of the verb and the adjective; — *sink, sunk, sunk;* — imperfect, because it denotes the continuance of the action; — intransitive, because it does not have a noun or pronoun for its object; — and belongs to *sun*. Participles relate to nouns or pronouns.

What is the rule respecting a singular and a plural nominative, connected by or or nor? *Examples. Respecting two or more nominatives of different persons, connected by* or or nor? *Examples.*

"*I will obey.*" — "*He has returned.*" — "*It is lost.*" — "*Strive* to improve." — "The *multitude pursue* pleasure." — "*Time* and *tide wait* for no man." — "The *intellect*, and not the heart is *concerned.*" — "Neither the *time* nor the place *was known.*" — "The *origin* of the city and state of *Rome is involved* in *great* uncertainty."

§ 234. "In *civilized* life, where the *happiness*, and indeed almost the *existence* of man, *depends* so much *upon* the opinion of his *fellow* men, *he is* constantly *acting* a *studied* part."—*Irving.* "That great critic and philosopher *endeavors to palliate* this *imperfection* in the *Greek* poet."—*Addison.* "*This*, and this *alone*, *constitutes the* worth and importance of the sacrifice."—*Channing.* "A *shady grove*, a green pasture, a stream of fresh water, *are sufficient to attract a colony* of sedentary *Arabs.*"—*Gibbon.* "*Africa*, as well as *Gaul, was* gradually *fashioned* to the imitation of the capital."—*Ibid.*

"Like the *leaves* of the *forest* when summer *is green*,
  That *host* with *their* banners, at sunset *were seen.*"—*Byron.*

"The *almost unobserved* advancement and *diffusion* of knowledge *were paving* the way for discoveries."—*Mackintosh.* "The iron, as well as the *wood, was taken* from the wreck of the *same ship.*"—*Southey.* "*It has been* frequently *observed* by writers on physiognomy, *that every* emotion *and* every *operation* of the mind *has* a *corresponding* expression of the countenance."—*Dugald Stewart.*

Rule XII.— Verbs.— Government.

§ 235. Transitive verbs govern the objective case; as, "*I have heard him;*" — "*Honor* thy *father* and thy *mother.*"

Rem. 1.— A verb in the infinitive, a sentence, or a phrase, often supplies the place of a noun or pronoun in the objective case; as, "You see *how few of these men have returned.*"

Rem. 2. — An intransitive verb may be used to govern an objective, when the verb and the noun depending upon it are of kindred signification; as, "*To live* a blameless *life;*" — "*To run* a race."

What is the rule respecting transitive verbs? Examples. *What of an intransitive verb followed by a noun of kindred signification? Examples.*

OBS.— Idiomatic expressions sometimes occur in which intransitive verbs are followed by objectives depending upon them; as, "Perhaps we have wanted the spirit, and manliness, to *look* the *subject* fully in the face." —*Channing*. "They *laughed him* to scorn."—*Matt.* 9: 24. "We have stopped a moment *to breathe* our *horses*."—*Longfellow*.
"The broken soldier, kindly bid to stay,
Sat by the fire, and *talk'd* the *night* away."—*Goldsmith*.

REM. 3.— Transitive verbs of *asking, giving, teaching,* and some others, are often employed to govern two objectives;* as, "*Ask him* his *opinion*." — "This experience *taught* me a valuable *lesson*." —"*Spare me* yet this bitter *cup*."—*Hemans*. "I thrice *presented him* a kingly *crown*."—*Shakspeare*.

REM. 4.— Verbs of *asking, giving, teaching,* and some others, are often employed in the passive voice to govern a noun or pronoun in the objective.

Examples: — "He *was asked* his *opinion*."—*Johnson*. "The pupil, in more advanced life, *is taught* the *science* in its strictly logical form." —*N. A. Review*. "He *was denied admission* to the most important public repositories."—*Prescott*. "He had *been refused shelter*."— *Irving*. "They *were denied* the *indulgence*."—*Macaulay*. "Am I to be *asked* such a *question*?"—*Cooper*.

OBS.— This form of expression is anomalous, and might, in many cases, be improved.† Thus, instead of saying, "He was offered a seat

---

Transitive verbs of asking, teaching, etc.? Examples. How are verbs of asking, teaching, etc., often employed in the passive voice? Examples.

---

* Many grammarians supply a preposition to govern one of the objectives following this class of verbs; but such a mode of parsing is, in many cases, arbitrary, and does violence to an important and well established idiom of the language. In the expressions, "*Teach them* to obey the laws," and "*Teach them* obedience to the laws," it is manifest that the grammatical influence of the verb *teach* upon the pronoun *them*, is the same in both examples. Why then parse the word *them* as governed by the *verb* in one example, and in the other by a *preposition understood?*

The rule for the government of two objectives by a verb, without the aid of a preposition, is adopted by Webster, Weld, Alexander, Frazee, Nutting, Perley, Goldsbury, J. M. Putnam, Hamlin, Flower, Crane, Brace, Greenleaf, C. Alexander, Burr, Cornell, Cutler, Fowler, and many others.

† G. Brown, Sanborn, Murray, Wright, and several other grammarians condemn this usage altogether; while, on the other hand, it has the sanction of a still larger class of authors, including Dr. Crombie, Flower, D'Orsey, Crane, Frazee, R. C. Smith, Emmons, Hamlin, Lennie, Hendrick, Ainsworth, Arnold, Greene, Weld, Fowler, and Nutting.

"Examples of the application of this rule are furnished by the best writers. Phrases such as these,—'She was asked the question,' 'She was taught her lesson,' 'They were offered a pardon,' 'They were denied their request,' etc., are of frequent occurrence; and it seems better, after the example of the Latin, to provide for them by a special rule, than to condemn them as inaccuracies."—*Pond's Murray*.

in the council," it would be preferable to say, "A seat in the council was offered [to] him."

REM. 5. — The passive voice of a verb is sometimes used in connection with a preposition, forming a *compound passive verb*.

Examples: — " He *was listened to* without a murmur."—*A. H. Everett* " Nor is this enterprise *to be scoffed at*."—*Channing*. " This is a tendency *to be guarded against*."—*Paley*. " A bitter persecution *was carried on*."—*Hallam*.

REM. 6. — Idiomatic expressions sometimes occur in which a noun in the objective is preceded by a passive verb, and followed by a preposition used adverbially.

Examples: — " Vocal and instrumental music *were made use of*."—*Addison*. " The third, fourth, and fifth, *were taken possession of* at half past eight."—*Southey*. " The Pinta *was* soon *lost sight of* in the darkness of the night."—*Irving*. " It ought never *to be lost sight of*."—*N. A. Review*.

OBS. — This idiom is anomalous; but it has the sanction of many good writers, and is therefore shielded from the unqualified condemnation of the critic. It would, however, generally be better to avoid it.

REM. 7. — There are some verbs which may be used either transitively or intransitively; as, " He *will return* in a few days;" " He *will return* the *book;*" — " The wind *blows* violently;" " The wind *blows* the *chaff*."

REM. 8. — The verb *learn* is often improperly used for *teach;* as, " It is of little utility *to learn* scholars that certain words are signs of certain modes and tenses." Insert *teach* in the place of *learn*.

REM. 9. — The verbs *lay* and *set* should not be confounded with *lie* and *sit*. *Lay* is properly transitive; *lie*, intransitive. *Set*, is either transitive or intransitive; *sit*, always intransitive. See the *principal parts* of these verbs, in the list of irregular verbs, pp. 96, 97.

Correct Examples: — " He fasted and *lay* in sackcloth." — 1 Kings 21 : 27. " He *laid* his robe from him."—*Jonah* 3 : 6. " I have *sat* for hours at my window."—*Irving*. " Thou hast *set* a bound that they may not pass over."—*Ps.* 104 : 9. " They have forsaken my law which I *set* before them."—*Jer.* 9 : 13. " We say, a thing *lies* by us until we bring it into use; we *lay* it by for some future purpose; we *lie* down in order to repose ourselves; we *lay* money down by way of deposit."—*Crabb*.

False Syntax: — " My old friend sat himself down in the chair." —*Addison*. " The mate of a British vessel then laying at anchor in Boston harbor."—*Sparks's Am. Biog.*

What of the verbs lay *and* set*? Correct the false syntax, and show why it is false.*

"Even now, where Alpine solitudes ascend,
I sit me down a pensive hour to spend."—*Goldsmith.*
"For him through hostile camps I bend my way,
For him thus prostrate at thy feet I lay."—*Pope.*

REM. 10.—A verb in the infinitive is often preceded by a noun or pronoun in the objective, which has no direct dependence on any other word.*

Examples:—"One error is that of concluding the *things* in question *to be* alike."—*Whateley.* "Columbus ordered a strong *fortress* of wood and plaster *to be erected.*"—*Irving.* "Its favors here should make *us* tremble."—*Young.*

REM. 11.—Idiomatic expressions sometimes occur, in which the active form of a transitive verb is used in a sense nearly allied to the passive; as, "The goods *sell* rapidly;"—"The cloth *tears;*"—"Mahogany *planes* smooth;"—"These lines *read* well."

REM. 12.—The imperfect participle of a transitive verb is sometimes employed in a passive sense.†

Examples:—"The spot where this new and strange tragedy was *acting.*"—*E. Everett.* "An attempt is *making* in the English Parliament to provide by law for the education of the poor."—*Daniel Webster.* "The fortress was *building.*"—*Irving.* "We must pass to a rapid notice of the magnificent church, now *erecting* in the city of New York."—*N. A. Review.* "While this necessary movement was *making.*"—*Cooper.* "While these things were *transacting* in England."—*Bancroft.*

What peculiar use is sometimes made of the imperfect participle of a transitive verb? Examples.

---

* "The infinitive has sometimes a subject in the objective case; as, 'I believe *him* to be an honest man;'—'He commanded the *horse* to be saddled;'—'I confess *myself* to be in fault;'—'Let *him* be punished.' *Him*, in the first sentence quoted, is not the object of the verb *believe*, but the subject of *to be.* In the second sentence, *horse* is not the object of *command;* —it is not meant that a command was given to the horse.'—*Butler.*

"The agent to a verb in the infinitive mode must be in the objective case."—*Nutting.*

See also Nixon's English Parser.

† Different opinions have long existed among critics respecting this passive use of the imperfect participle. Many respectable writers substitute the compound passive participle; as, "The house is *being built;*" "The book is *being printed.*" But the prevailing practice of the best authors is in favor of the simple form; as, "The house is *building.*"

"The propriety of these imperfect passive tenses has been doubted by almost all our grammarians; though I believe but few of them have written many pages without condescending to make use of them. Dr. Beattie says, 'One of the greatest defects of the English tongue, with regard to the verb, seems to be the want of an imperfect passive participle.' And yet he uses the imperfect participle in a passive sense as often as most writers."— *Pickbourn's Dissertation on the English Verb.*

"Several other expressions of this sort now and then occur, such as the

Rule XIII.—Predicate Nominative.

§ 236. Intransitive and passive verbs have the same case after them as before them, when both words refer to the same person or thing; as, "*Society* is the true *sphere* of human virtue;"—"*They* wished *him* to be their *king;*"—"*He* soon became the *leader* of his party;"—"*He* was chosen *librarian;*"—"*Homer* has been styled the *prince* of poets."

Rem. 1.—In some instances the words so agreeing in case are both placed either before or after the verb; as, "Are *they friends?*"—"*Friends* they cannot be."

Rem. 2.—When the nominative after a verb forms a part of the predicate, it is called the *predicate nominative*. The nominative employed as the subject of a verb, is called the *subject nominative*.

Rule XIV.—Government of the Infinitive.

§ 237. The infinitive mode may be governed by a verb, a noun, or an adjective;* as, "*Strive to improve;*"—"I am in *haste to return;*"—"The ship was *ready to sail*."

Rem. 1.—The infinitive is often governed by *than* or *as*. The following are examples:—"An object so high *as to be* invisible;"

What is the rule respecting the same case? Examples. Respecting the government of the infinitive? Examples. *What conjunctions are frequently employed to govern the infinitive? Examples.*

---

new-fangled and most uncouth solecism, 'is being done,' for the good old English idiomatic expression is doing,'—an absurd periphrasis, driving out a pointed and pithy turn of the English language."—*N. A. Review.*

* Several respectable grammarians treat the infinitive particle *to* as a *preposition*, governing the verb. See Comly, G. Brown, Bell, Snyder, and Fowle.

"If *to* is here a preposition, it differs at least in one respect, from every other English preposition, and from the same word in other situations, in giving entire generality to the verb,—an effect which no preposition, as such, ever has, either on the verb, or any other part of speech. That it should assume this peculiarity in this particular connection only, is remarkable; and that it should do this and at the same time retain the usual properties of a preposition, seems very improbable."—*Everest.*

— "It is sometimes better to submit to injustice, *than to resort to judicial proceedings.*"

REM. 2. — The infinitive is sometimes governed by an adverb; as, "The shipmen were *about to flee.*"

REM. 3. — The infinitive is sometimes governed by a phrase or a sentence; as, "*Too ready* ever *to have* leisure for attempting to execute any great and worthy design." — *Southey.*

"In age, in infancy, *from others' aid*
Is all our hope, *to teach* us to be kind." — *Young.*

REM. 4. — The infinitive is sometimes used *absolutely*, having no dependence on any other word; as, "It was, so *to speak*, a branch of the Executive Power." — *N. Y. Review.*

REM. 5. — A verb in the infinitive usually relates to some noun or pronoun.* Thus, in the sentence, "He desires to improve," the verb *to improve* relates to the pronoun *he* while it is governed by *desires.*

REM. 6. — When the infinitive follows the active voice of the verbs *bid, dare, feel, see, let, make, need,* and *hear*, the sign *to* is usually omitted; as, "I *felt* my strength *return;*" — "Nothing *need be said;*" — "We *heard* the thunder *roll;*" — "Pride guides his steps, and *bids* him *shun* the great."

REM. 7. — The sign of the infinitive is also omitted, in some instances, after the verbs *have, behold, perceive, know,* and *help;* as, "Would they *have* us *reject* such an offer?"

RULE XV. — TENSES.

§ 238. In the use of verbs, those tenses should be employed which express correctly the sense intended.

What of infinitives having no dependence on other words? Examples. To what do infinitives relate? Examples. After what verbs is the sign of the infinitive usually omitted? Examples. Give the rule for the employment of the tenses. *Illustrate its application.*

---

* Some teachers pay little attention to the *government* of the infinitive, while they direct their pupils to point out in all cases the noun or pronoun to which it *relates.* Others require their pupils to designate both government and relation. See Sanborn's Grammar, p. 144.

"An infinitive refers to the noun which is the agent or subject of the action expressed by the infinitive. The reference is precisely of the same nature as that of a participle to its substantive, or of a finite verb to its nominative." — *Parkhurst.*

REM 1. — This rule is somewhat indefinite, but when taken in connection with the definitions and illustrations of the tenses given under Etymology, it will, in most cases, be a sufficient guide to the learner. It is violated in the following example: — "I expected *to have seen* you." The verb *to have seen* cannot here relate to a time prior to that denoted by the verb *expected*. It should not therefore be in the past perfect tense. Corrected: — "I expected *to see* you."

False Syntax: — "When I was in France, I have often observed, that a great man has grown so insensibly heated by the court which was paid him on all sides, that he has been quite distracted."—*Steele*. "Columbus had fondly hoped, at one time, to have rendered the natives civilized, industrious, and tributary subjects of the crown."—*Irving*. "As Dr. Wallis hath long ago observed." — *Lowth*. "They continue with me now three days." — *Matt*. 15 : 32.

REM. 2. — The present tense is often employed in expressions that relate to the future; as, "The world *to come*;" — "He *leaves* in half an hour;" — "I am about *to write*."

OBS. — When a finite verb in the present tense, occurs in a sentence denoting futurity, it is generally preceded by *before, as soon as, when, till*, or *after*; or accompanied by an adverb or modifying phrase denoting future time; as, "*When* the mail *arrives*, the letters will be delivered;"—"*Hold* you the watch *to-night?*" "*We do* my lord;" — "*Ring* the bell, *at a quarter before eight*."

REM. 3. — When the infinitive present is connected with another verb, it generally relates to the same time as the verb with which it is joined; as, "He began *to write;*" — "He will begin *to write*." In the first of these examples *to write* corresponds in time with *began*, and is therefore past in respect to the time of speaking. In the other example, it relates to the same time that is expressed by *will begin*.

OBS. — Sometimes, however, the infinitive denotes time subsequent to that expressed by the verb with which it is connected; as, "He *is to engage* in teaching;" — "Æneas went in search of an empire which *was* one day *to command* the world."

REM. 4. — In animated narrations, the present tense is occasionally used for the past; as, "After the lapse of eight precious days, they again

---

Correct the false syntax, and show why it is false. Give examples of verbs in the present tense, used in expressions that relate to the future. What of the infinitive present, used in connection with other verbs? Illustrate.

weigh anchor; the coast of England recedes; already they are unfurling their sails on the broad ocean, when the captain of the Speedwell, with his company, dismayed at the dangers of the enterprize, once more *pretends* that his ship is too weak for the service." — *Bancroft.*

REM. 5. — The future tense is frequently employed for the future perfect; as, "I *shall finish* my letter before the mail closes."

REM. 6. — When a verb in the present perfect tense is preceded by *before, as soon as, when, till,* or *after,* it usually performs the office of the future perfect; as, "When he *has finished* his engagement, he shall be rewarded."

REM. 7. — The hypothetical form of the verb *to be* is used to express either present or indefinite time; as, "If he *were* present, he would convince you of your error." See p. 84.

OBS. — The past subjunctive of other verbs is often employed in a similar manner; as, "If he *regarded* his own interest, he would be more faithful to his employer."

REM. 8. — The past perfect subjunctive is often employed to express indefinite past time; as, "I should have walked out if it *had* not *rained.*"

REM. 9. — In expressing general propositions which have no direct relation to time, the present tense of the verb should be employed; as, "The passion for power and superiority *is* universal."— *Channing.*

REM. 10. — The perfect participle of an irregular verb should not be used for the past tense, nor the past tense for the perfect participle. The following expressions are therefore incorrect: — "The storm *begun* to subside;" — "I *done* it in great haste;" —" He was displeased to receive a letter *wrote* with so little care." Corrected: — "The storm *began* to subside;" — "I *did* it in great haste;" — "He was displeased to receive a letter *written* with so little care." This rule is also violated when the past tense of an irregular verb is used with an auxiliary. Thus, instead of saying "The sun *has rose,*" we should say, "The sun *has risen.*"

False Syntax: — "We are not condemned to toil through half a folio, to be convinced that the writer has broke his promise." — *Johnson.* "The champions having just began their career, the king stopped the combat." — *Goldsmith.*

"Rapt into future times, the bard begun." — *Pope.*

What tense is employed in general propositions, having no direct relation to time? Examples. What is said respecting the use of the perfect participle and the past tense of an irregular verb? Illustrate. Correct the false syntax, and show why it is false.

Rule XVI.— Participles.

§ 239. Participles relate to nouns or pronouns; as, "He stood *leaning* on his spade, and *gazing* at the brightness in the west."

Rem. 1. — When the participle is preceded by the negative particle *un*, it becomes an adjective, unless the verb from which it is formed admits the same prefix. The words *untiring, unsought, unseen,* and *unknown*, are examples of this class of adjectives. But the words *unbinding, unfolded, undone,* etc., when used in the verbal sense, are to be regarded as participles, since they are formed regularly from the verbs *unbind, unfold, undo,* etc.

Rem. 2. — Participles are often used in the sense of nouns; as, "There was again the *smacking* of whips, the *clattering* of hoofs, and the *glittering* of harness." — *Irving.*

Rem. 3. — Participles often perform, at the same time, the office of a noun and a verb; as, "I could not avoid *expressing* my concern for the stranger." As a noun, *expressing* is in the objective case and governed by *avoid*. As a transitive verb, it governs the word *concern*.

Rem. 4. — A participle is sometimes used *absolutely*, having no dependence on any other word; as, "Properly *speaking*, there is no such thing as chance;" — "This conduct, *viewing* it in the most favorable light, reflects discredit on his character."

Rem. 5. — A participle sometimes relates to a sentence or phrase; as, "He had been strictly secured and guarded, *owing* to his former escape." — *Walter Scott.*

"To do aught good never will be our task,
But ever *to do ill* our sole delight,
As *being* the contrary to his high will
Whom we resist."—*Milton.*

Rem. 6. — There are certain adjectives which are derived directly from verbs, and supply the place of passive participles. Their use is mostly confined to poetry.

Examples: — "Regions *consecrate* to oldest time."— *Wordsworth.*
"'T is *dedicate* to ruin."—*Coleridge.*

Give the rule for the agreement of participles. Examples. *Participles preceded by the negative particle* un. *Examples of each class. Give examples of participial nouns. What double office do participles often perform? Examples. Give examples of participles used absolutely.*

"To save himself and household from amidst
A world *devote* to universal wreck."—*Milton.*

[For one of the uses of the imperfect participle, see Rule 12, Rem. 12.]

EXERCISES IN COMPOSITION.

§ 240. Write exercises containing objectives governed by transitive verbs; — *intransitive verbs governing objectives of kindred signification;* — verbs having the same case after them as before them; — verbs in the infinitive governed by verbs, nouns, and adjectives — verbs in the infinitive used without the sign *to*, — imperfect and perfect participles; — *participial nouns.*

EXERCISES IN PARSING.

§ 241. "*Evil* communications *corrupt* good *manners.*"—"Thy name *shall be Abraham.*"—"He *shall be called John.*"—"I *heard him relate* the anecdote."—"I *have written* exercises, *containing* all the *examples required.*"—"Conversation *enriches* the *understanding,* but solitude *is* the *school* of genius."—*Gibbon.* "*Napoleon was* never *known to change* his *opinion* on *any* subject."—*Alison.* "The *Puritans* were *men whose* minds *had derived* a peculiar character from the *daily* contemplation of superior beings and *eternal* interests."—*Macaulay.*

§ 242. "The daily press *first instructed* men in their wants, *and soon found that* the eagerness of curiosity *outstripped* the *power* of *gratifying it.*"—*Story.* "He that *teaches us* any *thing which* we *knew* not before, *is* undoubtedly *to be reverenced* as a master."—*Johnson.* "*This universal* pacification *has* hardly *been thought of.*" —*Channing.* "It *formed* so important and singular a *feature* of *their* social economy, *as to merit* a *much* more particular notice than it *has received.*"—*Prescott.* "He *was offered* an *employment.*"— *Campbell.* "He *lay* like a warrior *taking* his *rest.*"—*Wolfe.* "In the *beginning* they *may be assailed by* the clamor of self-interest, and *frowned upon* by the worshippers of expediency."—*N. A. Review.* "Many approximations *have been made,* and are now *making,* to the truth."—*Lockhart.* "We make *provision* for this life, as though it *were* never *to have* an end; and for the *other* life, as though it *were never to have* a *beginning.*"—*Addison.* "The desire *that* our country *should surpass all others, would* not *be criminal, did* we *understand* in what respects *it is most honorable* for a nation *to excel.*"—*Channing.* " To keep always *praying* aloud is plainly impossible."—*G. Brown.*

Rule XVII.—Adverbs.

§ 243. Adverbs modify verbs, adjectives, and other adverbs; as, "Men *frequently* contend for trifles;"— " It was *very thankfully* received."

Rem. 1.— An adverb is frequently used to modify a sentence or phrase.*

> *Examples:* — "Which is *so at war*† with nature."—*Prof. Haddock.* " The final debate on the resolution was postponed for *nearly a month.*"—*Wirt.* "They introduced the Deity to human apprehension, under an idea more personal, more determinate, *more within its compass.*"—*Paley.* " The other productions of this indefatigable scholar, embrace *a large circle of topics independently* of his various treatises on philology and criticism."—*Prescott.* " *Verily I say unto you*, they have their reward."—*Matt.* 6: 2.

Rem. 2.— An adverb is sometimes used to modify a preposition;‡ as, "He sailed *nearly round* the globe;"—"He was wounded *just below* the ear."

Rem. 3.— *Adjectives* should be employed to qualify *nouns* and *pronouns*, and *adverbs* to modify *verbs, adjectives,* and other *adverbs.* It is therefore incorrect to say, " She writes *elegant.*" " Thine *often* infirmities."

Obs.— There are, however, certain forms of expression in which adverbs bear a special relation to nouns or pronouns;∥ as, "Behold, I,

---

Give the rule for adverbs. Examples. *What are adverbs frequently used to modify, besides verbs, adjectives, and other adverbs? Examples. What distinction should be observed in the use of adjectives and adverbs? Illustrate.*

---

* " The adverb does not always belong to any one single word; nothing being more common than the relation of an adverb to a clause, all of whose words are taken as one word; and almost or quite as frequently, an adverb stands in relation to a whole sentence."—*Smart.*

† " Sometimes a preposition and a noun together have the signification of an adjective; and, as such, the phrase may be qualified by an adverb; as, *doubly in fault*,—*doubly criminal.*"—*Parkhurst.*

‡ See Sanborn, Parkhurst, J. M. Putnam, Wilbur, Bruce, Emmons, Goldsbury, and Goodenow.

∥ See Bullions, Allen and Cornwell, Bruce, Butler, Badgley, and Webber.

even *I*, do bring a flood of waters."—*Gen.* 6: 17. "For our gospel came not unto you in *word only*, but also in power."—1 *Thess.* 1: 5.

REM. 4.— The adverbs *yea, yes, nay, no,* and *amen,* are generally used independently; as, "Will you go?" "*No.*"—"Has the hour arrived?" "*Yes.*"

REM. 5.— *Never* is sometimes improperly used for *ever;* as, "They might be extirpated, were they *never* so many." Corrected:—"They might be extirpated, were they *ever* so many."

REM. 6.— The adverbs *hither, thither,* and *whither,* are now seldom employed except in grave discourse, their places being supplied, in common writings, by *here, there,* and *where;* as, "It was dangerous to go *there.*"—*Irving.* "Traders flocked *there* as to a fair."—*Prescott.* "Without knowing *where* to go."—*Paley.* "When you come *here.*"—*Willis.*

REM. 7.— Adverbs are sometimes used to supply the place of nouns.

Examples:—"Till *now* they had paid no taxes."—*A. H. Everett.* "On the following day Columbus came to *where* the coast swept away to the northeast for many leagues."—*Irving.* "Save *where* the beetle wheels his droning flight."—*Gray.* "Till *then* who knew the force of those dire arms?"—*Milton.* "The several sources from *whence* these pleasures are derived."—*Addison.* "From *hence* I was conducted up a staircase."—*Irving.*

OBS.— *At once,* and *by far,* are in general use; and the adverbial phrases *from hence, from thence, from whence,* constitute an authorized idiom. But such expressions as *from where, from there, to here,* are seldom employed by the best prose writers. In poetry, their occurrence is more frequent.

REM. 8.— *Where,* an adverb of place, is sometimes improperly employed without reference to place, for the phrase *in which;* as, "They framed a protestation, *where* [*in which*] they repeated all their former claims."

REM. 9.— The adverb *there* is often used for the sake of euphony, without any reference to *place;* as, "*There* is an hour of peaceful rest."—*W. B. Tappan.* "*There* came to the beach a poor exile of Erin."—*Campbell.* When used in this sense, *there* is called an *expletive* adverb.

REM. 10.— The word *all* is frequently used as an adverb, in the sense of *wholly;* as,

"Yet our great enemy,
All incorruptible, would on his throne
Sit unpolluted."—*Milton.*

What of the adverbs yea, yes, nay, no, *and* amen? *Examples. What part of speech are adverbs sometimes used to represent? Examples. Which of the different forms of expression named are authorized, and which are objectionable?*

REM. 11. — A negation is properly expressed by the use of one negative only. The following sentence is therefore erroneous:—

"I never did repent for doing good,
Nor shall *not* now."—*Shakspeare*.

OBS. 1. — Two negatives in the same clause are generally equivalent to an affirmative, and are sometimes elegantly employed to express a positive assertion; as, "The pilot was *not unacquainted* with the coast"—"*Nor* did he pass *unmoved* the gentle scene."

"*Nor* did they *not* perceive the evil plight
In which they were, or the fierce pain not feel."—*Milton*.

The intervention of *only*, or some other word of kindred meaning preserves the negation; as, "He was *not only illiberal*, but covetous."

OBS. 2. — A repetition of the same negative renders the negation more emphatic; as, "I would *never* lay down my arms;—*never—never —never*."—*Pitt*.

REM. 12. — The adverb *no* is sometimes improperly used for *not*; as, "Whether he will or *no*, he must be a man of the nineteenth century."—*Macaulay*.

REM. 13. — Two or more words are sometimes used in connection, as a *compound adverb*, or *adverbial phrase*.

Examples:—"We will see about this matter *by and by*."—*Irving*.
"Ishmael went forth to meet them, weeping *all along* as he went."—*Jer.* 41: 6. "If we hope for what we are not likely to possess, we act and think *in vain*."—*Addison*.

REM. 14. — Adverbs should be placed in that situation which contributes most to the harmony and clearness of the sentence, and which accords best with the usage of the language. This rule is violated in the sentence, "Thoughts are *only* criminal, when they are first chosen and then voluntarily continued." As it stands, the adverb *only* properly qualifies *criminal*, whereas the author intended to have it qualify that portion of the sentence which follows the comma. Corrected: — "Thoughts are criminal, *only* when they are first chosen and then voluntarily continued."

False Syntax:—"In following the trail of his enemies through the forest, the American Indian exhibits a degree of sagacity, which almost appears miraculous."—*Alison*. "There are certain miseries in idleness, which the idle can only conceive."—*Johnson*. "It not only has form but life."—*N. A. Review*.

How is a negation properly expressed? Give examples of the violation of this rule. What is an adverbial phrase? Examples. What rule should be observed respecting the position of adverbs? Illustrate. Correct the false syntax, and show why it is false.

OBS. 1. — An adverb should not be placed immediately after the infinitive particle *to*.* This rule is violated in the following sentence : — " Teach scholars to *carefully* scrutinize the sentiments advanced in all the books they read."

False Syntax : — " To make this sentence perspicuous it would be necessary to entirely remodel it." — *Newman's Rhetoric.* " It costs the pupil more to simply state the examples in such a form, than it does to perform them without any statement at all." —*N. A. Review.*

OBS. 2. — The adverb *enough* is placed after the adjective which it modifies, and both the adjective and the adverb are placed after the noun; as, " A house *large enough* for all."

REM. 15. — The words *howsoever, whichsoever,* and *whatsoever,* are sometimes divided by the intervention of another word ; as, " But surely this division, *how* long *soever* it has been received, is inadequate and fallacious." —*Johnson.* " By *what* manner *soever.*" — *Wayland.*

RULE XVIII. CONJUNCTIONS.

§ 244. Conjunctions connect words or sentences ; as, " Idleness *and* Ignorance are the parents of many vices ; " — " He fled *because* he was afraid."

REM. 1. — Relative pronouns and conjunctive adverbs are also employed to perform the office of connectives.

OBS. 1. — In the compound sentence, " He *who* expects much, will often be disappointed," the relative *who* is the subject of the verb *expects* in one clause, and relates to the pronoun *he*, which is the subject of *will be disappointed* in the other clause. The connection expressed by *who* in this example, and by relative pronouns generally, is quite as close as that expressed by conjunctions. See § 77, Rem. 2.

OBS. 2. — Many conjunctive adverbs modify the two verbs embraced in the different clauses which they connect ; as, " *When* he

---

What of the position of adverbs modifying infinitives? Correct the false *syntax, and show why it is false.* Give the rule respecting conjunctions. Examples. *What other classes of words are also employed as connectives? Illustrate the connective office of a relative pronoun. Two-fold modifying power of many conjunctive adverbs. Examples.*

---

* See Davis, Parkhurst, Perley, and Kennion.

had delivered his message he *departed;*" — " Fame *may* give praise, while it *withholds* esteem."

OBS. 3. — A conjunctive adverb used to supply the place of a preposition and a relative pronoun, is called a *relative adverb;* as, " The shepherd leaves his mossy cottage, *where* [*in which*] he dwells in peace;" — " The colonies had now reached that stage in their growth, *when* the difficult problem of colonial government must be solved."

REM. 2. — There are certain idiomatic forms of expression in which the connection between different clauses is implied in the relation which they bear to each other in sense; as, " In this last case, the more apt and striking is the analogy suggested, the more will it have of an artificial appearance." — *Whately.* " Whatever was his predominant inclination, neither hope nor fear hindered him from complying with it." — *Johnson.* " Sad as his story is, it is not altogether mournful." — *Southey.*

REM. 3. — The conjunction *that* often performs the office of a pronoun or substitute. Thus, in the sentence, " I know *that* he will return," *that* represents the clause *he will return*, and is the object of the transitive verb *know*. See Rem. 11.

OBS. 1. — The conjunction *that* is often suppressed when the connection of the different clauses is obvious; as, " But Brutus says he was ambitious." — *Shakspeare.*

OBS. 2. — When, however, the connection of the clauses is less intimate, the omission of *that* is objectionable; as, " His ingenuity was such [that] he could form letters, make types and wood cuts, and engrave vignettes in copper." — *Bancroft.*

REM. 4. — Two or more words are sometimes used together as a *compound conjunction* or *conjunctive phrase.*

Examples: — " It has been observed that happiness, *as well as* virtue, consists in mediocrity." — *Johnson.* " The writer, by whom the noble features of our scenery shall be sketched with a glowing pencil, and the peculiarities of our character seized with delicate perception, cannot mount so entirely and rapidly to success, *but that* ten years will add new millions to the number of his readers." — *E. Everett.*

OBS. — Many expressions of this class are elliptical; but it is generally better not to attempt to supply the words omitted, unless they are obviously implied.

CORRESPONDING CONJUNCTIONS.

REM. 5. — Some conjunctions are composed of two corresponding words. The following list embraces most of this class of connectives, and exhibits the correct mode of employing them: —

What is a relative adverb? Examples. Compound conjunctions Examples. Corresponding conjunctions.

Both — and: "It is the work of a mind fitted *both* for minute researches *and* for large speculations." — *Macaulay.*

Though, although — yet, still, nevertheless : " *Though* deep, yet clear, *though* gentle, *yet* not dull ;" — " *Though* a thousand rivers discharge themselves into the ocean, *still* it is never full."

Whether — or : " *Whether* it were I *or* they."

Either — or : " No leave ask'st thou of *either* wind *or* tide."

Neither — nor : " *Neither* act *nor* promise hastily."

OBS. — The poets frequently use *or — or* for *either — or,* and *nor — nor* for *neither — nor ;* as,

"Not to be tempted from her tender task,
Or [*either*] by sharp hunger, *or* by smooth delight." — *Thomson.*

" *Nor* [*neither*] eye *nor* listening ear an object finds." — *Young.*

REM. 6. —Some conjunctions are used in correspondence with adverbs or adjectives. The following are the principle connectives of this class : —

As — as, so : " She is *as* amiable *as* her sister ; " —" *As* he excels in virtue, *so* he rises in estimation."

So — as : " No riches make one *so* happy *as* a clear conscience." — " Speak *so as* to be understood."

So — that, expressing a consequence : " She speaks *so* low *that* no one can hear what she is saying."

Not only — but, but also : " He was *not only* prudent, *but also* industrious."

Such — as : " There never was *such* a time *as* the present."

Such — that : " *Such* is the emptiness of human enjoyment, *that* we are always impatient of the present."

More, sooner, etc. — *than :* " They have *more than* heart could wish ; " — " The Greeks were *braver than* the Persians."

OBS.— *Than* should be used to correspond with *rather* and with all *comparatives ;* as, " Receive knowledge *rather than* choice gold ; "

What conjunction is used to correspond with both *? Give an example.* The teacher should proceed in a similar manner through the list of corresponding conjunctions, and repeat the exercise till the pupils are able to distinguish readily the terms which properly correspond with each other. *What words are employed by the poets to correspond with* or *and* nor *? Examples. With what words does* than *properly correspond ? Examples.*

—" Wisdom is *better than* rubies." The clause following *other* * is also more properly introduced by *than*, though good writers occasionally employ some other term.

REM. 7. — The negatives *no, not*, etc., may be followed by either *or* or *nor*. The use of *nor* serves to repeat the negation; and there are many cases in which it is decidedly preferable to *or*.†

Examples: — " There are *no* more continents *or* worlds to be revealed." — *E. Everett.* " It is *not* by accuracy *or* profundity, that men become masters of great assemblies." — *Macaulay.* " I know *not* where to begin, *nor* where to end." — *E. Everett.* " He *never* convinces the reason, *nor* fills the imagination, *nor* touches the heart." — *Macaulay.* ." Let *not* your fancy, *nor* your excited feelings lead you captive." — *B. B. Edwards.* " The exiles of New England saw *not* before them *either* a home *or* a country." — *Story.*

REM. 8. — The conjunction *as*, used in connection with an adjective or adverb in the positive degree, is sometimes improperly coupled with a comparative, and followed by *than;* as, " The latest posterity will listen with *as much*, or even *greater* pleasure *than* their contemporaries." — *A. H. Everett.* Corrected : — " The latest posterity will listen with as much pleasure as their contemporaries, or even greater."

Correct Example: — " I am as well as you have ever known me in a time of much trouble, and even better." — *Cowper.*

False Syntax: — " A vision came before him, as constant and more terrible than that from which he had escaped." — *Dickens* " I have proceeded in the revisal, as far, and somewhat farther than the fifteenth book." — *Cowper.*

REM. 9. — The conjunction *or* is sometimes employed to connect words that are in apposition; as, " No disease of the mind can more fatally disable it from benevolence, than *ill-humor* or *peevishness.*" *Peevishness* is not here a distinct thing from *ill-humor*, but merely another term for the same idea.

REM. 10. — The word *as* has a variety of uses, some of which deserve particular notice. It is employed, —

1. In connection with certain prepositions; as, " It would have

---

Improper use of than *to correspond with* as. *Correct the false syntax and show why it is false. What peculiar office does* or *sometimes perform? Illustrate. What peculiar uses of* as *are mentioned? Give examples of each kind.*

---

* " In the book of Common Prayer, we have, ' Thou shalt have no *other Gods but* me;' and the same expression occurs in Addison, Swift, and other contemporary writers. Usage, however, seems of late to have decided almost universally in favor of *than*." — *D. Crombie.*

† See Burns's Grammar.

been idle for the philosopher to form conjectures, *as to* the direction which the kindling genius of the age was to assume." — *E. Everett.* "*As for* the rest of those who have written against me, they deserve not the least notice." — *Dryden.*

2. To connect nouns and pronouns which are in apposition; as "Nor ought we, *as** citizens, to acquiesce in an injurious act." — *Channing.* See also Rule 2, Rem. 7.

3. To connect adjectives and participles with the nouns or pronouns to which they belong; as, "The infantry was regarded *as* comparatively worthless." — *Macaulay.* "Their presence was of great moment, *as* giving consideration to the enterprise." — *Prescott.*

REM. 11. — The conjunction *that* is often employed to introduce a sentence or clause, which is used as a noun in the nominative or objective case; as, "*That the idea of glory should be associated strongly with military exploits*, ought not to be wondered at." — *Channing.*

REM. 12. — The conjunction *so* is occasionally used in the sense of *if*, or *provided that*; as, "It signifies little whether it be very well executed or not, *so* it be reasonably well done, and without any glaring omissions or errors." — *Brougham.*

REM. 13. — The word *than* was formerly employed as a preposition, and still retains this character in the phrase *than whom*;† as, "There sat a patriot sage, *than whom* the English language does not possess a better writer." — *E. Everett.*

"Which, when Beëlzebub perceived, *than whom*,
Satan except, none higher sat, with grave
Aspect he rose." — *Milton.*

"Felon unwhipp'd! *than whom* in yonder cells
Full many a groaning wretch less guilty dwells." — *Sprague.*

OBS. — The phrase *than which* is also sometimes used in a similar manner; as, "A work, *than which* the age has certainly produced none more sure of bequeathing its author's name to the admiration of future times." — *J. G. Palfrey.*

REM. 14. — The word *both* should not be used with reference to more than two objects or classes of objects. The following example is therefore erroneous: — "He paid his contributions to literary undertakings, and assisted *both* the Tatler, Spectator, and Guardian." — *Johnson.* *Both* should be omitted.

What care should be observed in the use of the word both *? Illustrate.*

---

* Several respectable grammarians entertain the opinion that *as* in this and similar examples is a preposition, governing the following noun. See Fuller, J. M. Putnam, Sanborn, Cobb, and Emmons.

† "The comparative agreeth to the parts compared, by adding this *preposition, than*." — *Ben Johnson; London,* 1640. See also Crombie, Priestley, Wm. Ward, Bicknell, Meikin, and Lindsay.

REM. 15. — The conjunctions *than* and *as* are frequently followed by an ellipsis of one or more words required to complete the construction; as, "More *than* one [ ] of his plays are devoted exclusively to its illustration." — *Prescott.* "He was the father of all such *as* [ ] handle the harp and organ." — *Gen.* 4 : 21.

OBS. — Examples sometimes occur in which it is impossible to supply the ellipsis satisfactorily, while the sense is clearly conveyed by the expression in its abridged form. In parsing such examples, it would be better for the pupil to refer to the foregoing remark, and not attempt to supply words which are altogether rejected by the idiom of the language. Thus, in the first example above, the word *one* may be parsed as the subject of a verb understood, without naming any particular word to complete the construction. But in the second example, the ellipsis is more readily supplied. "He was the father of all such as [those who] handle the harp and organ." In parsing examples of this class, it is better to supply the ellipsis. See § 300.

RULE XIX. — PREPOSITIONS — RELATION.

§ 245. Prepositions connect words and show the relation between them.

REM. 1. — In parsing a preposition, both terms of the relation expressed by it should be pointed out. One of these terms is always the object of the preposition; the other may be a verb, an adjective, a noun, or an adverb. In the sentence, "He travelled *for* pleasure," *for* shows the relation between *pleasure* and the verb *travelled.* In the sentence, "They were destitute *of* food," *of* shows the relation between *food* and the adjective *destitute.* In the sentence, "This is an age *of* improvement," *of* shows the relation between *improvement* and the noun *age.* In the sentence, "Ambassadors were sent previously *to* the declaration," *to* shows the relation between *declaration* and the adverb *previously.*

OBS. — There are certain elliptical forms of speech in which the antecedent term of relation is omitted; as,

"O *for* the voice and fire of seraphim,
To sing thy glories with devotion due!" — *Beattie.*

REM 2. — A preposition and its object should be so placed as to leave no ambiguity in regard to the words which the preposition is intended to connect. The following sentence is faulty in this res-

---

By what are the conjunctions than *and* as *frequently followed? Examples. Give the rule for the relation expressed by prepositions. Illustrate. What rule is given respecting the position of a preposition and its object?*

pect:—"The message was communicated by an agent, who had never before discharged any important office of trust, *in compliance with the instructions of the executive.*" *In* is here intended to show the relation between *was communicated* and *compliance;* whereas the present arrangement indicates that it expresses the relation between *had discharged* and *compliance.* Corrected:—"The message was communicated *in compliance* with the instructions of the executive, by an agent who had never before discharged any important office of trust."

REM. 3.—The use of two prepositions before a single noun, though inelegant, often contributes to perspicuity and brevity, and has the sanction of many good writers.

Examples:—"Men's passions and interests mix *with,* and are expressed *in,* the decisions of the intellect."—*Channing.* "They were never revealed *to,* nor confronted *with,* the prisoner."—*Prescott.* "We have never uttered a word in this Journal, either in advocacy *of,* or in opposition *to,* any particular religious sect, or political party amongst us."—*Horace Mann.*

OBS.—The same remark applies also to the use both of a preposition and a transitive verb before a single object.

Examples:—"It was created to *influence,* and not solely to be influenced *by,* the opinions of the community."—*N. A. Review.* "And may readily associate *with,* and *promote* either."—*Dr. Hopkins.* "We are so made as to be capable, not only of *perceiving,* but also of being pleased *with,* or pained *by,* the various objects by which we are surrounded."—*Wayland.*

REM. 4.—Two or more words are sometimes used together as a *compound preposition;* as, "*From between* the arcades, the eye glances up to a bit of blue sky, or a passing cloud."—*Irving.* "*Over against* this church stands a large hospital."—*Addison.*

REM. 5.—Care should be taken to employ such prepositions as express clearly and precisely the relations intended.

Correct Examples:—"He went *to* New York;"—"He arrived *at* Liverpool;"—"He rode *into* the country;"—"He resides *in* London;"—"He walks *with* a staff *by* moonlight;"—"The mind is sure to revolt *from* the humiliation *of* being thus moulded and fashioned, *in* respect *to* its feelings, *at* the pleasure *of* another."—*Whately.*

False Syntax:—"We differ entirely with Lord Brougham."—*N. Y. Review.* "The posthumous volumes appeared in considerable

---

Illustrate. Give examples of compound prepositions. What care should be observed in the choice of prepositions? Correct the false syntax, and show why it is false.

intervals." — *Hallam.* "It was not evident what deity or what form of worship they had substituted to the gods and temples of antiquity." — *Gibbon.*

Rule XX. — Prepositions. — Government.

§ 246. Prepositions govern the objective case; as, "They came *to us in* the *spirit of kindness;*" — "*From him* that is needy, turn not away."

Rem. 1. — A preposition should never be introduced to govern a word which is properly the object of a transitive verb. Thus, instead of saying, "We delight to contemplate *on* the wonders of creation," we should say, "We delight to contemplate the wonders of creation."

Rem. 2. — Respecting the *ellipsis* of prepositions, no definite rule can be given. Care should be taken to conform to the usage of good writers. In the following sentence the preposition is improperly omitted: — "Chemistry and Botany will be studied the Spring term." — Corrected: — "Chemistry and Botany will be studied *during* the Spring term." The following is also objectionable: — "It is worthy the consideration of all." — *N. A. Review. Of* should be inserted after *worthy*. See § 293.

Rem. 3. — A noun or pronoun following *like, unlike, near,* or *nigh,* is often governed by a preposition understood;* as "Solomon, in all his glory, was not arrayed *like* [to] one of these;" — "The house stands *near* [to] a river."

Rem. 4. — The word *save* is frequently used to perform the office of a preposition; as,

"And all desisted, all *save* him alone." — *Wordsworth.*

Rem. 5. — *But*† is sometimes employed as a preposition, in the sense

---

What do prepositions govern? Examples. *Nouns and pronouns following the words* like, unlike, *and* nigh. *Examples. The word* save. *Examples.*

---

* *Like, unlike, near* and *nigh,* are classed by some grammarians with prepositions.

"We have not placed them with the prepositions, for *four* reasons; (1.) because they are sometimes *compared;* (2.) because they sometimes have *adverbs* evidently relating to them; (3.) because the preposition *to* or *unto* is sometimes expressed after them; and, (4.) because the words which *usually* stand for them in the learned languages, are clearly *adjectives.*" — *G. Brown.*

† The use of *but* as a preposition is *discountenanced* by G. Brown, Sanborn, Murray, S. Oliver, and several other grammarians. See also an able article in the Massachusetts Common School Journal, vol. ii., p. 19.

The use of *but* as a preposition is *approved* by J. E. Worcester, John Walker, R. C. Smith, Pickett, Hiley, Angus, Lynde, Huli, Powers, Spear, Farnum, Fowle, Goldsbury, Perley, Cobb, Badgley, Cooper, Jones, Davis, Beall, Hendrick, Hazen, Goodenow, Weld, Pinneo, Spencer, and others.

"It is a preposition where we say, 'I saw no one *but him;*' yet we may by an ellipsis still explain it as a conjunction, — 'I saw no one *but* [I saw] him;' — or, by another ellipsis, as an adverb, — 'I saw no one [I saw] *but* him, that is, *only* 'him.' The simplest explanation, or that which dispenses with the contrived ellipsis, is the best." — *Smart.*

of *except;* as, "No one can appreciate the beauty and majesty of the heavens, *but* him who has been shut out from every other prospect for days and weeks together." — *Graham's Magazine.*

"The boy stood on the burning deck,
Whence all *but* him had fled." — *Hemans.*

Rem. 6. — "*O'clock*" is an elliptical expression, contracted from "*Of the clock.*"*

Rule XXI. — Interjections.

§ 247. Interjections have no grammatical relation to the other words of a sentence; as, "These were delightful days; but, *alas!* they are no more."

EXERCISES IN COMPOSITION.

§ 248. Write exercises containing examples of adverbs; — conjunctions; — *conjunctive adverbs modifying verbs in two different clauses;* — *a relative adverb;* — *several examples of corresponding conjunctions;* — examples of prepositions and interjections.

EXERCISES IN PARSING.
Model.

§ 249. "He came *in* haste, *and* soon returned.

In is a preposition, expressing the relation of the noun *haste* to the verb *came.* Prepositions connect words and show the relation between them.
And is a conjunction, connecting the two clauses. *He came* and [*he*] *returned.* Conjunctions connect words or sentences.
Soon is an adverb, modifying the sense of the verb *returned.* Adverbs modify verbs, adjectives, and other adverbs.

"He is *very cautious.*" — "Health *and* plenty cheer the laboring swain." — "The *weakest* kind *of* fruit *drops soonest to the ground.*" — *Shakspeare.* "*If* men *see* our faults, they *will talk* among *themselves, though* we *refuse* to let them *talk to us.*" — "War is *to be* ranked among the *most* dreadful calamities *which* fall on a guilty *world.*" — *Channing.*

"*O Solitude! where* are the charms
That sages *have* seen in thy *face?*" — *Cowper.*

What is the rule respecting interjections? Examples.

* "At seven *of the clock.*" — *Spectator.* "By five *of the clock.*" — *Shakspeare.*

§ 250. "*It* is *not* true, *that* the state of public morals and virtue is *as elevated as that* of the individuals *who* compose a community." — *B. B. Edwards.* "*When* a great principle is *at* stake, we *must learn* to dismiss *all* minor differences." — *Ibid.* "*Now* Moses kept the *flock* of *Jethro,* his *father-in-law.*" —*Exodus* 3 : 1. "*How* little *opportunity for* mental improvement *do even* * they *possess!*" — *E. Everett.* "He *did* not, like a *leader, get up on* an eminence, and *from thence survey* the subject *in all its bearings.*" — *Brougham.* "Their road lay *through* the beautiful land *where* they *had been so long lingering.* — *Prescott.* "The sanctity of private property *was recognized,* as the surest *guaranty* of order and abundance." — *Bancroft.* "*Doth* he come from *where* the swords flashed high ?" — *Hemans.*

"We took our seats
By *many* a *cottage-hearth, where* he received
The welcome of an inmate *come from far.*" — *Wordsworth*
"*Nor* pride *nor* poverty *dares come*
Within that *refuge-house,* the *tomb.*" —*Croly.*

"Liberty, *as well as* religion, *has too* deep an interest in the change *which is to be effected.*" — *Prof. C. Dewey.* "*As* to the question of abstract right, I *should hardly undertake* its discussion *at* this time." — *Dana.* "*I have all along gone* on the ground of the mutual influence *of the private upon* the public, and the *public* upon the private *relation.*" — *Ibid.* "Nor is this enterprise *to be scoffed at as hopeless.*" — *Channing.* "*It* was my good *fortune* to meet *in* a dinner party, *with* more *men of* celebrity *in* science or polite literature, *than are* commonly *found collected round* the *same table.*" — *Coleridge.*

Rule XXII. — General Rule.

§ 251. The different parts of a sentence should be made to harmonize with one another; and the several clauses should be so constructed and arranged as to express clearly the various relations, connections, and dependences intended, according to the best usages of the language.

Repeat the general rule of Syntax.

* See Rule 17, Rem. 3, Obs.

REM. 1.— This rule is sufficiently comprehensive to embrace all the different forms of construction in the language. It is, however, too general to afford special guidance to learners, and should be applied only in cases for which no definite rule is given.

REM. 2.— The abverbs *rather* and *better* are often used in connection with the auxiliary *had;* as, "I *had rather* remain;"—"He *had better* return." These forms of expression are anomalous, but their use in the familiar style is too well established to be controverted. Good authors sometimes employ them also in elevated writings, but this practice is not to be recommended.

Examples:—"You are therefore to consider whether you *had rather* oblige than receive an obligation."—*Spectator.* "Practices which *had* much *better* be inferred from general rules."—*N. A. Review.* "They *had rather* part with life, than bear the thought of surviving all that made life dear to them."—*Hazlitt.*

REM. 3.— The expressions, "had as lief," "had like," and "had ought," are anomalous and inelegant, and should be carefully avoided. *Erroneous examples:*—"More serious consequences *had like* to have resulted."—*Prescott.* "*I had as lief* the town-crier spoke my lines."—*Shakspeare.*

False Syntax, under the General Rule.

"It belonged to that peculiar class of poetry, which never has, and never will awaken sympathy in the universal heart."—*N. A. Review.*

"Among all the animals upon which nature has impressed deformity and horror, there is none whom he durst not encounter."—*Johnson.*

"The sun looketh forth from the halls of the morning,
And flushes the clouds that begirt his career."—*W. G. Clark.*

"The manner in which these essays were given to the world, on separate sheets, and with an interval of a few days between the publication of each, distinguished them from every thing of the kind which had preceded them."—*N. A. Review.*

"Domestic society is the seminary of the social affections, the cradle of sensibility, where the first elements are acquired of that tenderness and humanity which cement mankind together; and which, were they entirely extinguished, the whole fabric of social institutions would be dissolved."—*Hall.*

"Deliver me from the hand of strange children, whose mouth speaketh vanity, and their right hand is a right hand of falsehood."—*Ps.* 144:11.

"I have only touched on these several heads, which every one

Correct the false syntax, and show why it is false.

who is conversant in discourses of this nature will easily enlarge upon in his own thoughts, and draw conclusions from them which may be useful to him in the conduct of his life." — *Spectator.*

"The perplexity that attends a multiplicity of criticisms by various hands, many of which are sure to be futile, many of them ill-founded, and some of them contradictory to others, is inconceivable." — *Cowper.*

"The greatest masters of critical learning differ among one another." — *Spectator.*

"Thus, oft by mariners are shown
Earl Godwin's castles overflown." — *Swift.*

GENERAL EXERCISES IN PARSING.

§ 252. "The happiness of life *is made up of an infinite number* of little things, *and not of startling* events *and* great emotions; *and he* who daily and hourly diffuses pleasure *around* him *by* kind offices, frank salutations, and cheerful *looks, deserves as well of* his *species, as he, who,* neglecting *or despising all these,* makes *up for it* by occasional acts of generosity, justice, or benevolence." — *G. S. Hillard.*

"*It were, indeed,* a bold *task to venture* to draw *into* comparison *the* relative merits of *Jay* and Hamilton." — *Dr. Hawks.*

"*Success* being now *hopeless,* preparations *were made for* a retreat." — *Alison.*

"The *name* of a mother; — *what* a long *history does* it bring with it *of* smiles and words of mildness, of tears *shed* by night and of *signings* at the *morning* dawn, of love *unrequited, of* cares *for which* there can be no recompense on earth." — *Prof. E. A. Park.*

"*How feeble* were the attempts at *planting towns, is evident* from the nature of the tenure *by which* the lands *near the Saco* were held." — *Bancroft.*

"The language and literature, *as well as* the history of Spain, have, *till* within *a few* years *past, attracted* little attention in the *United States;* a *neglect* which would be a *subject of the* greater reproach to us, *if we could not find* some apology *for it* in the *less pardonable* indifference of other nations, *who have* more leisure *to indulge* themselves *in* the pleasures of literature *than falls* to the lot of the *ever busy* inhabitants of the United States." — *N. Y. Review.*

"When events *are made familiar* to us by history, we are *perhaps* disposed to undervalue the wisdom *that* foretold them."—*Th. Campbell.*

"*Fortune,* friends, kindred, home,— *all were gone.*"—*Prescott.*

"This spirit of *knight-errantry* might lead us to undervalue his talents *as a general,** and *to regard* him † *merely in* the light of a lucky adventurer."—*Ibid.*

"There leviathan,
Hugest of living creatures, *on* the deep
Stretched like a *promontory,* sleeps or swims,
And *seems* a moving *land.*"—*Milton.*

"But now the door *is open'd soft* and *slow.*"—*Prof. Wilson.*

"We *all* of us feel, *that* virtue is not *something adopted* from necessity."—*Channing.*

"*Sir William Berkley* was elected *governor.*"—*Bancroft.*

"I have little doubt, *but that* the contempt *with* which a ploughman *would look down* upon me for not *knowing oats* from barley, *would transcend that* of an astronomer at *my* not *being able to distinguish* between Cassiopeia and Ursa Major."—*Prof. Wilson.*

"*No* farther steps for *procuring* his *release* were taken at this *time;* either *because* the means for defraying the legal expenses *could* not *be raised; or, which* is *quite as probable, because it* was *certain that* Bunyan, thinking *himself in* conscience bound to preach in defiance of the law, *would* soon *have made his* case *worse* than it *then* was."—*Southey.*

"This court was composed of *three* officers, *than whom none* are more distinguished in our naval service."—*N. A. Review.*

"*Of what* immense benefit *had it been to* England in all subsequent ages, *if* her *Elizabethan* era *had been* a Christian *era;* if the great men who then toiled in the fields of knowledge, had *all* been Boyles and *Miltons.*"—*B. B. Edwards.*

"*If Christianity may be said to have given* a permanent elevation to *woman as an* intellectual and moral *being; it* is as *true, that* the present age, *above* all *others,* has given play *to* her genius, and *taught us* to reverence *its* influence."—*Story.*

"The private wars of the nobles *with each other, were* the *first* cir-

---

* See Rule 2, Rem. 7   † Cortes.

cumstance which *renewed* the courage and revived the energy of the feudal barons."— *Alison.*

" *To be* a *foreigner,** was* always in England a reason of dislike.'
— *Johnson.*

" The mind courses *to and fro through* the *past*, and casts *itself* into the *future.*" — *Am. Quart. Review.*

    " The rill is *tuneless to* his ear *who* feels
    No harmony *within;* the south wind steals
    As silent as unseen, amongst the leaves.
    Who has *no* inward beauty, *none perceives,*
    Though all around is beautiful."—*Dana.*

" Nine *times* the *space* that measures day and night
To mortal men, he with his horrid crew
Lay *vanquished.*" — *Milton.*

---

* See Rule 4, Rem. 2.

PUNCTUATION.

§ 253. Punctuation treats of the points or marks inserted in written composition, for the purpose of showing more clearly the sense intended to be conveyed, and the pauses required in reading.

§ 254. The principal points or marks employed in punctuation, are the comma (,), the semicolon (;), the colon (:), the period (.), the note of interrogation (?), the note of exclamation (!), and the dash (—).

REM. 1. — The comma requires a momentary pause; the semicolon, a pause somewhat longer than the comma; the colon, a pause somewhat longer than the semicolon; and the period, a full stop. The note of interrogation, or the note of exclamation, may take the place of any of these, and accordingly requires a pause of the same length as the point for which it is substituted.

REM. 2. — The duration of these pauses depends on the character of the composition; the grave style requiring much longer intervals than the lively or impassioned.

§ 255. The sense of a passage often requires a pause in reading, where usage does not allow the insertion of a point in writing; as, " He woke | to die; "— " Our schemes of thought in childhood | are lost in those of youth." On the other hand, points are sometimes inserted merely to indicate the syntactical construction, without requiring the suspension of the voice in reading; as in the phrase, " No, Sir."

§ 256. — THE COMMA.

RULE 1. — When a relative and its antecedent are separated from each other by one or more words, a comma should generally be inserted before the relative; as, " Think not *man* was made in vain, *who* has such an eternity reserved for him." — *Spectator.*

Of what does punctuation treat ? What are the marks chiefly employed in punctuation ? *What pauses do they severally require ? What departure from the grammatical punctuation of a sentence is often required in reading ? Examples.*

'There is a *pleasure* in poetic pains,
Which only poets know." — *Cowper.*

RULE 2. — When two or more words come between the adjective and its noun, a comma is placed after the intervening words; as, "To dispel these errors, and to give a *scope* to navigation, *equal* to the grandeur of his designs, Prince Henry called in the aid of science." — *Irving.*

RULE 3. — When the subject of a sentence consists of several nominatives, or of a single nominative followed by an adjunct consisting of several words, a comma should be inserted before the following verb.

Examples: — "The effect of this universal diffusion of gay and splendid light, *was* to render the preponderating deep green more solemn." — *Dwight.*

"The golden sun,
The planets, all the infinite host of heaven,
Are shining on the sad abodes of death."

RULE 4. — When a sentence or clause is used as the nominative to a preceding or following verb, it should be separated from the verb by a comma; as, "how dearly it remembered the parent island, *is told* by the English names of its towns." — *Bancroft.*

RULE 5. — Two successive words in the same construction, without a conjunction expressed, are generally separated by a comma; as, "An *aged, venerable* man."

"Has Nature, in her *calm, majestic* march,
Faltered with age at last?" — *Bryant.*

REM. 1. — An apparent exception to this rule often occurs in the case of two successive adjectives; as in the expression, "A venerable old man." But the two adjectives, in this example, are not in the same construction, since *old* qualifies *man,* while *venerable* qualifies the phrase *old man.*

REM. 2. — A comma may also be inserted before a conjunction expressed, if either of the words connected is followed by an adjunct consisting of several words; as, "Intemperance destroys the vigor of our bodies, and the strength of our minds."

RULE 6. — Three or more distinct, successive words in the same

---

[The teacher may repeat an example under each of the rules for the use of the several points, and require the pupil to give the rule that applies to it. Pupils should also be required to select examples from other works, illustrating all the rules of punctuation.]

construction, with or without a conjunction expressed, should be separated by commas; as,

> "Beside the bed where parting life was laid,
> And sorrow, guilt, and pain, by turns dismayed,
> The reverend champion stood." — *Goldsmith.*

> "How poor, how rich, how abject, how august,
> How complicate, how wonderful, is man!" — *Young.*

REM. — The same apparent exception occurs in this rule as in the last. In the expression, "A light bluish green tint," *bluish* modifies *green*, and *light* modifies the phrase *bluish green;* while the three words *light bluish green*, taken together, qualify *tint*.

RULE 7. — Successive pairs of words should be separated from each other by commas, as, "The authority of *Plato* and *Aristotle*, of *Zeno* and *Epicurus*, still reigned in the schools."

RULE 8. — When the different members of a compound sentence contain distinct propositions, they are generally separated from each other by commas.

> *Examples:* — "They shrunk from no dangers, and they feared no hardships." — *Story.* "And thus their physical science became magic, their astronomy became astrology, the study of the composition of bodies became alchemy, mathematics became the contemplation of the spiritual relations of number and figure, and philosophy became theosophy." — *Whewell.*

RULE 9. — When the different members of a sentence express a mutual comparison, contrast, or opposition, they should generally be separated from each other by commas.

> *Examples:* — "The more I reflected upon it, the more important it appeared." — *Goldsmith.* "The quaker revered principles, not men; truth, not power." — *Bancroft.* "As the heart panteth after the water brooks, so panteth my soul after Thee." — *Ps.* 42: 1.

RULE 10. — To prevent ambiguity in cases of ellipsis, a comma is sometimes inserted in the place of the word or phrase omitted.

> *Example:* — "As a companion, he was severe and satirical; as a friend, captious and dangerous; in his domestic sphere, harsh, jealous, and irascible."

RULE 11. — When two or more successive clauses end with words sustaining a common relation to some word in the following clause, a comma should generally be inserted after each.

> *Examples:* — "The truest mode of enlarging our benevolence, is not to quicken our sensibility towards great masses, or wide-spread evils, but to *approach, comprehend*, sympathize *with*, and act *upon*, a continually increasing *number* of individuals." — *Channing.*
> "Such compulsion is not merely incompatible with, but impossible in, a free or elective government." — *H. Mann.*

Rem. — When, however, the word in the following clause, is not accompanied by several words, the comma before it is often omitted; as, "We *may*, and often *do employ* these means."

Rule 12. — When several words intervene between the verb of a principal clause and the commencement of a subordinate clause, the clauses should be separated from each other by a comma; as, "Had we stopped here, it might have done well enough." — "He was nineteen years of age, when he bade adieu to his native shores." — *Prescott.*

Rule 13. — When the connection of a sentence is interrupted by one or more words, not closely related in construction to what precedes, a comma should generally be inserted both before and after the word or words introduced; as,

"He, like the world, his ready visit pays
Where fortune smiles." — *Young.*

Rule 14. — The independent case, and the infinitive absolute, with their adjuncts, should be separated from the rest of the sentence by commas.

Examples: — "To foster industry, to promote union, to cherish religious peace,—these were the honest purposes of Lord Baltimore during his long supremacy." — *Bancroft.* "The playwriters, where are they? and the poets, are their fires extinguished?" — *H. More.*

"Wept o'er his wounds, or, tales of sorrow done,
Shouldered his crutch, and showed how fields were won."
Goldsmith.

"Rejoice, you men of Angiers, ring your bells!" — *Shakspeare.*

Rule 15. — When either of two words in apposition is accompanied by an adjunct, the latter of them, with the words depending upon it, should be set off from the rest of the sentence by commas; as, "The following is a dialogue between Socrates, the great Athenian philosopher, and one Glaucon, a private man."

Rule 16. — When a word or phrase is repeated for the sake of emphasis, a comma should be inserted both before and after it; as, "Here, and here only, lies the democratic character of the revolution." — *Bancroft.*

"Where are the flowers, the fair young flowers, that lately sprang and stood,
In brighter light, and softer airs, a beauteous sisterhood!" — *Bryant.*

Note. — When the word or words to be set off according to the three preceding rules, stand at the beginning or end of a sentence, one of the commas is of course unnecessary.

§ 257.—THE SEMICOLON.

RULE 1.—When a sentence which is complete in construction, is followed by a clause containing a reason, an explanation, an inference, or a contrast, the latter clause should generally be preceded by a semicolon; as, " The past seems to promise it; but the fulfilment depends on the future." — " To the latter it is a double advantage; for it diminishes their pain here, and rewards them with heavenly bliss hereafter." — *Goldsmith.*

RULE 2. — When several successive clauses have a common connection with a preceding or following clause, a semicolon is generally inserted after each.

> *Examples:*—" Children, as they gamboled on the beach; reapers, as they gathered the harvest; mowers, as they rested upon the scythe; mothers, as they busied themselves about the household; — were victims to an enemy who disappeared the moment a blow was struck, and who was ever present where a garrison or a family ceased its vigilance." — *Bancroft.* " Reason as we may, it is impossible not to read, in such a fate, much that we know not how to interpret; much of provocation to cruel deeds and deep resentment; much of apology for wrong and perfidy; much of doubt and misgiving as to the past; much of painful recollections; much of dark forebodings." — *Story.*

RULE 3. — When several particulars are enumerated in a sentence, some of which are expressed in several words, they are often separated from each other by semicolons; as, " The Aragonese cortes was composed of four branches or arms; the *ricos hombres,* or great barons; the lesser nobles, comprehending the knights; the clergy; and the commons." — *Prescott.*

RULE 4. — Two or more successive short sentences having no common dependence, are often separated by semicolons instead of periods.

> *Example:* — " As we have already noticed, its bruised leaves afforded a paste from which paper was manufactured; its juice was formed into an intoxicating beverage, *pulque,* of which the natives to this day, are excessively fond; its leaves supplied an impenetrable thatch for the more humble dwellings; thread of which coarse stuffs were made, and strong cords, were drawn from its tough and twisted fibres; pins and needles were made of the thorns at the extremity of its leaves; and the root, when properly cooked, was converted into a palatable and nutritous food." — *Prescott.*

THE COLON.

§ 258. The colon is at present much less used than formerly;

its place being often supplied by the period, the semicolon, or the dash. There are, however, many cases in which no other point can with propriety be substituted. The following examples will give an idea of the circumstances under which the colon is most frequently employed: —

"The grant was absolute and exclusive: it conceded the land and islands; the rivers and the harbors; the mines and the fisheries." — *Bancroft.*

"There is only one cause for the want of great men in any period· nature does not think fit to produce them." — *Hallam.*

"Johnson puts the case thus: The Historian tells either what is false or what is true. In the former case he is no historian. In the latter, he has no opportunity for displaying his abilities." — *Macaulay.*

"The following are the names of the survivors, four of whom were seated on the platform from which this address was spoken: — Dr. Joseph Fiske, Messrs. Daniel Mason, Benjamin Locke, William Munroe," etc. — *E. Everett.*

"In Num. 14: 33, it is predicted, that Israel shall wander in the wilderness forty years." — *Biblical Repository.*

"The works of Wm. E. Channing, D.D., with an Introduction. Boston: James Munroe and Company."

The Period.

§ 259. The period is placed at the end of a complete sentence.

REM. — A period is sometimes inserted between two complete sentences, which are connected by a conjunction; as, "By degrees the confidence of the natives was exhausted; they had welcomed powerful guests, who had promised to become their benefactors, and who now robbed their humble granaries. But the worst evil in the new settlement was the character of the emigrants." — *Bancroft.*

The period should be used after all abbreviations; as, "Mass.," "N. Y.," "M. D.," "Aug.," "Esq.," "Mrs.," "Mr." Such expressions as 1*st*, 3*d*, 10*th*, 4's, 9's, 4*to*, 8*vo*, 12*mo*, do not require the period after them, since they are not strictly abbreviations, the figures supplying the place of the first letters of the words.

The Dash.

§ 260. The dash is used where a sentence is left unfinished, where there is a sudden turn, or an abrupt transition; and where a significant pause is required.

Examples: — "Let the government do this — the people will do the rest." — *Macaulay.*

"Ah, that maternal smile! it answers — Yes." — *Cowper.*

"He suffered,—but his pangs are o'er;
Enjoyed,—but his delights are fled;
Had friends,—his friends are now no more;
And foes,—his foes are dead."—*Montgomery.*

REM.—Modern writers often employ dashes in place of the parenthesis.

THE NOTE OF INTERROGATION.

§ 261. The note of interrogation is placed at the end of a sentence in which a question is asked; as, "What is to be done?"

THE NOTE OF EXCLAMATION.

§ 262. The note of exclamation is used after expressions of sudden emotion or passion, and after solemn invocations and addresses; as,

"Liberty! Freedom! Tyranny is dead:
Run hence, proclaim, cry it about the streets!"—*Shakspeare.*
"Hail, holy light! offspring of heaven first-born!"—*Milton.*

REM.—When the interjection *Oh* is used, the point is generally placed immediately after it; but when *O* is employed, the point is placed after one or more intervening words; as,

"Oh! my offence is rank, it smells to heaven!"—*Shakspeare.*
"But thou, O Hope! with eyes so fair,—
What was thy delighted measure?"—*Collins.*

The following characters are also employed in Composition:—

§ 263. The *parenthesis* ( ) generally includes a word, phrase, or remark, which is merely incidental or explanatory, and which might be omitted without injury to the grammatical construction; as,

"The tuneful Nine (so sacred legends tell)
First waked their heavenly lyre these scenes to tell!"—*Campbell.*
"Know then this truth, (enough for man to know,)
Virtue alone is happiness below."—*Pope.*

REM.—The parenthesis is now employed less frequently than formerly; commas or dashes being used to supply its place; as, "The colonists—such is human nature—desired to burn the town in which they had been so wretched."—*Bancroft.*

§ 264. *Brackets* [ ] are used to enclose a word, phrase, or remark, which is introduced for the purpose of explanation or correction; as, "Putting off the courtier, he [the king] now puts on the philosopher."

REM.—The parenthesis is often used to supply the place of brackets, and brackets are occasionally used to supply the place of the parenthesis

The parenthesis. Examples. Brackets. Examples.

§ 265. The *apostrophe* (') is used to denote the omission of one or more letters; as, *o'er*, *tho'*. It is likewise the sign of the possessive case, being used instead of a letter which was formerly inserted in its place; as, *man's* for *manes* or *manis*.

§ 266. *Marks of quotation* (" ") are used to indicate that the exact words of another are introduced; as, "In my first parliament," said James, "I was a novice."

REM.—When a quotation is introduced within a quotation, it is usually distinguished by single inverted commas; as, "I was not only a ship-boy on the 'high and giddy mast,' but also in the cabin where every menial office fell to my lot." If both quotations commence or terminate together, this commencement or termination is indicated by the use of three commas; as, "In the course of this polite attention, he pointed in a certain direction and exclaimed, 'That is Mr. Sherman of Connecticut; a man who never said a foolish thing in his life.'"

When a point is inserted immediately after a quotation, it should be placed within the quotation marks.

§ 267. A *small dash* (¯) is sometimes placed over a vowel to denote that it is long; as, *nōble*. A breve (˘), placed over a vowel, shows that it is short; as, *respĭte*.

§ 268. A mark of accent (') is sometimes placed over a syllable to denote that it requires particular stress in pronunciation; as, *dóing*.

§ 269. A *diæresis* (¨) is sometimes placed over the latter of two successive vowels to show that they do not form a diphthong; as, *coöperate*.

§ 270. The *cedilla* (¸) is a mark which is sometimes placed under the letter *c* to show that it has the sound of *s*; as in "façade."

§ 271. The *asterisk* (*), the *obelisk* (†), the *double dagger* (‡), and *parallels* (‖), as well as letters and figures, are employed in referring to notes in the margin, or at the bottom of the page.

§ 272. The *ellipsis* (* * *) or (———) is used to denote the omission of some letters or words; as, "H * * * y M * * * * * l," "C——s K——g." See also an example in the note on p. 151.

§ 273. The *brace* { is used to connect words which have a common application.

The apostrophe. Examples. Marks of quotation. Examples. How are long vowels distinguished? — short vowels? The diæresis. The asterisk, obelisk, etc. Marks of ellipsis. Examples. The brace. Examples.

§ 274. The *caret* (∧) is employed in writing, to show that some word or letter has been omitted; as, "Washington uniformly treated Mr. Sherman with great respect ∧ attention." (and)

§ 275. The *hyphen* (-) is used after a part of a word at the end of a line, to show that the remainder is at the beginning of the next line; and to connect the simple parts of a compound word, as, *all-absorbing*.

NOTE.—In dividing a word at the end of a line, the break should always be made between two syllables, and not between different letters of the same syllable. See § 37.

§ 276. The *index* (☞) refers to some remarkable passage.

§ 277. The *section* (§) is used to distinguish the parts into which a work or a portion of a work is divided.

§ 278. The *paragraph* (¶) is used in the Old and New Testaments to denote the beginning of a new subject. In other books paragraphs are distinguished by commencing a new line farther from the margin than the beginning of the other lines. This is called *indenting*.

[For exercises in punctuation, the teacher may write on a blackboard some portion of a well pointed book or other piece of writing, omitting all the points; and then require the pupil to transcribe and punctuate it. When this is done, the several copies may be compared and corrected. The teacher may also read one or more paragraphs aloud, and require the pupils to write and punctuate what is read, without seeing the printed copy. Exercises of this description should be repeated till the pupils become familiar with all the common principles of punctuation. Pupils should also be required to devote careful attention to this subject, in connection with their ordinary exercises in composition.]

The caret. Examples. The hyphen. Examples. Division of a word at the end of a line. The index. Examples. The section. Examples. The paragraph. Examples.

PART IV.

PROSODY.

§ 279. PROSODY treats of accent, quantity, and the laws of versification.*

§ 280. *Accent* is the stress which is laid on one or more syllables of a word, in pronunciation; as, rever*ber*ate, under*take*.

The term *accent* is also applied, in poetry, to the stress laid on monosyllabic words; as,

"Content is *wealth*, the riches of the *mind*." — *Dryden.*

§ 281. The *quantity* of a syllable is the relative time occupied in its pronunciation. A syllable may be *long* in quantity, as *fate*; or *short*, as *let*. The Greeks and Romans based their poetry on the quantity of syllables; but modern versification depends chiefly upon accent, the quantity of syllables being almost wholly disregarded.

§ 282. A *pause* is a brief suspension of the voice in reading or speaking.

There are two pauses which are peculiar to poetry;—the *cæsural* and the *final*. The *cæsura* is a pause which is introduced into a line to render the versification more melodious; as,

"Not half so swift | the trembling doves can fly."
"Thrones and imperial powers, | offspring of heaven."

REM. 1.—The cæsural pause generally occurs after the fourth, fifth, or sixth syllable; but it occasionally takes place after the third or the seventh.

REM. 2.—When the cæsura occurs after the *fourth* syllable, the verse is lively and spirited; as,

"Her lively looks | a sprightly mind disclose,
Quick as her eyes | and as unfixed as those."

Of what does prosody treat? *What is accent? Examples. What is said of quantity? What is a pause? What pauses are peculiar to poetry? Give an account of each. Examples.*

---

* Emphasis, Tone, Pitch, and Inflection, which are often treated of under the head of Prosody, belong more properly to Elocution.

Rem. 3. — When the cæsura occurs after the *fifth* syllable, the verse loses its brisk and lively air, and becomes more smooth, gentle, and flowing; as,

"Eternal sunshine | of the spotless mind,
Each prayer accepted | and each wish resigned."

Rem. 4. — When the cæsura occurs after the *sixth* syllable, the verse becomes more solemn and its measure more stately; as,

"The wrath of Peleus' son, | the direful spring
Of all the Grecian woes, | O Goddess, sing."

The final pause is that which occurs at the end of a line.

In reading poetry, careful attention should be given to the final and cæsural pauses.

VERSIFICATION.

§ 283. *Versification* is a measured arrangement of words, in which the accent is made to recur at certain regular intervals.

Rem. — This definition applies only to modern verse. In Greek and Latin poetry, it is the regular recurrence of long syllables, according to settled laws, which constitutes verse.

§ 284. — There are two kinds of verse; — *rhyme* and *blank verse*.

Rhyme is the correspondence of sounds in the last words or syllables of verses;* as,

"Thus to relieve the wretched was his *pride*,
And even his failings leaned to virtue's *side*." — *Goldsmith.*

Rem. 1. — For two syllables to form a full and perfect rhyme, it is necessary that the vowel be the same in both; that the parts following the vowel be the same; that the parts preceding the vowel be different; and that the syllables be accented.†

Blank verse is verse without rhyme; as,

"So live, that when thy summons comes to join
The innumerable caravan that moves
To that mysterious realm, where each shall take
His chamber in the silent halls of death,
Thou go not, like the quarry-slave, at night,
Scourged to his dungeon, but, sustained and soothed
By an unfaltering trust, approach the grave,
Like one that draws the drapery of his couch
About him, and lies down to pleasant dreams." — *Bryant.*

What care should be observed in reading poetry? What is versification? What different kinds of verse are there? Define rhyme. Examples. Define blank verse. Examples.

---

* The lines of poetry are properly called *verses*. † Latham.

REM. 2. — Blank verse possesses, in many respects, important advantages over rhyme. It allows the lines to run into one another with perfect freedom, and is hence adapted to subjects of dignity and force, which demand more free and manly numbers than can be commanded in rhyme. Rhyme, on the other hand, is undoubtedly the most important *ornament* of English versification.

REM. 3. — Blank verse is always written in lines of ten syllables. Rhymed verses may consist of any number of syllables.

§ 285. A *foot* is a rhythmical division of a verse; as,

"Our thoughts | as-bound | less, and | our souls | as free."

§ 286. A *couplet*, or *distich*, consists of two verses making complete sense; as,

"Indulge the true ambition to excel
In that best art, — the art of living well."

§ 287. A *triplet* consists of three verses which rhyme together; as,

"Of many things, some few I shall explain,
Teach thee to shun the dangers of the main,
And how at length the promised land to gain." — *Dryden*

§ 288. *Alliteration* is the frequent recurrence of the same letter; as,

"The *l*ordly *l*ion *l*eaves his *l*onely *l*air."
"*W*eave the *w*arp and *w*eave the *w*oof."

§ 289. A *stanza* is a combination of several lines, or verses, constituting a regular division of a poem.

REM. — In popular language, stanzas are frequently called verses.

§ 290. *Scanning* is the resolving of verses into the several feet of which they are composed.

§ 291. The principal feet used in English poetry are, —

1. The *Iambus*, which consists of two syllables; the first unaccented, and the second accented; as, *con-ténd*.

2. The *Trochee*, which consists of two syllables; the first accented, and the second unaccented; as, *nó-ble*.

3. The *Anapest*, which consists of three syllables; the first two unaccented, and the last accented; as, *in-ter-céde*.

§ 292. The following feet are employed less frequently : — (1.) The *spondee*, which consists of two accented syllables; (2.) the *pyrrhic*, which consists of two unaccented syllables; (3.) the *dactyle*, consisting of three

---

What is a foot? Examples. What is a couplet? Examples. What is a triplet? Examples. What is alliteration? Examples. Define a stanza. What is scanning? What kind of feet are principally used in English poetry? Examples of each.

syllables, of which the first only is accented; (4.) the *amphibrach*, consisting of three syllables, of which the second only is accented; (5.) the *tribrach*, consisting of three unaccented syllables.

Iambic Verse.

§ 293. *Iambic* verse is composed of iambic feet, and has the accent on the even syllables. The most common forms are the following: —

1. Four iambuses, or eight syllables in a line; as,

"And máy | at lást | my weá | ry áge
Find oút | the peáce | ful hér | mitáge."

REM. 1.—This measure is sometimes varied, to adapt it to light subjects, by taking an additional unaccented syllable; as,

"Or if | it bé | thy will | and pléas | ure,
Diréct | my plough | to find | a treás | ure."

REM. 2.—In some cases, a syllable is cut off from the first foot; as,

"Praise | to Gód, | immór | tal práise,
For | the love | that crówns | our dáys."

2. Five iambuses, or ten syllables in a line; as,

"For mé | your tríb | utá | ry stóres | combíne."

REM. 1.— This is usually called the *heroic* measure, and is the most elevated and dignified kind of English verse. It frequently admits of some variety, particularly at the beginning or end of a line. A trochee is sometimes employed instead of an iambus, and an unaccented syllable is occasionally attached to the last foot; as,

"His house she enters; there to be a light
Shining within, when all without is night;—
A guar | dian-an | gel, o'er | his life | presid | ing,
Doubling | his pleas | ures, and | his cares divid | ing." — *Rogers.*

REM. 2.— A verse of six feet, or twelve syllables, called an *Alexandrine*, is occasionally introduced into heroic poetry, especially at the close of a passage; as,

"Time writes no wrinkle on thine azure brow; —
Such as | Crea | tion's dawn | beheld, | thou roll | est now."

REM. 3. — Heroic verse may be written either with or without rhyme. Milton's Paradise Lost, Thomson's Seasons, Cowper's Task, and Pope's Translation of Homer, are examples of heroic verse.

REM. 4.—The four lined stanzas of Psalmody often consist of alternate verses of four and three feet; as,

"Thou didst, | O might | y God! | exist
Ere time | began | its race;
Before | the am | ple el | ements
Fill'd up | the void | of space."

What is iambic verse? What are the principal forms of iambic verse? Examples of each.

REM. 5. — A single syllable is sometimes added at the end of a line, for the sake of variety; as,

"Waft, waft, | ye winds, | his sto | ry;
And you, ye waters roll,
Till like | a sea | of glo | ry,
It spreads from pole to pole."

§ 294. The following forms of iambic verse are also occasionally employed: —

(1.) One iambus, with an additional syllable; as,

"Consent | ing,
Repent | ing."

(2.) Two iambuses, with or without an additional syllable; as,

"What place | is here!
What scenes | appear!"

"Upon | a moun | tain,
Beside | a foun | tain."

(3.) Three iambuses, with or without an additional syllable; as,

"A charge | to keep | I have,
A God | to glo | rify."

"Our hearts | no long | er lan | guish."

Trochaic Verse.

§ 295. *Trochaic* verse is composed of trochaic feet, and has the accent on the odd syllables. The principal forms of Trochaic verse are the following: —

1. Three trochees in a line; or three trochees and an additional syllable; as,

"Wó is | mé, Al | háma."

"Haste thee, | Nymph, and | bring with | thee
Jest, and | youthful | Jolli | ty." — *Milton.*

2. Four trochees; as,

"Round us | roars the | tempest | louder."

3. Six trochees; as,

"On a | mountain | stretch'd be | neath a | hoary | willow

The following forms are sometimes employed: —

(1.) One trochee, with an additional syllable; as,

"Tumult | cease,
Sink to | peace."

What are the principal forms of trochaic verse? Examples of each.

(2.) Two trochees; or two trochees, with an additional syllable, as.

"Wishes | rising,
Thoughts sur | prising."

"Give the | vengeance | *due*
To the | valiant | *crew*."

(3.) Five trochees; as,

"Virtue's | bright'ning | ray shall | beam for | ever."

Anapestic Verse.

§ 296. *Anapestic* verse has the accent on every third syllable. The following are the principal forms: —

1. Two anapestic feet; or two anapests and an unaccented syllable; as,

"They renew | all my joys."
"For no arts | could avail | *him*."

2. Three anapestic feet; as,

"I am out | of human | ity's reach,
I must fin | ish my jour | ney alone." — *Cowper.*

3. Four anapestic feet; or four anapests and an additional syllable; as,

"For a field | of the dead | rushes red | on my sight;
And the clans | of Cullo | den are scat | ter'd in flight." — *Campbell.*

"On the cold | cheek of death, | smiles and ro | ses are
blend | ing." — *Beattie.*

REM. — Iambic, trochaic, and anapestic feet, admit of occasional intermixture.

Trochaic and Iambic.

'Týrant | and sláve, | those námes | of háte | and féar."

Iambic and Anapestic.

"My sŏr | rows I thén | might assuáge."

POETIC LICENSE.

§ 297. Custom has given sanction to certain modes of expression in poetry, which are not conformable to the ordinary rules of grammar. The following are the most important of these peculiarities: —

What are the principal forms of anapestic verse? Examples of each. What peculiarities of expression are allowed in poetry. Examples of each class.

1. Poetry admits of many antiquated expressions and irregular forms of construction; as,

> "Let each, as *likes him best*, his hours employ."
> "*Long were* to tell what I have seen."
> "He *knew to sing* and *build* the lofty rhyme."

2. Many words sometimes undergo changes in spelling, that the number of syllables may be made greater or less; as, *'gan*, for *began*; *e'er*, for *ever*.

3. The arrangement of words frequently departs from the ordinary requirements of syntactical rules; as,

> "In saffron robe with taper *clear*." — *Milton.*
> "No *hive hast thou* of hoarded sweets." — *Gray.*
> "*A transient calm* the happy scenes bestow." — *Ibid.*
> "When first thy sire *to send* on earth
> Virtue, his darling child, *designed*." — *Ibid.*
> "Heaven trembles, *roar* the mountains, *thunders* all the ground."
> "Thee, chantress, oft the *woods among*,
> I woo, to hear thy even song." — *Milton.*

4. Adjectives are often used for nouns or adverbs; as,

> "*Gradual* sinks the breeze into a perfect calm."

5. The conjunction *nor* is often used for *neither*, and *or* for *either*; as,

> "To them *nor* stores *nor* granaries belong."
> "He riches gave, he intellectual strength,
> To few, and therefore none commands to be
> *Or* rich, *or* learned." — *Pollok.*

6. Intransitive verbs are often used transitively; as,

> "He *mourned* no recreant friend."
> "Yet not for thy advice or threats, I *fly*
> These wicked tents devoted." — *Milton.*

7. Poetry admits of a great variety of elliptical expressions; as,

> "The brink of [a] haunted stream."
> "For is there aught in sleep [which] can charm the wise?"
> "To whom thus Adam" [spake.]
> [He] "Who does the best his circumstance allows,
> Does well, acts nobly,—angels could [do] no more." — *Young.*

APPENDIX.

FIGURES OF SPEECH.

§ 298. A FIGURE of speech is a departure from the ordinary *form* of words, from their regular *construction*, or from their literal *signification*.

Departures from the usual *form* of words are called *figures of Etymology*.

Departures from the regular *construction* of words are called *figures of Syntax*.

Departures from the literal *signification* of words are called *figures of Rhetoric*.

Figures of Etymology.

§ 299. The figures of Etymology are *Aphæresis, Syncope, Apocope, Prósthesis, Paragóge, Synæresis, Diaresis,* and *Tmésis*.

1. *Aphæresis* is the taking of a letter or syllable from the beginning of a word; as, *'neath,* for *beneath, 'gainst* for *against.*

"But his courage *'gan* fail,
For no arts could avail."

2. *Syncope* is the elision of one or more letters from the middle of a word; as, *ling'ring,* for *lingering; lov'd* for *loved.*

3. *Apocope* is the elision of one or more letters from the end of a word; as, *thro'* for *through; th'* for *the.*

4. *Prosthesis* is the addition of one or more letters to the beginning of a word; as, *beloved,* for *loved; enchain* for *chain.*

Define a figure of speech. Wat are figures of Etymology? — of Syntax? — of Rhetoric? Define Aphæresis. Examples. Syncope. Examples. Apocope. Examples. Prosthesis. Examples.

5. *Paragoge* is the addition of one or more letters to the end of a word; as, *awaken*, for *awake*; *bounden*, for *bound*.

6. *Synæresis* is the contraction of two syllables into one; as, *alienate*, for *aliënate*, *learned*, for *learn-ed*.

7. *Diæresis* is the separation of two vowels standing together, so as to connect them with different syllables; as, *coöperate*, *aerial*.

8. *Tmesis* is the separation of a compound word into two parts, by introducing another word between them; as, " Thy thoughts which are *to* us *ward*," for " Thy thoughts which are *toward* us;" —" *How* high *soever*," for " *Howsoever* high."

Figures of Syntax.

§ 300. The principal figures of Syntax, are *Ellipsis*, *Pleonasm*, *Enállage*, and *Hypérbaton*.

1. *Ellipsis* is the omission of one or more words which are necessary to complete the grammatical construction. The following examples will serve to illustrate this figure: —

(1) *Nouns;* as, " St Paul's " [church]; " The twelve " [apostles].

(2) *Adjectives;* as, " Every day and [every] hour;" " A gentleman and [a] lady."

(3) *Pronouns;* as, " I am monarch of all [which] I survey;"— " He left in the morning, and [he] returned the same day."

(4) *Verbs;* as, " to whom the angel " [spoke]; — [Let] " No man eat fruit of thee."

(5) *Adverbs;* as, " He spoke [wisely] and acted wisely."

(6) *Prepositions;* as, " He was banished [from] England;"— " He lived like [to] a prince."

(7) *Conjunctions;* as, " I came, [and] I saw, [and] I conquered."

(8) *Phrases and entire clauses;* as, " The day has been considered as an image of the year, and a year [has been considered] as the representation of life." —*Johnson.*

Paragoge. Examples. Synæresis. Examples. Diæresis. Examples. Tmesis. Examples. What are the principal figures of Syntax? Define Ellipsis. Examples of the omission of nouns; — adjectives; — pronouns; — verbs; — adverbs; — prepositions; — conjunctions. Give examples of the omission of phrases and clauses.

2. *Pleonasm* is the use of more words to express ideas, than are necessary; as, "What we have seen *with our eyes*, and heard *with our ears*."

REM.— The repetition of a conjunction is termed *Polysyndeton;* as, "We have ships *and* men *and* money *and* stores."

3. *Enallage* is the use of one part of speech for another; as, "*Slow* rises worth by poverty depressed."

4. *Hyperbaton* in the transposition of words; as, "All price beyond," for "Beyond all price."

Figures of Rhetoric.

§ 301. The principal figures of Rhetoric are *Simile, Metaphor, Allegory, Antithesis, Hyperbole, Irony, Metonymy, Synecdoche, Personification, Apostrophe, Interrogation, Exclamation, Vision,* and *Climax.*

1. A *Simile* is a direct and formal comparison; as, "He shall be like a tree planted by the rivers of water."

"As, down in the sunless retreats of the ocean,
Sweet flowrets are springing, no mortal can see;
So, deep in my bosom, the prayer of devotion,
Unheard by the world, rises silent to thee." — *Moore.*

2. A *Metaphor* is an implied comparison; as, "What are the sorrows of the young? Their growing minds soon close above the wound."

3. An *Allegory* is a continued metaphor. In the following beautiful example found in the 80th Psalm, the people of Israel are represented under the symbol of a vine: —

"Thou hast brought a vine out of Egypt; thou hast cast out the heathen and planted it. Thou preparedst room before it, and didst cause it to take deep root, and it filled the land. The hills were covered with the shadow of it, and the boughs thereof were like the goodly cedars. She sent out her boughs unto the sea, and her branches unto the river. Why hast thou then broken down her hedges, so that all they which pass by the way do pluck her? The boar out of the wood doth waste it, and the wild beast of the field doth devour it."

4. An *Antithesis* is an expression denoting opposition or contrast; as, "The wicked flee when no man pursueth, but the righteous are bold as a lion."

"Tho' deep, yet clear; tho' gentle, yet not dull."

Define Pleonasm. Examples. Enallage. Examples. Hyperbaton. Examples. Simile. Examples. Metaphor. Examples. Allegory. Examples. Antithesis. Examples.

5. An *Hyperbole* is an exaggeration in the use of language, representing objects as greater or less, better or worse, than they really are. Thus, David, speaking of Saul and Jonathan, says, "They are swifter than eagles; they were stronger than lions."

6. *Irony* is a mode of speech expressing a sense contrary to that which the speaker or writer intends to convey. The prophet Elijah employed this figure when he said to the priests of Baal: "Cry aloud, for he is a god; either he is talking, or he is pursuing, or he is in a journey, or peradventure he sleepeth, and must be awaked."

7. *Metonymy* is a figure by which one thing is put for another; as, "I have been reading *Milton;* that is, his *poems* or *works.*—" *Gray hairs* [*old age*] should be respected."

8. *Synecdoche* is a figure by which the whole is put for a part, or a part for the whole; as, "*Man* returneth to dust;" that is, his *body*.—" This *roof* [*house*] shall be his protection."

9. *Personification* or *Prosopopeia*, is a figure by which we attribute life and action to inanimate objects; or ascribe to irrational animals and objects without life, the actions and qualities of rational beings; as, "The ground thirsts for rain."

"See, *Winter* comes, *to rule* the varied year,
Sullen and *sad*, with *all* his rising train." — *Thomson*.

10. *Apostrophe* is a figure by which a speaker or writer turns from the party to which his discourse is mainly directed, and addresses himself to some person or thing present, or absent; as, "Death is swallowed up in victory. *O Death! where is thy sting? O grave! where is thy victory?*" — 1 *Cor.* 15 : 54, 55.

REM. — In modern usage, the term *Apostrophe* is applied to any address made to an inanimate object, an irrational animal, or an absent person; as, "Hail, holy light, offspring of Heaven, first-born!" — *Milton*.

"Sail on, thou lone, imperial bird,
Of quenchless eye and tireless wing." — *Mellen*.

"Alas! my noble boy! that thou shouldst die!
Thou, who wert made so beautifully fair!
That death should settle in thy glorious eye,
And leave his stillness in this clustering hair!
How could he mark thee for the silent tomb!
My proud boy, Absalom." — *Willis*.

Hyperbole. Examples. Irony. Examples. Metonymy. Examples. Synecdoche. Examples. Personification. Examples. Apostrophe. Examples.

11. *Interrogation* is a figure by which a question is asked for the purpose of expressing an assertion more strongly; as, "Do we mean to submit to the measures of Parliament, Boston Port Bill and all? Do we mean to submit, and consent that we ourselves shall be ground to powder, and our country and its rights trodden down in the dust? I know we do not mean to submit. We never shall submit." — *Webster.*

12. *Exclamation* is a figure employed to express some strong emotion; as,

"O wretched state! O bosom, black as death!" — *Shakspeare.*
"Ah! how unjust to nature and himself,
Is thoughtless, thankless, inconsistent man!" — *Young.*

13. *Vision*, or *Imagery*, is a figure by which past or future events are represented as passing before our eyes. The following is a beautiful example of this figure: —

"Methinks I see it now, that one solitary, adventurous vessel, the Mayflower of a forlorn hope, freighted with the prospects of a future state, and bound across the unknown sea. I behold it pursuing, with a thousand misgivings, the uncertain, the tedious voyage. Suns rise and set, and weeks and months pass, and the winter surprises them on the deep, but brings them not the sight of the wished-for shore. I see them now scantily supplied with provisions, crowded almost to suffocation in their ill-stored prison, delayed by calms, pursuing a circuitous route; — and now driven in fury before the raging tempest, on the high and giddy waves. The awful voice of the storm howls through the rigging. The laboring masts seem straining from their base; — the dismal sound of the pumps is heard; — the ship leaps, as it were, madly from billow to billow; — the ocean breaks, and settles with engulfing floods over the floating deck, and beats with deadening weight against the staggered vessel." — *E. Everett.*

14. *Climax* is a figure in which the ideas rise or sink in regular gradation; as, "Giving all diligence, add to your faith, virtue; and to virtue, knowledge; and to knowledge, temperance; and to temperance patience; and to patience, godliness; and to godliness, brotherly kindness; and to brotherly kindness, charity." — 2 Pet. 1:5 — 7. "What a piece of work is man! how noble in reason! how infinite in faculties! in form and moving, how express and admirable! in action, how like an angel! in apprehension, how like a god!" — *Shakspeare.*

Define Interrogation. Examples. Exclamation. Examples. Vision. Examples. Climax. Examples.

INDEX.

A, peculiar uses of this letter, 159.
Abstract nouns, 37.
Accent, 202, 204.
Adjectives, 14, 22, 51, 154.
Adverbs, 19, 100, 178.
Adverbial phrases, 180.
Adjuncts, 109.
Agreement, 109, 163.
All, 155, 179.
Allegory, 213.
Alliteration, 206.
Alphabet, 26.
Amen, 179.
Analysis, 110.
Anapestic verse, 206, 209.
Antithesis, 213.
Aphæresis, 211.
Apocope, 211.
Apostrophe, 202, 214.
Apposition, 143, 184.
Articles, 14, 53, 158.
As, 184, 186.
Asterisk, obelisk, etc., 202.
Auxiliary verbs, 76.

Blank verse, 205.
Both, 185.
Brace, 203.
Brackets, 201.
But, 188.

Capital letters, 27.
Caret, 20.
Case, 47.
Catalogue of grammars, 6.
Cedilla, 202.
Clauses, classification of, 120
Climax, 215.
Close vowels, 32.
Cognate sounds, 33.
Collective nouns, 38, 164.
Colon, 199.
Comma, 195.
Common and proper nouns, 37.
Comparison of adjectives, 54.
Comparison of adverbs, 100.
Composition, exercises in, *passim*.
Compound conjunctions, 182.
Compound prepositions, 187.
Compound words, 34.
Conjugation of verbs, 76, 93.
Conjunctions, 20, 23, 102, 181.
Conjunctive adverbs, 100, 181.
Connection, 63, 100, 134, 181–186.
Consonants, 31
Corresponding conjunctions, 182.
Couplet, 206.

Dash, 200.
Declension of nouns, 50.
Declension of pronouns, 59–61, 64.

INDEX.

Synecdoche, 214.
Syntax, 108.

Tenses, 73, 173.
Than, 183-186.
Than whom, 185.
That, 63, 64, 150, 182, 185.
There, 179.
This and *that*, 155.
Thither, 179
Thou, 60.
Tmesis, 212.
To be, 81.
To-day, to-night, etc., 100.
Triphthongs, 32.
Triplet, 206.
Trochaic verse, 206, 208.

Unipersonal (impersonal) verbs, 99.

Verbs, 15, 22, 66, 163.
Versification, 205.
Vision, 215.
Voice of verbs, 67, 68.
Vowels, 31.

We, applied to one person, 149.
What, 64, 65, 151.
Where, 179.
Which, 63-65.
Whither, 179.
Who, 63, 64, 150.
Whose, possessive of *which*, 64, 150.
With, used as a connective, 165
Words, 33.
Worth, 102.

Yes and *no*, 179.
You, sometimes singular, 60.

www.ingramcontent.com/pod-product-compliance
Lightning Source LLC
Chambersburg PA
CBHW031827230426
43669CB00009B/1250